Peacemaking

Peacemaking
in the 1990s
A GUIDE FOR
CANADIANS

Edited by Thomas L. Perry, M.D.

Gordon Soules Book Publishers Ltd.
West Vancouver, Canada
Seattle, U.S.A.

Canadian Cataloguing in Publication Data

Main entry under title:

Peacemaking in the 1990s

ISBN 0-919574-93-9

1. Peace. 2. Disarmament. I. Perry,
Thomas L. (Thomas Lockwood), 1916-

JX1953.P42 1991   327.1'72   C91-091408-7

Published in Canada by
Gordon Soules Book Publishers Ltd.
1352-B Marine Drive
West Vancouver, B.C.
Canada V7T 1B5

Published in the U.S.A. by
Gordon Soules Book Publishers Ltd.
620 - 1916 Pike Place
Seattle, WA 98101

Typesetting by Joy Woodsworth and The Typeworks
Printed and bound in Canada by Hignell Printing Limited

Table of Contents

Acknowledgments

I thank all of the contributors to this new book, *Peacemaking in the 1990s: A Guide for Canadians*, for their generosity in providing their expertise to the Canadian peace movement. All of the authors, and the editor, have worked on this book with the understanding that no payment or royalties would be received for work done. We all wanted to produce at a reasonable price a book that would give Canadians new factual information and ideas to make their efforts for peace and multilateral disarmament more productive. For me, as editor, it has been a rewarding experience to receive such friendly responses from chapter authors, when I have often demanded complicated essays on very short notice.

Thanks are also due to my publisher, Mr. Gordon Soules, whose enthusiasm for getting this book out rapidly has all along been that of a person seriously concerned with preventing war. I am indebted to the hard work of his staff, especially to Mrs. Joy Woodsworth, the typesetter of the manuscript.

I am particularly grateful to Mr. Ryoji Inoue who took the initiative of bringing me his English translation of Mitsue Kubo's account of her experiences in the atom bombing of Nagasaki. That account, which forms Chapter 2 of this book, stimulated me to ask my friends to contribute their ideas in sufficient numbers to produce a new book on peacemaking. Thanks are also due to Ms. Louise Hader for helping in the translation of Mitsue Kubo's story.

I also thank my long time scientific associate, Mrs. Shirley Hansen, for drawing the figures which appear in chapters 4 and 15, and for much other help which made my editing duties easier. My wife, Claire L. Perry, gave me excellent constructive criticism both on my own writing, and on the editors' choices in polishing the contributions of the other authors. Where things are expressed awkwardly, it is likely due to my not having heeded her advice.

The publishing of *Peacemaking in the 1990s: A Guide for Canadians* was materially aided by generous financial contributions from Ryoji Inoue, Mitsue Kubo, Public Education for Peace Society, Vancouver, and End the Arms Race, Vancouver. We wish to acknowledge a financial contribution by the Peace and Security Competitions Fund of the Canadian Institute for International Peace and Security. This project should not, however, be taken to represent the views of the Institute.

Canadians marching for peace. Photo courtesy of Vancouver Province news-paper.

7

Professor Thomas L. Perry, M.D.

CHAPTER 1

Introduction: How to Use This Book and Lessons of the Gulf War

PROFESSOR THOMAS L. PERRY, M.D.

Five years ago we published a book entitled *End the Arms Race: Fund Human Needs,* Eds. T. L. Perry and J. G. Foulks, Gordon Soules Book Publishers Ltd., West Vancouver, 1986. The book contained the full proceedings of the Vancouver Centennial Peace and Disarmament Symposium, which was held in April 1986 to celebrate Vancouver's 100th birthday. The book sold 8000 copies, and had a significant effect in educating Canadians about the importance of working to prevent nuclear war, and of beginning to divert tax funds from armaments to meeting social needs.

Thomas L. Perry, M.D. received his education at the Universities of Harvard and Oxford (as a Rhodes scholar). Born in the United States, he served in combat in the American army in France and Germany during World War II. When he understood the unnecessary mass slaughter inflicted on Japanese citizens by the atomic bombing of Hiroshima and Nagasaki in 1945, he became an outspoken opponent of the development and testing of nuclear weapons. This led to his being hounded by McCarthyite committees in the United States and eventually being forced to emigrate to Canada in 1962.

For the last 28 years, he has worked in the Department of Pharmacology and Therapeutics at the University of British Columbia where he is a professor, and where he conducts medical research on biochemical causes of mental and neurological diseases. Perry has been active in the peace movement in Canadian Physicians for the Prevention of Nuclear War (CPPNW) and in Veterans Against Nuclear Arms (VANA). He was one of the organizers of Vancouver's Centennial Peace and Disarmament

The world has changed markedly since 1986. Enormous social and economic changes have taken place in eastern Europe, the Warsaw Pact no longer exists, conventional weapons arsenals have been substantially reduced by the Soviet Union, and the Cold War has ended. Yet the world as a whole is spending even more preparing for war (1000 billion U.S. dollars a year, compared to 800 billion in 1986), and Canada's military expenditures have also increased, despite the fact our country has no military threat directed against it.

Meanwhile many Canadians have been taking one or the other of two political positions, each of which seems equally illogical to me. Some Canadians have concluded that "the peace movement is dead," because there is no longer a need for it. We have heard this siren song from the press in each of the last few years, especially immediately before Vancouver's annual Walk for Peace in late April. Perhaps some incredibly optimistic people might have believed that there was no longer a need for peace activism prior to August 2, 1990. Saddam Hussein's invasion of Kuwait ought to have destroyed this fatuous daydream.

Other Canadians who have done useful work in the peace movement complain of "burn-out." They say that all the activities they have participated in over the last few years—attending meetings, walking for peace, signing petitions and writing letters—have accomplished nothing. The juggernaut preparing for war continues unabated, despite their personal protest. I think that such premature personal surrender in the struggle for peace ignores the lessons of history, namely that it takes a long time to accomplish really important changes such as outlawing slavery, or even beginning to achieve equality of opportunity for women. And to give up on working for peace when results are not apparent after a few years is incredibly dangerous. What better way is there to increase the likelihood of people's suffering and death in war?

Symposium in April 1986, and a co-editor of the Symposium Proceedings (End the Arms Race: Fund Human Needs, *Gordon Soules Book Publishers Ltd., 1986).*

In recent years, Professor Perry has worked actively to promote friendship and better understanding between Canada and the Soviet Union. He was one of six Canadian Physicians invited to Moscow to participate in an International Forum for a Nuclear-Free World, For the Survival of Humanity, called together by Mikhail Gorbachev in February 1987. For the last five years he has served as an appointed member of Vancouver City Council's Special Committee on Peace, and he was recently named first recipient of Vancouver's Citizen's Peace Award.

Thomas L. Perry

OUTLINE OF CONTENTS

In any case, this new book, *Peacemaking in the 1990s: A Guide for Canadians,* is intended to help rejuvenate a vigorous peace movement in Canada, and to dispel harmful notions such as "burn-out" or an imagined lack of need for peace activism. The idea for this book was born in May 1990, when Mr. Ryoji Inoue brought me the manuscript of a very moving personal account of the atom bombing of Nagasaki. He had translated into English the story written by his friend, Mrs. Mitsue Kubo, of her survival of the atom bombing of Nagasaki on August 9, 1945. Mitsue Kubo's account, which had been published in Japanese in 1987, was printed privately in English under the title *Hibaku: Recollections of A-Bomb Survivors* in August 1990. But it seemed to me so important for Canadians to understand fully the horror of nuclear attack on a city, that I thought reading this very personal account of a young teen-aged girl who became a Hibakusha should serve as the beginning of this book, and ought to reach as many Canadian readers as possible. So Mitsue Kubo's story, "A Survivor's Personal Account of the Atom Bombing of Nagasaki," forms Chapter 2 of this book. It should be read by everyone, and should remind us what faces each of us if we, and peace-minded people elsewhere in the world, let down our guard before all nuclear weapons have been destroyed in all countries.

Chapter 3, "Lanterns for Peace," by Dr. Dorothy M. Goresky, describes the response of one Canadian community to commemorate the suffering of the hundreds of thousands of innocent Japanese people who experienced the nuclear holocausts of Hiroshima and Nagasaki. History has made it clear that there was *no* legitimate military reason to subject either city to atom bombing in order to insure a victory for the allies over Japan in the summer of 1945. We westerners should feel profound shame for this deliberate cruelty, and Dr. Goresky's description of Canadian Physicians for the Prevention of Nuclear War's (CPPNW) efforts to educate children as to the immorality of nuclear war is a small step to make amends.

Chapter 4, entitled "The Social Ruin and Continuing War Danger Caused by the Arms Race," was prepared by myself. I have emphasized the enormous sum spent by the world as a whole (1000 billion U.S. dollars a year, or 1.9 million U.S. dollars a minute) preparing for war, and have contrasted this wastage with the unmet social needs of most of the world's inhabitants. Details are given in four tables in the chapter, most of them relating to unmet needs for health care. In Table 4, I present some examples of important health problems which could be solved by trivial reductions in arms expenditures. I argue that it is not only for humanitarian reasons that we in the developed countries should curb our profligate arms spending. The 20 per cent of us who live in wealthy countries con-

11

sume 80 per cent of the world's energy supply, leaving 20 per cent of total energy production for the 80 per cent of people living in developing countries. How long do we imagine it will be before these 4 billion poor demand their just share of the riches of the world and begin taking them from us by military force? In the concluding section of my chapter, I make some specific suggestions for steps Canada should now take to promote peace. These include reduction of our current defence expenditures ($12.36 billion annually) by 50 per cent; an end to all arms exports from Canada; vigorous support by Canada for a Comprehensive Nuclear Weapons Test Ban in the United Nations; and an end to low-level bomber training flights and to flight testing of the American stealth cruise missile over Canadian territory.

Chapter 5, by C. G. "Giff" Gifford, D.F.C., and Founding Chairman of Veterans Against Nuclear Arms (VANA), is entitled "Canada's Military after the Cold War." Gifford presents a detailed analysis of the sort of armed forces and military equipment which he and the leadership of VANA believe Canada requires in the 1990s. He emphasizes that Canada's military role must become one of strengthening the United Nations to provide negotiated settlements to long-standing military conflicts, to provide peacekeeping forces to maintain truces, and to provide "fire-brigade" use of military blockade and economic sanctions to end aggression and threats to peace. Giff recommends that Canada (and other nations) abolish all nuclear and other weapons of mass destruction, as well as military capability for invasion, and of major offensive weapons: tanks, bombers, medium and long range (strategic) missiles, long range artillery, and submarines. The *raison d'être* of the Canadian military should no longer be to "win wars," but rather to block aggression and achieve stalemate, and to create the conditions for negotiated non-violent solutions. Giff estimates that a sensible Canadian defence policy, cognizant of *real* rather than *imaginary* enemies, could save Canadian taxpayers $2.5 billion in capital expenses, and at least $500 million in annual operating costs, starting immediately. On reading Chapter 5, I am struck by what a bargain he is offering officials of our Department of National Defence. Instead of spending many millions of dollars repeating research for the hawkish 1987 White Paper on Defence, they can have most of what they need for the purchase price of this book!

Chapter 6, "Canadian Foreign Policy in the 1990s," by Professor Michael D. Wallace, is a companion piece to Chapter 5. Wallace emphasizes the need for a complete revision of the 1987 White Paper on defence to bring Canada's foreign policy into line with post-Cold War realities. He stresses the need for our country to strengthen the role of the United Nations, to promote multilateral free trade rather than free trade beneficial only to the United States, to expand development assistance to Third

12

World countries (see also suggestions in Chapter 4), and to promote human rights in Central America, in Israeli-occupied Palestine, in Southeast Asia, and in countries like Romania, which buy Canadian nuclear reactors, while flagrantly violating the human rights of their own people.

Chapter 7, "Arms Control: Promises and Reality," has been prepared by Professor James G. Foulks, and in many ways it is the key section of the book. Dr. Foulks, an important peace activist in Canada for the last 40 years, masterfully surveys the histories of efforts to work out arms control and disarmament agreements between the United States and the Soviet Union, together with other major powers. Foulks reviews the SALT and START negotiations, as well as more recent efforts to reduce arsenals of conventional weapons, and to limit the spread of chemical and biological warfare agents. He directs major attention to the need for establishing a comprehensive nuclear weapons test ban treaty, expertly verified, as the single most important step that can be taken to prevent once and for all the danger of nuclear war, and to create an international climate favourable to major disarmament. Professor Foulks ends his paper with a wish list for disarmament measures highlighted by the outbreak of the war in the Persian Gulf. Originally, Rear Admiral Eugene J. Carroll Jr. (Ret.), Deputy Director of the U.S. Center for Defense Information, had agreed to write this chapter. But his very heavy duties trying to prevent the war in the Persian Gulf made it impossible for him to carry out this assignment. We have retained the title for Chapter 7 originally provided by Admiral Carroll, and hope that when he reads the book, he will feel that Jim Foulks has done a superb job and deserves a position on his staff!

Three chapters in this book describe in some detail the horrors of the small wars, the "low-intensity" wars, that have killed 20 million people, and wounded more than twice that many since the end of World War II in 1945. Almost all of these casualties have occurred in Third World countries, in some 127 different wars. The contributors to this book are just as committed to preventing these small wars as to preventing global nuclear war, and the suffering of the victims of these small wars is just as intense as that described by Mitsue Kubo for Nagasaki.

In Chapter 8, Dr. Joanna Santa Barbara gives a dramatic description of the suffering of a young woman who is a victim of the civil war in Somalia. Chapter 9, by Dr. Derek Summerfield and Leslie Toser, gives details of the harmful psychiatric effects on young adults in a rural community in Nicaragua of the war waged by the United States-backed Contras to overthrow the Sandinistas. "Low intensity" warfare is defined as total war at the grass roots level, with population, not territory, the target. The aim of "low intensity" warfare is to terrorize a population to silence individuals and communities, and to convince people that personal struggle for justice can never bring fruit. Chapter 10, by Peter Davies, a Canadian now living in Cyprus, describes the miseries of people who have been victims of small wars, as seen through the eyes of a British soldier serving for 26 years in Israel, Lebanon and Cyprus.

The last two thirds of Dr. Santa Barbara's Chapter 8, entitled "Children and War, Children and Peace," discusses in great detail the steps which Canadian parents and teachers can take to educate children as to the need for non-violent solutions to international disputes. Readers especially interested in peace education will want to take advantage of this child psychiatrist's expertise in this area, as well as to read the descriptions of peace education for school children given by Dr. Dorothy Goresky in Chapter 3.

Chapter 11, "Letter to Tessa, Born Canadian, September 1990," is an imaginative and poetically written essay dealing with the ethical aspects of preparing for war. It was written by Ms. Meredith Wadman, a young woman who is both an advocate for peace and justice issues, and a devoutly religious Christian. The moral issues she raises will interest churchgoers, and should make it easier for them to work effectively to build an active peace movement within church congregations of many faiths.

Chapter 12, contributed by Libby Davies, a prominent member of Vancouver's City Council, is entitled "Peacemaking: A New and Powerful Role for Cities." Councillor Davies provides readers of this book with some excellent suggestions of activities they can undertake to change Canadian Government policies to ones more conducive to fulfilling Canada's traditional international role as a peacemaker. She argues that new ways of thinking are beginning to take hold in municipal governments. As more and more of us live in cities, and the quality of life becomes harder to sustain, we are challenged to address questions and problems that previously were not considered part of the civic agenda. Citizens are concerned about air and water quality and creeping pollution. We have to make important choices about our future growth, including transportation, health care, housing, lack of agricultural land, and needed urban repairs. All of these decisions are intimately dependent upon our not wasting tax funds on preparations for war.

Councillor Davies also makes the important point that it is generally easier for citizens to speak to, and be heard by, municipal governments than to communicate effectively with the Federal Government. She reviews numerous examples of effective peace initiatives taken by the City of Vancouver, and some important recent municipal government activities undertaken in eastern Canada by the cities of Montreal, Ottawa, London and Toronto. Readers of this book, eager to start peace initiatives in their own communities, cannot afford to miss studying Councillor Libby Davies' contribution.

Thomas L. Perry

One of the features of this new book which I hope readers will find appropriate and useful, is the considerable amount of attention some of the contributors have placed on environmental questions, and the interconnectedness between preventing war and preserving the environment. I believe there is no longer any legitimate reason for having separate peace and environmental movements. Unless we stop the international arms race, we shall never have available the public funding we need to begin correcting damage already done to the environment.

Chapter 13, by Professor Alan F. Phillips, M.D., is entitled "Nuclear Power: A Difficult Question," and it addresses one part of the complex scientific dispute over nuclear energy, and its relationship to peace and preserving the environment. Professor Phillips, a highly trained physicist as well as a physician, explains how the generation of electrical energy in nuclear power plants can lead to the production of tritium or of weapons grade plutonium. Therefore, as long as nuclear weapons continue to be manufactured and tested, and are not completely and permanently eliminated from the arsenals of the nuclear powers, secret and illicit misuse of tritium and plutonium adds to the dangers of nuclear war. On the other hand, the use of fossil fuels as our current main source of electrical energy is causing increasing pollution of the atmosphere with CO_2, and will endanger our planet from the greenhouse warming effect early in the 21st century. (In this connection, readers will also want to consult Chapter 15 by Professor Michael Pentz.) Alan Phillips also carefully lists the human and economic costs of generating electricity from nuclear fuels as compared to coal or oil generation. He points out that casualties from nuclear power generator accidents, like those at Three Mile Island and Chernobyl, have been very small compared to those in coal mines and oil platforms at sea. Alan Phillips' wife has written informally that his balanced account of the pros and cons of nuclear power will displease the extremists on each side! That is the best reason for reading Chapter 13 carefully.

Chapter 14, by Professors George Spiegelman and Luis Sobrino, is entitled "A Revolution in Thinking: The Role of Science in the 21st Century." These two scientists, both active in Science for Peace and both dependable peace activists, point out that Canada spends very little of its public funds on research and development, and a correspondingly low proportion of its gross national product on war-related research. Spiegelman and Sobrino clearly oppose scientific research designed to produce new ways to kill people. But they are cautious about proposing specific scientific research projects designed for peaceful purposes. They fear that pursuit of technological solutions alone will lead to the proliferation of inappropriate technologies, unless it is guided by insights derived from basic scientific research. However, interested readers will note some examples of socially useful scientific research areas, derived from the

15

Brundtland report in 1987, that Spiegelman and Sobrino list early in their chapter.

Chapter 15, by Professor Michael Pentz, is entitled "Global Warning." It discusses in great detail the disastrous effects that global warming is going to cause our planet, global warming produced by the massive injection of carbon dioxide and other greenhouse gases into the atmosphere. Mike Pentz, who was formerly Dean of Science at Britain's Open University, considers global warming second only to global nuclear war as a threat to human health and survival. He points out in Chapter 15 that it is imperative that all countries, especially the developed countries, act now to reduce drastically the amounts of carbon dioxide, chlorofluorcarbons (CFCs) and methane being released into the atmosphere, if we are to avoid very serious climate changes in the early 21st century. The basic problem is that per capita income in the developing countries averages only one tenth that in the rich industrialized countries, with per capita energy use less than one sixth. Meanwhile population growth in the developing countries is far too high, and the impoverished people of the world are demanding their fair share of the world's riches. Professor Pentz believes that it is still not too late for us to avoid severe global warming, if we improve energy efficiency, stop all production of CFCs, and make more use of renewable energy sources. But these problems are not going to be solved in a world embroiled in wars and preparations for war, because their solution requires massive investments and international collaboration. The scholarly details given in Chapter 15 should convince Canadians that the problems of peace and environmental protection are intimately linked.

In Chapter 16, entitled "Recovering the Root: Militarism and the Ecological Society," Professor Michael M'Gonigle and Ms. Suzanne Rose masterfully bring together the issues of ending the arms race and beginning to solve the severe environmental problems our planet is faced with. They describe the long-continuing impacts of militarism on our physical environment, including the low-level NATO and American bomber flights over Labrador-Quebec and British Columbia, and the impacts on society of Canada's serving as the main supplier of uranium and tritium for nuclear weapons manufacture. They do not neglect the negative social impacts of secrecy and of export of weapons from Canada. And they discuss in detail what must be done to convert our economy from an overconsumptive and deformed one into an ecological and balanced society, one which consumes now only what it can maintain over the long term. Our security problem today is not a military problem. Rather a security problem exists with militarism itself—with its waste, its dominating institutions, and its resistance to change.

Thomas L. Perry

LESSONS OF THE PERSIAN GULF WAR

This new book, *Peacemaking in the 1990s: A Guide for Canadians,* was planned in May and June of 1990, and subjects for chapters and contributors had been selected well before any of us knew about the imminent invasion of Kuwait by Iraq. Many contributors might have presented different material if they had known that the Persian Gulf War was so close at hand. As things stand, the importance of working to promote both peace and environmental protection, in the various ways suggested in each chapter, has been given deadly emphasis by the Persian Gulf War. Hopefully, readers will find the messages of this book particularly urgent and useful for their work in the near future.

This introductory chapter was written between January and March 1991, during, and after, the agonizing countdown to a horrible war in the Persian Gulf between a massive United Nations force led and organized by more than 500,000 American soldiers, sailors and airmen, and hundreds of thousands of fanatic and supposedly experienced Iraqi troops. What started as a proper U.N. response to Iraq's invasion of Kuwait—to block any further invasion into Saudi Arabia, and to force Iraq's withdrawal from Kuwait by means of an economic embargo preventing sales of Iraqi oil—has now changed into a very dangerous effort by the Americans to destroy Saddam Hussein and Iraq's military potential permanently by offensive warfare. During the first two weeks of January 1991 we have seen first the United States Congress, and then Canada's House of Commons, debate and formally approve plans for an all-out military strike by the U.N. forces in the Persian Gulf area against Iraq. The sensible original option of economic sanctions to force—albeit slowly—Iraq to withdraw from Kuwait, has been abandoned in favour of massive warfare, in which tens of thousands of Americans and hundreds of thousands of Iraqis could die horrible deaths.

On January 16, 1991 came the long-feared news that the fighting had actually started. By the end of January, more than 20,000 sorties of the coalition's air forces had taken place over Iraq, and by late February, the number of sorties exceeded 100,000. Tens of thousands of innocent civilians in Baghdad and other Iraqi cities have been killed by aerial bombing and missiles. Photographs coming from Iraq and shown on television nightly show damage to civilian buildings in Iraqi cities at least as bad as the most heavily damaged German cities in World War II. The electrical and water supplies for Baghdad were destroyed in the first few days of the war, and epidemics of severe intestinal infections threaten the Iraqi civilian population imminently. Saddam Hussein has cruelly directed Scud missile attacks on Tel Aviv, where once again innocent people have been killed and wounded. Iraq also has deliberately poured a massive

17

amount of oil into the Persian Gulf from Kuwait in efforts, of questionable military value, to delay landings of coalition troops on the north coast of Saudi Arabia. In summary, every dirty trick in the books is being used by Iraq, and every violent action usual in air warfare is being carried out by the coalition military forces. The far more deadly ground war expected in this conflict seems ready to begin. And what was originally claimed to be a United Nations effort to force Iraq's withdrawal from Kuwait, seems more and more an American-led war to destroy Iraq as a military power and to establish a permanent American hegemony over the oil riches of Iraq, Kuwait and the Saudi Arabian peninsula.

Readers of this book need to be asking themselves what we in the peace movement, and what Canada as a traditional peacemaking nation, might have done to avoid this cruel and very dangerous war in the Persian Gulf. Why didn't we oppose the well-publicized international sales of arms and key machine tools to Iraq both during the Iraq-Iran war of 1980 to 1988, and since 1988? Will we continue to allow greed for profits from international arms sales to build up the military power of other dictators after this war has ended? Why have those of us active in peace and justice movements in Canada been so tolerant of Israeli brutalities towards Palestinians in the Intifada uprising during the last three years? Had we demonstrated a serious attitude toward elementary justice for the Palestinians in Gaza and on the West Bank, perhaps the climate of hatred between Israelis and Palestinian Arabs would not have reached its present peak. This hatred can intensify and prolong the present war, and can lead to horrible future confrontations between Arabs and westerners.

Why has the peace movement in Canada tended to drag its feet on preventing a military solution to the Iraqi occupation of Kuwait? There has been overwhelming evidence that continuation of the United Nations economic embargo of Iraq would ultimately force Saddam Hussein to capitulate and withdraw his troops from Kuwait. Without the ability to obtain foreign currency by selling its oil, or to import any of the replacements needed for its military and industrial machine, Iraq could only have capitulated. There is no question that economic privations would have been hard on the Iraqi people, but surely not so hard as the heavy bombing they are now suffering. Why did the government of Canada, and why did we in the peace movement, not work harder to support economic sanctions as the effective and least cruel way of solving the problem?

One very important lesson which the Persian Gulf War should have clarified for all of us is the intimate linkage between opposing militarism and protecting the environment. Towards the end of the war, the Iraqis released a massive amount of oil from Kuwaiti wells and storage tanks into the Persian Gulf. The amount of oil released was probably much larger than the record Exxon Valdez oil spill in Alaska in early 1989, and its environmental consequences may be consideraby worse due to ineffi-cient tidal flushing in the northern Persian Gulf. Far more damaging was the mischievous setting fire to Kuwait's oil wells shortly before Iraq's retreat from Kuwait. News reports indicate that some 500 oil wells are still burning, releasing massive amounts of black smoke into the atmo-sphere, and that it may take months or years for experts to extinguish these fires. Readers can calculate for themselves the probable amounts of CO_2 that will be released from this burning oil, and the likely acceleration of the greenhouse effect worldwide, by careful reference to the tables and figures in Chapter 15 by Professor Michael Pentz. A scientifically rea-sonable outcome of the Kuwaiti oil well fires burning for months or years would be accelerated global warming, with resultant rises in sea level worldwide. What will be the environmental consequences of that on low-lying cities like Kuwait, Tel Aviv, New York and London? These two dramatic environmental tragedies of the Persian Gulf War—the oil spill and the oil well fires—ought to convince us all of the correctness of the points made in Chapters 15 and 16 of this book that opposition to militar-ism and to environmental degradation must go hand in hand.

The Persian Gulf War ended very rapidly after the ground phase of the war commenced in late February, much more rapidly than the public ex-pected. Questions are now being raised that the coalition forces, and in particular their American command, had purposefully spread disinforma-tion as to the military capabilities of the Iraqis, exaggerating the morale and equipment of the Republican Guards, Saddam Hussein's "elite" troops. It turns out that the military strengths of the allied coalition, versus the Iraqis, were grossly unequal. Casualties of the war were fortunately miniscule for the Americans and their allies, but were very substantial for the Iraqis, especially for civilians living in Baghdad, Basra and other large cities. For uninformed North Americans, a disastrous re-sult of the rapid conclusion of the Gulf War, and of the totally unbalanced casualties resulting from it, could be public approval of massive rearma-ment and of aggressive decisions to take military action in the future. Ca-nadians concerned with peacemaking have plenty to worry about in the overwhelming American public approval for President Bush's conduct of the Persian Gulf War. The next time an irresponsible dictator in some other country tries invading a neighbour, could not a similar American response as uninvited military policeman have vastly different results, in-cluding far larger casualties for American soldiers and their allies?

Finally, I think the dilemma of the Persian Gulf War needs to bring home to Canadian activists the crucial need for them to become more po-litically effective. Isn't it a shame that at a time when there is great oppo-sition to the Persian Gulf War—demonstrated by the large turnouts at peace rallies called at short notice in many Canadian cities from Halifax to Victoria—we are saddled with a Federal Government which does not even listen to protest? Surely this is our fault. If we who support peacemaking had raised the issues of peace and disarmament in the weeks before the last federal election, we might now have in Parliament more members prepared to deal imaginatively with potential solutions to the situation in the Persian Gulf, rather than a bunch of cowardly legislators satisfied to take orders from Washington, D.C. My fervent hope is that readers of this book will firmly decide to ask their local candidates in the next federal election for detailed statements of what they propose to do to avoid future Gulf Wars. Peace activists, and everyone else concerned with improving the quality of human life, should make sure that the primary issue in the next federal election is peace and the protection of the environment.

CHAPTER 2

A Survivor's Personal Account of the Atom Bombing of Nagasaki

MITSUE KUBO
Translated from the Japanese by Ryoji Inoue

THE FATEFUL DAY: August 9, 1945

Forty-five years have passed since that fateful day, but the nightmarish memory of the atomic disaster in Nagasaki comes back to my mind, untarnished, on the ninth day of August every year. My blood chills every time I remember the horrendous scenes of that day. No human words could possibly describe that absolute devastation.

It all happened at two minutes after eleven o'clock on the morning of August 9, 1945. I was sixteen and in the fourth year at Nagasaki Girls' High School. Instead of attending school, I had been drafted to work at the Morimachi Factory of Mitsubishi Weaponry, and at the time of the explosion was working in my usual workshop located on the second floor of one of the buildings there. I was only 1.4 kilometres away from the hypocentre.

The month of August had started with frequent air-raid warning sirens; night after night they shrilled like mad. My landlady Mrs. Hirai, her daughter Chi-chan and I slept fully clothed in our monpes in a spacious room, on three mattresses called futons laid side by side. Dressed thus in our baggy wartime trousers, we were prepared to go out and take shelter at any time.

One night I was suddenly awakened by the shrill sound of a warning siren. We got up and, rubbing our sleepy eyes, hurried to the basement of the five-story building which stood next to our house. After a while, an all-clear sounded and we returned to our house. Disturbed in the middle of my sleep, I couldn't get to sleep again till almost dawn. On the morning of the ninth, Chi-chan and I did not wake up till Mrs. Hirai woke us.

"Chi-chan, Takeno-san (my maiden name), get up quick! I have fixed a lunch for you today."

"A lunch?" I jumped out of my futon. Dazzling morning sunlight was streaming into the room through a wide window facing the east. It commanded a good view of Nagasaki City, and I saw the roofs of the houses down below reflecting the morning light. On the table were two little lunch boxes with their lids off, and in them I saw glossy white rice balls—unmixed with barley—gleaming so deliciously.

"Wow! Aren't they gorgeous!" exclaimed both Chi-chan and I happily. "But where did you get the rice?" Mrs. Harai looked at us smilingly, but did not answer our question.

Where could she have gotten the white rice in this time of acute food shortage? To have rice balls of pure white rice for lunch was an almost unthinkable luxury at the time. For our hungry stomachs, even the mixture of rice and defatted soybeans served with cooked sweet-potato stems, which our factory gave us for lunch, was treat enough. The white rice balls made me so happy that I almost skipped around the room like a little child.

We left the house with our two war-time necessities hanging from our shoulders: an air-raid hood and a pouch containing a first-aid kit. Together with two other schoolmates who also lived in the district of Junin-cho, we headed for the nearby tram station. Each of us was wearing an armband labelled with the words "Prefectural Girls' High School Patriotic Volunteer Corps."

It was a very hot morning; the sun glared down on our heads. Most of the people walking hurriedly on the street seemed to be on their way to the military supply factories. We walked quickly to the tram station at Senba-cho, and stood in the rear of a long line of people waiting for a tram bound for Uragami.

I was wearing a soft rayon blouse and unmatching serge monpe. This monpe was of my own making, and I was rather proud to be wearing it. I had taken apart a serge kimono my grandmother had given me, and had sewn the pieces into the monpe just from having watched other people doing it. I had attached a bib to it, and liked it so much that I didn't even mind wearing it in the middle of summer. Over my right shoulder was slung diagonally the dark blue cotton pouch for the first-aid kit, and from the other shoulder hung the air-raid hood. The two straps crossed right on my chest, making the letter "X." Everybody, young and old, men and women, even small infants, bore this "X" mark on their chests when they went out. This outfit was our symbol of wartime.

"I'm not going to work today. I'll go back," said Chi-chan abruptly, and started to walk quickly toward her house. We were all taken by surprise, and, without stopping her, we just watched her walk away. It was not like her at all; she had never before done such a thing. I just could not figure out why she went back; she had been so happy about the rice-ball lunch.

After she had gone, I became more preoccupied with the silvery white rice-ball lunch. I had put it in the first aid pouch, and was happy to feel its warmth. I was sixteen, and my stomach craved food, but all that was available then was so-called substitute food. Besides, being just a boarder, I was not in a position to have my own way and to express my hunger frankly. As a result, I was so skinny that my friends nicknamed me "senko," which means "incense stick." The little tram, packed with passengers, rocked its way up north, and soon we arrived at the station near our factory. Because we each worked at a different section of the factory, we parted at the entrance.

The Mitsubishi Weaponry was located close to Ibinokuchi Tram Station. This was an industrial area, and there were rows and rows of long factory buildings on the west side of the station. On the east side were thousands of small houses standing wall to wall. Many bomb shelters had been dug horizontally into the rock wall on the roadside. When an air-raid warning siren sounded, we stopped our work and ran to the shelter for girl-students only, which was a little way up a hill. But whenever a full-scale alarm sounded suddenly, we had to go into the nearest shelter, together with many other people.

We had heard that at Mitsubishi Weaponry, where we were working, torpedoes and submarines were being manufactured. We never had a chance to see them with our own eyes, because armament factories kept secret what they were making. My workshop was on the second floor of a building where the finishing work was done; my job was to file some of the tiny parts of the torpedoes. Cranes moved to and fro above our heads, incessantly making a loud roaring sound. The grinders splashed golden sparks about, and hammers struck at metal pieces, producing sharp clangs. These deafening noises, together with the foul pungent smell of stale machine oil, had made me feel dizzy on my first day of work there.

A blackish work-table, about two metres long, stood in the middle of the long rectangular workshop which extended from east to west. It was a wooden table, but, being covered with a fine metal dust, it had acquired the dark colour of lead, and now looked as if it were made of metal. This table had drawers in which we put our personal things. I looked longingly for a while at my first aid pouch which contained the precious rice-ball lunch, and then placed it carefully in my drawer.

In front of the table was a long bench, and on it we sat, four high school girls, with files in our hands. We were working on the tiny parts, mostly nuts and bolts, of torpedoes. On my left was Miss K-san, from Tamagi Girls' High School, and the two girls on my right were my

Mitsue Kubo, seated right, a few months before the Nagasaki atom bomb explosion.

With classmates at the Nagasaki Arms Works, autumn 1944. Mitsue Kubo, seated left.

schoolmates. Usually Setsuko Nakamura, another schoolmate, was with us too, but on that particular day she was absent. Her house was in Mezame-cho, which was closer to the hypocentre than our factory was. The noises in the factory were so loud that we had no fear of being over-heard by the other male workers, no matter how loudly we talked or sang. Taking advantage of the loud noises, we often sat at work, moving our files busily. We sang Shinanoyoru, Soshuyakyoku, Aizenkatsura, etc. And without fail we sang the song of Students' Volunteer Corps:

> Young cherry trees we are
> With flowers still in bud,
> To their full height yet to grow,
> But ready we are to sacrifice our young lives
> For the need of our country.
> To the holy cause is the Students' Corps dedicated.
> Our hearts are afire with patriotism.

It was a time when nobody was sure whether or not she would be alive the next day. It was not a happy time for songs, but we sang all the songs we knew, one after another, in the middle of all the factory noises. We did not care about the harmony; we just sang together with loud voices, and we were happy enough. It was the only joy of youth, modest as it was, that we, high school girls who were forced out of school, could hope for.

Right beside us, there was a large square hole in the floor through which a crane went up and down, carrying heavy goods between the first and second floor. A high fence, as tall as a man's chest, surrounded the hole to ensure our safety. We would often look down over the fence at the men working below, around a large cylindrical object which we thought could be the body of a submarine.

Soon after we began the day's work, an air-raid warning siren shrilled. We stopped our work and started running toward the shelter immediately. We panted up what seemed endless stone stairs to the middle of the hill, to where our shelter was. Inside the shelter, which had a damp red clay wall, it was as hot as in a steam bath. Water was dripping from the round clay ceiling, making puddles here and there on the floor. I happened to meet Miss Hashimoto, who was senior to me in the same school.

"They say a new type of bomb was dropped on Hiroshima, did you know?" she whispered in my ear. I shook my head, admiring her quick acquisition of information of this nature. "The bomb exploded in mid-air. Hiroshima was totally wiped out, they say. Isn't that awful!" She continued in whispers using the Nagasaki dialect, to which she was not totally accustomed because she had just recently moved here from Yamaguchi Prefecture. Who could have known but God that we ourselves were doomed to be the next victims of the "new type of bomb"?

Soon an all-clear sounded, and we went back to work, glad to be out of the gloomy, damp shelter. Around eleven o'clock, I began thinking of my rice-ball lunch again. "I can hardly wait. . . . I wish it were already lunch time." Just then there was an extraordinary flash, an eye-crushing flash—purple, orange, yellow, red, blue—or a mixture of all of these. Then came the tremendous roar of an explosion, followed by a thundering sound of things being crushed, and an awful earthshaking tremor. It was so tremendous that I thought it was the end of the world. Being in wartime, we were prepared for almost anything, but this was something that defied description. It was far more enormous than a bomb, an ordinary bomb directly hitting us; it was tens of thousands of times greater than that. Its enormity was simply beyond all words. Immediately after the blinding flash, it suddenly turned as dark as dusk, and that was all I remember because the tremendous blast knocked me down to the floor and I lost consciousness.

I don't know how long I had been unconscious. The next thing I remember was the screaming of people, which pierced my consciousness and reached my ears. The usual loud noises of the factory were all gone. "Help! Mother, help!" "I don't want to die! Please help me!"

The ghastly screams and terrible groans brought me back to my senses. I was lying on my belly under heavy objects, unable to move; but strangely I felt no pain, nor fear. I moved my head and looked carefully around, but I was covered with debris, and it was so dark that I could not see anything. A sudden realization of the state I was in struck my mind: I was faced with death. It stopped my moving.

I lay still for a second, listening. But it was just for a second; I began to wriggle frantically. After a while I managed to get my right arm loose. My hand touched the floor beneath my head and felt something slimy. In the darkness I checked my head for an injury. Yes, I was injured, and it was my blood that was on the floor. But I felt no pain.

I reached out my hand as far as possible, and touched. . . oh, this must be K-san's foot! "K-san! K-san! K-san!" Under the debris of the building I pulled on her foot as hard as I could, and called her name at the top of my voice. But there was no response from her; she did not stir at all. She was still as stone.

It was getting quiet; the screaming voices were getting farther away, and smaller. I could hear running steps of various kinds passing by—feeble scurries, panicky stomps. They all passed me, and the footsteps died away in the distance. What was this that lay heavy on my body?

"Oh, how heavy! How dark! How quiet! I can no longer hear people screaming. Am I going to die this way, under this heavy thing? Is this the moment of death for me? No, I'm alive. I'm conscious. I'm breathing. No, I will not die. Never, never this way," I said to myself encouragingly. Lying unable to move, I held out, mustering up all the strength I had. The faces of my grandmother, parents, brother and sisters flashed across my mind.

"Oh, God and Buddha, please help me!" A picture of my grandmother chanting a Buddhist sutra in front of the Buddhist altar in our house, as she did every morning and every evening, now came to my mind. "Namuamidabutsu, namuamidabutsu. . . (I sincerely believe in Buddha, I sincerely believe in Buddha. . .)." I found myself almost instinctively chanting the prayer to Buddha again and again, and asking for his mercy.

"I must get out of this hell by any means. . . " I was determined, writhing alone in the silent darkness. With a desperate struggle, I tried to raise my body, putting forth every ounce of energy left in me. I tried again. And then again. Just then, the heavy object on my body slid aside a little, and light poured in through a hole which appeared above my head. Once more summoning all the strength I had, I managed to get my head through the small hole, and wriggled myself out of that living hell.

I felt joyful relief now that I was safely out of the heavy debris, but I was still in a panic in the face of this extreme adversity, and thus was not composed enough to check what it was that had fallen on K-san and myself.

"K-san! K-san!... ," I called again and again. But no answer came back. How I wish I had had enough courage at that time to stay longer and move the debris away to check whether or not she was alive! I had been left behind, alone, and had no time to lose. Yet to this day, whenever I think of her, I feel remorse in my conscience. This, I am sure, will stay with me as long as I live.

K-san had been unlucky from the start. She was a student at Tamagi Girls' High School, but she alone was drafted to work together with the students from Nagasaki Girls' High School. She had not been working in our section very long when she fell victim to the atomic bomb. She was a gentle and quiet girl, doing her work in silence, and she was not particularly friendly with anybody, perhaps because she alone was from a different school. I call her K-san in this account, but I am ashamed to say that I have forgotten her real name. I have tried hard to remember it, but somehow I have been unable to recall her actual name. It is very sad that time erodes our memory, our very last resort. One thing after another vanishes into oblivion and never comes back.

I looked around. There was nobody to be seen. The two girls that had sat on my right seemed to have fled already. I ran staggering to the door but stopped short there. "Oh, no! The stairs are gone!" The lower half of a long wooden staircase, which had been attached to the outer wall of the factory building, had been blown away by the blast. The upper part was torn and hanging loose, looking like teeth of a gigantic saw. About three feet away from the mid-air ending of the stairs hung a log; its lower portion had also been claimed by the blast. A fire had already started inside the building and clouds of smoke were coming out of it. There was another staircase at the eastern end of the long building, but I simply did not have time to run over there. There was no other choice left for me but to take a chance and jump over to the swaying log. I took a deep breath, made a desperate leap, and clutched at it. I clambered down halfway and jumped off the log to the ground.

Once on the ground, the feeling of relief triggered a surge of dreadful terror, and I was seized with an uncontrollable fit of sobs and moans coming deep from the bottom of my heart. My whole body was filled with terror. I staggered along a few steps over the debris of the factory buildings, and fell. I raised myself up and staggered along until I fell again. Repeating this over and over again, I made my way in the unusual quietness toward the main entrance of the factory. Just then I sensed the presence of somebody near me. It was Funatru-san, from Chinzei Middle School.

I had never talked with him before, but his name and face were quite familiar to me because he had often come during lunchtime to see a friend of his, who was working in our factory building. In those days, middle schools were for boys only and it was considered improper to talk in a friendly way with female students, even if they were working in the same place. But in this extremely disastrous situation, he made an exception and spoke to me.

"Don't cry. Don't cry. You have to hurry up and get the wound on your head treated at once. There's a dispensary just a little way beyond the main gate."

All I could do was nod, suppressing my sobs momentarily. He said these words before running swiftly away. But how glad I was to have heard his words, the voice of another human being, in this solitary abyss of fear. It gave me tremendous encouragement. "I'm not alone; there's another person. . . a man I know." Thanks to his kind words of consolation, I began gradually to have my composure restored.

He had not seemed injured, but because he was not a youth of strong build, I have been apprehensive about his health afterward. The radioactivity from the bomb has deprived so many uninjured people of their lives; the evil hands of the atomic bomb may be reaching out for us at this very moment, and may take us by surprise tomorrow. I wonder what has become of him. Every time I think of that fateful day, his kind words, and the consolation and immense encouragement they gave me, come back clearly to my mind. I sincerely pray for his good health.

If only I could get out of the main gate, I could get some treatment for my head injury. I urged myself to hurry up, but my feet did not obey. Billows of smoke, getting more and more violent, were closing in on me. Although I did not feel any pain, blood was trickling down, not only from my head, but from my neck and shoulders as well. I must have been injured when I struggled out of the wreckage. My thin rayon blouse, which had been clean and white, was now smeared all over with blood, torn to tatters, exposing my bare shoulders. The legs of my monpe trousers were also tattered, hanging in shreds like seaweed from my knees.

The flames from the factory adjacent to ours were reaching toward me. In the thick smoke, I stumbled again and again, but kept on running in a desperate effort to escape the imminent danger. Finally I passed through the main gate and looked around to see where I might find the dispensary. However, what I saw there was not the town I knew; it was a world utterly different. There were no traces of what had been before. It was a catastrophe beyond all words. Around me spread an endless sea of roof tiles. Every single house had been crushed to the ground, leaving only the tiles to be seen. As far as the eye could see, everything that had stood on the ground was now lying flattened.

I could not believe my eyes. What on earth had happened? What, in a single blow, could possibly bring about such a horrendous disaster of this magnitude? In the face of this unbelievable sight, it was only natural that I had thought that it was the end of the world at the moment of that blinding flash and the terrible roar. But I had survived it. I had escaped the rubble of the burning factory, managed to get to the gate, and had begun to believe that it was after all a bomb that had been dropped somewhere in the factory. But no, it was not. It was not just a bomb dropped on the factory. It could not be. The whole town of Nagasaki had been turned into a scene of destruction and carnage. It was nothing but Hell itself.

Corpses were lying all over the place. People still alive were crouching together, their whole bodies burnt black. Terrible screams came from under the roofs of crushed houses. "Help me! Help me!. . . " They were desperate cries. They were the agonies of death. Even now I can hear them echoing deep in my ears.

This must be what Hashimoto-san had whispered about in the shelter this morning—the same terrible bomb that was dropped on Hiroshima. The treatment of my injuries was no longer an important matter; it was dangerous to be walking around in the town. I decided to seek refuge immediately.

"Help! Please help me!" Cries were coming from everywhere. I was unable to do anything for them; I felt like covering my ears. Repeating, "I'm sorry, I'm sorry," from within my heart, I headed with unsteady steps for the mountains. Those seeking refuge were all weak and desperate themselves; dragging their own heavy feet was all they could do. They could not even turn their heads towards the heart-rending cries for help.

By sheer coincidence I met Hashimoto-san again on a road rising toward the mountains. "Oh, you're safe!" we both cried out and wept, embracing each other tightly. I cannot describe how glad and how encouraged I was to meet her. I had been so lonely, but not any more. I am sure she was feeling the same way. Then we continued to stagger our way up the hill, holding each other's hand, and encouraging each other.

While gasping our way up a narrow footpath between terraced fields, we heard from the sky that awful buzzing sound of airplanes approaching us. "Enemy planes!" people were shouting. I was terrified, remembering that terrible blinding flash and awful roar. "I'm scared!" We fled about on the open fields, screaming loudly. There was no place to hide.

"Come over here. It's a little safer here." A young man taking shelter in the shade of an embankment beckoned to us. Oh, thank God, we thought and ran to his side and crouched down. To our relief the buzzing sound thinned out into the distant sky.

"They must have been our planes," the young man said, reassuring two very terrified girls. He looked like a dauntless young man, wearing a hairband with a red mark of the rising sun tied tightly around his head. From then on, we followed behind him silently, regarding him as our reliable protector. Human beings are weak; we seem unable to get along alone at a time of crisis. The meeting with Hashimoto-san and this young man greatly eased my fear and anxiety; their support was invaluable to me.

In Nagasaki there are a number of small mountains that lead up to Mt. Konpira. We climbed along a narrow path between terraced fields, towards the top of one of these mountains, to a little grove we knew of. Finally we were there, and could rest our terror-beaten bodies and spirits. It was cool and calm in the grove, peacefully quiet, not even the sound of a breeze. The lush green trees, unaware of the hellish devastation below, soothingly embraced us. Most of the people who had come up to this grove to take refuge seemed to have escaped with only minor injuries. We stood looking down at the sea of fire below, speechless.

"We've lost the war," muttered a half-naked young man, as he glared down at the sea of fire, arms folded. He was the only one to spit out the words which surely everyone else was thinking.

I had narrowly escaped the infernal depth of disaster, but would not be able to live long after all, because we were sure to lose the war. I had a threatening sense of doom, for I believed then that to lose the war meant death. We stood facing the incredible view of Nagasaki City; as far as the eye could see spread a sea of fire. The city had been totally destroyed by a single blow. Who could possibly witness this inferno, and still believe in victory?

People were just standing there, bewildered and speechless, gazing down at the blazes billowing everywhere; the roaring sound of the flames broke the silence of the ruined city. What thoughts were passing through everyone's minds? Thoughts of their houses, their loved ones, and our inevitable defeat in the war? By an enormous power of destruction unprecedented in human history, Nagasaki had become a huge melting pot; the ravenous flames were consuming everything that had existed on the ground, sending it all smoking into the sky. As we watched, thousands of people were being burnt in the spreading sea of fire.

Most of the wooden electric poles that had stood in a line at the base of one of the nearby mountains had been blown down. A cable hanging from a tilting pole lashed about at enormous speed as it emitted tremendous sparks, and then was blown away. The poles still standing were being devoured by the fire one after another, writhing as they burnt red-hot. They reminded me of the furious writhing of a huge snake called "Yamata-no-orochi," which appeared in a Japanese myth I had studied in primary school. Fires were breaking out in the area of the Mitsubishi Weaponry; towering pillars of flame rose up all over the place, widening until they united with others to form an ever-expanding sea of raging fire.

The people screaming for help from beneath the collapsed roofs, crowds of burnt people crouching unable to move, and K-san, who did not answer. . . all of them were being incinerated in those roaring and ravenous flames.

The place around Mezame-cho, where Setsuko Nakamura lived, was also in flames. Was she in that fire? She must have been crying and begging for help from inside the crushed house. She might even now be burning alive. "Oh! How sorry I am, Setsuko!" I called the name of my best friend in a choked voice. I learned later that, as I had feared, both she and her mother were burnt to death under their collapsed house. If it had not been for the war, people would not have faced such tragedies. "War! You inhuman devil!" I wanted to yell aloud; "If only we lived in peace!" I wanted to shout. The white rice balls I had been so happy about, so looking forward to, were also gone in the fire. I crouched down to the ground, no longer able to bear watching the blazing hell below.

The young man who had led us here was wiping his sweat with the hairband he had been wearing. I thought that it had been a mark of the red rising sun printed on it, but to my surprise I saw now that it was actually a red bloodstain from an injury to his forehead. "It is nothing serious. It has already stopped bleeding," he said, noticing our surprised looks, and, refolding the cloth in a strip, he tied it tightly around his head again. He told us that he was from Tokyo, as I had suspected from his accent, and that he had been drafted to work at the Nagasaki factory of Mitsubishi Steel Works. He had been working there when the bomb was dropped. This factory stood beside the Mitsubishi Weaponry factory where we had been working. It was a time when the war was reaching a stage of desperate intensity and almost every young man able to fight had been sent to the battlefields. The fact that he was drafted to work in an armament factory in Nagasaki showed, I conjectured, that he was a very important person with a high technical knowledge.

Turning my eyes to the ground, I happened to notice the bodies of dead cicadas lying all about. What a pity! I collected a countless number of them and covered them with sand. The sand felt emptily warm in my palms. While we rested in the grove for about an hour, the greenery and calmness soothed our tortured minds, and gradually we regained our composure. The young man with the hairband, who I will call A-san, persuaded us to leave the grove.

After walking a while we came across a scene so ghastly that our breath caught in our throats. Along the path between the fields lay people with totally burnt bodies, their faces disfigured beyond recognition. More people huddled everywhere, on the sloping banks, in the shade of tall grass, in pits on the ground. They all extended their hands and begged in faint gasping voices, "Water... give me some water, please... " They had escaped this far but seemed to have used up every bit of strength in their search for water. Along the paths and grassy banks silent processions of victims trudged wearily along, staring blankly as if in a trance. They were all practically naked, their exposed skin a dark reddish brown. Patches of burnt skin hung from their hands. The women, whose long hair hung dishevelled over their faces, moved like a funeral procession of somnambulists. One, moving like a phantom, held the charred body of her dead baby tightly in her arms as she followed the others.

Her steps are weak
But strong are the mother's arms
holding her dead little baby.
What are they seeking,
these trudging people?
Processions of red burnt bodies, all in a line,
go on through the grass and along the paths.
With mouths shut, heads sagging, the processions go on.
Their hollow hearts feel no more sorrow, no more pain,
no trace of spirit left in their vacant eyes,
no tears left to shed.
They are just following the people ahead
with feeble steps
not caring where they lead.

Water! Water! Water, please!
Water! Water! Water...
people begging from the roadside,
shaking, worn-out hands extended,
opening the slits of eyes
hidden beneath burnt, swollen lids.

For the people begging for water,
for the people who have lost their souls,
for the people with burnt skin hanging...
at least, for their last hours,
oh clouds, please... cover the glaring sun!
Oh, sun, if you have mercy, please soften your brilliance;
too harsh are your rays on their burnt bodies.

What are these cruel tortures for?
Are these not innocent people, free of blame?

Out of Death I am walking,
out of Death I am running, and pushing through,
holding on to the hope of Life.

Oh, War, what a merciless devil you are! I was filled with wrenching anger at the atrocious war which threw a countless number of people literally into infernal hell. With their clothes blown away by the blast, their near-naked bodies burnt all over, burnt skin hanging from their bodies, the victims were wandering everywhere. "Water, water, please!" they all kept begging, but not a drop of water was given to them, and, with their burnt bodies exposed to the relentless sun, they breathed their last, one after the other. Forty-five years have passed since then, but I still clearly remember the pitiful voices, and the unspeakable plight of these people.

I was not aware where we walked, where we ran, in our flight. We had come down the mountain to a house with a well in front of it. The lady of the house was serving the cold well water to the lucky people who happened to pass by. If only we could take this water back to those who were begging for water to quench their thirst before their death. This thought crossed my mind, but I was not brave enough nor good-hearted enough to go back. I feel sad about it and am ashamed of my heartless weakness at that time, but people were all, including myself, desperate about protecting their own life only, in constant fear of air-raids which might begin again at any moment.

The water was delicious beyond words; it penetrated to every cell of the marrow. But my pleasure was momentary; soon after I drank it, I began to feel nauseous and was unable to walk as before. A-san and Hashimoto-san, who were having no such symptoms, stopped walking and anxiously watched as I knelt on the ground and vomited. I walked a little way and vomited again, and had to repeat this again and again. It became a continuous agony. I lost my mental strength to run; all I could do was silently follow behind them, exercising what little strength I had left.

The busiest section of Nagasaki City was spared destruction because a mountain range extending from Mt. Konpira juts out nearly as far as the middle of the city, and the Nakauma River, which runs through the center of the city, stopped the further expansion of the fire. The house of Hashimoto-san was in Okeya-machi, which was located along the Nakajima River close to the city centre. Her house was right on the street we had been taking. After we parted from Hashimoto-san in front of the gate of her house, I told A-san that I could go back alone, but he kindly told me that he would not just leave me alone, because I was throwing up. How grateful I was for his kindness!

The house I was boarding at was in Junin-machi, which was located in an elevated section of the city with stone-paved streets that wound up the slopes, and numerous flights of stone steps that led to every corner. We took Teramachi-dori, which we thought might be a little safer. My nausea did not stop. I ran and threw up, ran and threw up, along a graveyard there.

Again I heard the buzzing sound of planes coming from the distant sky. I ran, watching the sky, filled with fear that I might again experience that awful blinding flash and the ear-splitting roar. A-san took my hand and we ran desperately, but I had exhausted every bit of energy. I was terribly afraid of the sound of planes, but was completely worn out, with no will-power left to make myself run.

"I just can't run any more. It's all over with me. Leave me here and please go on alone," I said to A-san in a strained voice. I really wished him to do so, but he just stood there watching the distant sky. The buzzing sound was fading away, taking the threat of danger with it. I sat on the grass in the graveyard and kept on vomiting. There was nothing left in my stomach, yet it strained with excruciating spasms to produce a frothy milky liquid. I wanted to lie down right there in the grass, abandon myself to fate. If I had been alone, I would have been so unable to move that I would have spent the night there in the graveyard.

"Now cheer up. We're very close to Junin-machi." A-san pulled me up by the arm, and encouraged me to go on walking. The excruciating spasms were very painful but, in retrospect, throwing up everything in my stomach after drinking the water may have done more good than harm, because it helped to rid my body of contaminated substances.

Mrs. Hirai and Chi-chan will be waiting for me anxiously, I thought. I must make it to the house by any means. Climbing up the long flights of stone steps, helped by A-san, I finally found myself standing, head drooping, at the front door of the house. Mrs. Hirai came dashing out, with Chi-chan close behind her. "Oh, you've come back alive! I've been so worried about you. I would not have known what to tell your parents if something had happened to you, and only my daughter were safe. I've been waiting and waiting for you to come back." She let out in one breath all the anxieties piled heavily on her mind, and burst into tears.

"I'm so sorry I came back alone," cried Chi-chan, putting her arm around my shoulder. A-san stood by silently while we embraced, then spoke. "Please take good care." With just these brief words and a deep bow, he left and disappeared into the darkening dusk. He had not even told me his name. "Thank you very much," was all I could say as he turned away, though my heart was filled with more gratitude than even a million words could express.

In that time of extreme hardship, when people cared about protecting only their own lives, A-san showed me true tenderness and real kindness, coming in and out of my life like a refreshing breeze. He appeared to be twenty-five or -six years old, so he would be in his early seventies now. I hope he is still in good health and living happily somewhere. On August 9th every year I pray for his health and happiness.

Chi-chan, who escaped the calamity because she suddenly returned home from the station, told me that she had had some sort of premonition and could not bring herself to continue on to work that morning. The factory at which she had been working suffered especially heavy damage; a great number of students and workers died there. I shudder at the thought that she might have otherwise been one of them. Mrs. Hirai was a devout Buddhist and never failed to chant sutras in the morning and evening. Both she and her daughter believed that Dainichi Buddha had saved her daughter and myself, and they were therefore offering even more pious prayers.

Half of the kitchen in the house had been destroyed, rendering it useless, so Mrs. Hirai went to the basement of the concrete building next door, which was serving as a refuge, to make some rice gruel. She served it to me along with some pickled ume (Japanese apricot). Although I had not eaten anything since the morning, I had no appetite at all. I tried just a little bit of the gruel, but it brought back the nausea. I then tried a piece of the pickled ume and found that its salty sourness appealed to me and refreshed me. I tried another and another, sipping on tea between bites. That was supper for me that day, and for the next few days as my stomach accepted nothing else. I believe pickled ume saved my life. That night we went to the shelter of a relative of Mrs. Hirai, near Kassenba.

THE NIGHT IN THE SHELTER

All through the night, the rising flames seared the skyline; the scarlet red sky over Uragami blazed as bright as day. Loud booming sounds occasionally echoed in the night air as gas tanks exploded. The fires, burning all night and all day, reduced to ashes all of Nagasaki City north of the dividing Nakajima River.

Mrs. Hirai's house at Junin-machi stood on a cliff with nothing hindering a panoramic view. Therefore it also had nothing to protect it from direct exposure to the devastating power of the blast, which left it in a miserable state, practically on the verge ,of collapse. All the windows which had faced northeast towards Nagasaki City were smashed into fragments, panes, frames, and all. The eaves were tilted; my desk was crushed beyond repair, under a fallen pillar. The only thing salvageable was my rucksack. Every time the air-raid warning siren had sounded, I had strapped it over my shoulders before running for shelter. It now lay undamaged in a corner of the closet.

The Nakajima River would prevent the fire from spreading beyond it over to Junin-machi, we thought, yet we were evacuated. Fortunately, my nausea had at long last subsided. Through the silent darkness I laboured to follow Mrs. Hirai and Chi-chan along deserted streets. Down sloping stone-paved roads I panted, dragging my heavy painful feet, the rucksack on my back. The building of Kaisei Middle School, silhouetted against the slate-gray sky, high on a little hilltop, seemed serenely nonchalant, as if nothing had happened today.

We arrived at last at the shelter of Mrs. Hirai's relative, near Kassenba. The small shelter was packed full; people were lying without enough room to properly stretch their legs. Three of us made the place even more crowded. I could not complain, of course; I felt sorry that I was making it more uncomfortable for the others.

Although I was utterly exhausted, physically and mentally, I was too agitated to sleep. The horrible scenes of the day, the indescribable carnage, were kaleidoscoping around in my mind and I feared that were I to fall asleep, these scenes would haunt my dreams. Unable to sleep, I walked out of the shelter.

It was the middle of summer, yet the winds at midnight felt refreshingly cool. The little stars twinkling in the western sky over my native Goto Islands kindled within me a yearning for home. Grandmother, parents, sisters... what were they doing now? Were they sleeping without knowing what had happened? Or were they in a state of confusion at the news that Nagasaki was almost annihilated by an extraordinary bomb? I wished I could inform them of my being safe and alive. It was, of course, an impossibility.

I noticed that I was still in my torn, bloodstained blouse and shredded monpe. From my rucksack I took clean clothes and in the darkness changed into them. I threw away the clothes soiled with blood, sweat and dirt, pushing them deep into the bush by the stone wall.

Neither Mrs. Hirai, nor Chi-chan, nor their relatives came out of the shelter. I did not know whether they were asleep or lying sleepless. I was all alone in the darkness, wide awake, lost in thought, gazing up alternately at the red sky over Uragami and the western sky in the direction of my hometown.

"I have survived. I'm glad I'm alive," I reassured myself about my existence. I felt the joy of being alive gushing out of my heart, although I knew quite well that it was not an appropriate time for joy, since a huge number of people had perished. At the same time various worrying thoughts passed through my mind. What would become of Japan? How long would I have to live in this shelter at Kassenba? We would most certainly lose the war. Then what would happen? How many days more would we live in restless suspension? I also felt sorry that I was being such a burden for Mrs. Hirai and Chi-chan.

But nothing could be done about that. There was not even a slim chance that the boat service to the Goto Islands was in operation under such extraordinary circumstances. I was feeling joy, resignation, uneasiness, and impatience as the awful scenes kept turning around in my mind.

It was quiet, except for the occasional roaring sounds of explosions piercing the stillness. These exploding gas tanks sounded symbolically like the ominous signals of a long funeral march. For the first time that August, no air-raid warning sirens were heard that night. Despite the desolate silence, the city of Nagasaki was in anguished turmoil. The scarlet of the distant sky was expanding toward us, as the fire spread nearer and nearer, gathering greater force as it went. It was a night almost as bright as day, a very long night.

IN THE BRIGHT SUNSHINE
Since that day we have had no more air raids. No buzzing sounds of airplanes have been heard in the sky over Nagasaki. From our refuge on the hill of Kassenba, we greeted the dawning of the third day after the terrible explosion.

My braided hair, left as it had been on the day of the disaster, had hardened tight with blood and sweat and dirt. The foul smell from my unclean body made me almost sick. Every part of my body, bruised by the things that had fallen on it, ached so much that I could hardly move. I decided that I had better get a medical examination at a hospital. Leaving the shelter, I began walking step by step down the hill of Kassenba along the sloping road which was made alternately of stone paving and stairs of stone. At every step a cry of pain escaped through my clenched teeth, but I went on in the summer heat, exerting myself to the utmost.

Finally I reached the hospital at the foot of the hill, but I found it packed with people suffering from horrible burns and injuries. Groans of agony filled the air. People injured beyond any possible treatment were lying about everywhere like lifeless objects. An offensive odour stung my nose. The sight was so horrible, so shocking, so painful that I could barely stand to look at it.

Compared with their serious injuries, my suffering was minor. I was luckily in the middle of a large factory at the time of the explosion, so was not directly exposed to the initial radiation of the bomb. Besides, being buried under the rubble, unable to go out immediately after the explosion, it was quite a while later that I went out of the building. This was good for me because I was exposed to less of the residual radiation.

After a while members of the Women's Association began to hand out rice balls, carrying them in a wide wooden box. They were the pure white rice balls, the same as those I missed so much—those taken away by the cruel fires. They were moving to and fro in front of me, shining silver-white.

Hand after hand reached out, scrambling for them. It was a sad pitiful sight, people groveling for food. There was no human dignity, no compassion, no generosity, no warm-heartedness, no tenderness. There was only egoistic, shameless audacity. I saw war had changed even the human heart, depleting it of its warmth, to replace it with intensified desires. "Wow! Rice balls!" I cried from my heart, extending my hands. But it was too late. The box was already empty. How miserable I felt. When I recall the meanness of myself at that time, I cannot help giving a wry smile. But I was only human.

I had been waiting patiently for about two hours when I decided that I could no longer stand waiting there and that I had better give up getting any treatment and go back. I began walking up the long stone steps, dragging my legs. On the way I dropped by at my deserted old residence.

It was actually a large stone house accommodating three families, and I had been living with Mrs. Hirai and Chi-chan in a suite on the east side of the main building where the landlord's family lived. There was another building on the south, occupied by another family, extending from our suite and facing the main building. A hallway connecting the south building and our suite was our vestibule. The sliding doors to the half-collapsed main building were left open. The key would not work on the broken doors, I thought.

I sat in the hallway, reflecting on various things. How frustrating it was to have pain in every part of the body and not to be able to move about as I liked! When would it be that I would become able to move about freely as before? It would be only a matter of time before we would lose the war. Then what would happen, to Japan and to me, to my life? I had been thinking about the same things over and over again since that fateful day. But it was just asking unanswerable questions of myself.

I kept on thinking, staring blankly into space, until I got tired of thinking any more. I stopped, and just looked vacantly at the kitchen of the landlord's house, which was exposed to view through the open doors. A row of kitchen furnaces in the unfloored section of the kitchen . . . the iron pots on the furnaces . . . the well right in front of my eyes! Looking at these things, I hit upon a wonderful idea. There was plenty of water in the well. There was a tub, too. Pieces of broken wood from the damaged house were scattered around all over. They were just right for firewood. Besides, as if everything had been arranged, there was a box of matches right beside the furnaces. There is nobody around; the houses around here are all empty. Why not take a bath in the tub, heating water in one of these big pots? It was a wonderful, somewhat wild, idea.

In the broad summer daylight, in the unfloored kitchen of the house that did not belong to her, a girl of sixteen was going to take a bath in the tub. Was it because my sense of modesty was paralyzed by the extreme confusion brought on by the atomic bomb? Or was it human wisdom in me, who had been brought up freely in the country where everything is true to nature, to adapt myself to the surroundings? I felt no sense of sin at all.

The sound of water splashing at the brim of the tub gave me the greatest relief. I felt an exquisite pleasure when I dipped my whole hair in the warm water. Lavishing the water, splashing it all over, I washed my hair again and again. I scrubbed my whole body painfully hard to cleanse it of all the loathsome filth of the bomb. The water running down my neck, chest, and back made me feel really good, so good and refreshed that my usual vigor gradually returned. Breezes coming in through the open glassless window played with my long hair, now soft and smooth. The brilliant rays of the sun coming through the window pouring over my body made me realize my nakedness. I stooped down out of shame.

The extraordinary happenings of the past few days had made me lose the sense of shyness typical of young girls. The gentleness of the great sun brought it back to me. A sense of human decency was restored to my shattered heart. At the same time, having washed away all the hideous filth from my body, I felt really refreshed and at ease both physically and mentally. It even felt as though the pain in my body had been somewhat alleviated. I was enjoying alone a luxurious moment of peace, completely oblivious to the grim reality of war. The poignant realization that I was alive came to my mind. I am alive, I am alive, I said to myself again and again in the bright sunlight. I also told myself that I must stay alive no matter what might happen.

LIKE A REFRESHING BREEZE
Life in the shelter at Kassenba was calm and peaceful, in complete contrast to the devastation of the city. It was a different world, with no information reaching us. I was gradually getting over the nightmarish experience, and the routine work in the noisy factory surrounded by the rugged, black machines was becoming a thing of the past. There was a lot of greenery around the shelter. Leaves fluttered and quivered; tall blades of summer grass rustled in the breeze. The little twigs chatting with each other in a soft voice consoled my lonely empty heart.

It would be nice to run about over the field in the bright sunshine. What would it be like to take a nap in the cool shade of the green trees? Such thoughts came up in my mind occasionally, but they were impractical thoughts for me. It was all I could manage to do to drag my aching body in and out of the shelter like a poor little mole. I whiled away my time, doing nothing in particular.

On the afternoon of the fourth day of my life in the shelter, Chi-chan called me from outside. "Takeno-san, you have a visitor, the young man who saw you home the other day."

I was almost too surprised to believe my ears. I ran out of the shelter, trying hard not to show my surprise. There I found none other than that same young man standing there, a broad smile on his face. The young man who had led Hashimoto-san and me out of those incredible scenes of devastation. The young man who was kind enough to see me to my boarding house, who held my hand and encouraged me when I was feeling too nauseous to go on. I was so dismayed by this totally unexpected visit that I was unable to utter any word. All I could manage to do was bob a quick bow.

"How are you feeling now? Have you stopped throwing up? I dropped by because I had an anxious feeling that you might still be in that terrible condition. I first went to your boarding house and found the little note at the entrance which gave the address here."

The masculine face, now wearing a patch of white gauze instead of the hairband with a round bloodstain, smiled again. I was too dismayed to know what to do at first, but as I recovered from the initial shock, I politely expressed my thanks, pretending self-composure.

"May I have your name, please?" I asked. "Well, that's not important. I am relieved to see you are fine." With this, he was already leaving. When we exchanged deep bows, I managed to catch a quick glimpse of his name written in sumi (Japanese ink) on his white canvas shoes. It said, "Honda."

I have never forgotten that name. So he is called Mr. Honda, I said to myself, and muttered his name again and again trying to engrave it in my memory. It was the last I saw of him. His visit was like a cool and serene breeze moving over the earth in the summer heat. He appeared in front of me all of a sudden, and a moment later was completely gone. How naive and childish I was then! I could not even ask him where he lived; asking his name was all I could do. His face appears in my thoughts every time August 9th comes around, every time I recollect the tragedy of the atomic bomb. As we say, "Ichigo ichie (every occasion of meeting someone is a special occasion that never recurs)." An encounter with a person is wonderful but evanescent at the same time. Our lives are indeed a countless repetition of encounters and partings. Each and every encounter and parting is woven into the tapestry which is weaving itself in our minds throughout our lives. Among the dark memories that come to my mind on August 9th every year, the memory of the encounter with Mr. Honda is the only one that continues to shine with unfading beauty. It will remain as a precious treasure in my heart forever.

For a few years after the war, I kept in touch with Hashimoto-san, with whom I fled to the grove in the mountain on that fateful day, but now I do not know her whereabouts. The letter I sent her in care of her parents in Yamaguchi Prefecture twenty-odd years ago, was returned with a tag which gave a new address at Minato Ward in Osaka. I immediately sent a letter to that address, saying that I wanted to see her, but I received no answer. Mrs. Hirai and Chi-chan emigrated to Brazil in 1955, and I have not heard from them since.

A passage from a poem, whose author I do not remember, goes like this:

They came near me and were holding my hands
before I knew it.
But they left and were gone forever before I knew it.

I cannot agree with this more strongly. How I wish I could have a chance to meet Mr. Honda again and to fully express my gratitude! My wish will likely never be fulfilled, yet I have decided that I must repay his profound and selfless kindness through someone else. His sincere and pure heart made an indelible impression upon me. I therefore made it my motto in my daily life to be always "kind and sincere."

PLAYING TAG ON LOGS

Five days had passed since that horrible A-bomb day. I must say I was very lucky that I did not suffer any burns from direct exposure to the extreme heat of the atomic bomb, because I happened to be working inside that building at the time of the explosion. The terrible pain in the whole of my body had abated somewhat, and I was able to walk about with much less difficulty. The injuries to my head, shoulders, neck and legs were also healing naturally. What a strong and tough body I had! I was amazed at the unyielding strength of my own body. Perhaps I owed my physical strength to the natural surroundings in my home town. I spent my childhood just playing out of doors, making a companion of nature, running about in the fields and on the hills, and swimming all day long in summer. This communion with nature in my childhood was a very precious experience for me. I thank my parents for bringing us up freely in natural surroundings.

My home town is a small seaside village called Takasaki on one of the Goto Islands, in the westernmost part of Nagasaki Prefecture about 120 km west of Nagasaki City. It is about 40 km away from Fukue City, the biggest town on our island.

In front of my house extended the white seashore and the deep blue sea. On a moonlit night in early spring, the sea would be packed with schools of kibinago, a kind of sardine.

Once caught, these fish were first boiled, then dried in the sun on racks made of bamboo. Rows and rows of these racks lined the seashore and roadsides near the shore. In the peak season, hundreds of thousands of boiled kibinago lay packed on the nets placed over the racks. When it was off-season, however, the bamboo racks were all taken off the frames below and stored away safe from exposure to the elements. What was left behind was a checkerboard of frames, made of logs which were from 15 to 20 cm in diameter, about a metre apart from each other.

These logs provided a lot of fun for children when I was a little girl. On them we, girls and boys together, played tag. We ran about barefoot on the logs, jumping from one log to another with loud shouts of joy. Sometimes we slipped and fell off a log, inevitably resulting in skinned, or even bleeding, knees. We would make nothing of it and keep on playing. Our parents, knowing that it could involve more serious injury, scolded us severely every time they caught us playing on the logs. This only added more thrill to the game, and we went on playing whenever we thought we were safe from our parents' watch.

Who could have known that the experience of this rough game in my childhood would turn out to be of crucial help to me later in my life? When I had finally extricated myself from the hellish wreckage of the factory buildings, only to find the lower half of the stairs blown off, I had to make the decision to jump over to a swinging log nearby, from the top platform of the stairs. It was the only way down, but what helped me muster up that courage to jump, more than anything else, was the experience of playing on logs in my childhood.

From what I heard later, one of my schoolmates, O-san, who was working in the same factory building, managed to get herself out of the debris safely, but then she jumped off to the lower floor through the crane hole, dying on the spot. The safety fence must have been blown away like a feather by that awful blast. O-san had been a calm, self-composed intellectual, the last person one would expect to do such a reckless thing. Possibly she became desperate when she found the stairs blown off and hanging loose. In an extreme situation, human beings may lose not only the power to reason, but also their intuition. She too was a victim of the atomic bomb, the worst demon in human history, which made no scruples in its mass indiscriminate killing.

RETURNING HOME

"The emperor's announcement will be broadcast at noon today. Everybody is requested to gather around the radio and listen." The voice sounded from the megaphone through the quiet atmosphere on the hill at

Kassenba on the morning of August 15th. At noon we gathered around the radio and listened closely to the broadcast, but the voice was drowned by radio interference. We could not very well make out what it was saying, but we had never heard the emperor's voice before, so we all listened intently, our heads bent down. When it was finished, we looked at each other, our faces serious, trying to comprehend what we had just heard.

After a while, the word "cease-fire" and remarks like, "the war's over," began to spread around. Nobody referred to the word "surrender." "The war is over." How good those words sounded! "The war is over," I repeated to myself again and again, and shed tears of relief at the thought that we would all be safe and could live in peace. But the truth was secretly being whispered by people: we have been defeated in the war, having accepted unconditional surrender. The government avoided the use of the term "surrender" or "defeat" and simply used the word "shu-sen" which meant the "end of war."

It had been in the hope of victory that students from all over the country, under the slogan of full national mobilization, had left their schools to work in the war factories, or even to fight at the front. It had all been for naught, futile before the unbelievable enormity of power shown by the two atomic bombs.

When I knew that we were, in truth, defeated, I was not very surprised or even shocked. Since the day the bomb was dropped, I had been thinking that our losing the war was just a matter of time. The defeat seemed only natural to me. I had even felt anger when I thought that if we would eventually be defeated anyway, why had we not surrendered much earlier, before the atomic bombs were dropped on Hiroshima and Nagasaki? (I understand now that this question involves intricate problems, both military and political.)

On the morning of the third day since the end of the war, although I still had pain in various parts of my body, I went down to the wharf to get information about ships to the Goto Islands. The sound of waves slapping against the floating pier, and the smell of the sea, made me feel so good, kindling within me a yearning for home. At the wharf I chanced to meet H-san from Kashiwago, a town close to my home town, and she told me that a ship was soon leaving for the Goto Islands. What good news! I was so happy that I wanted to dance about. Beyond this vast stretch of sea lies my home town. I am going back to my home town! These thoughts caused my elation to grow.

I went in high spirits to my boarding house, where Mrs. Hirai and Chi-chan were busily cleaning up the wreckage of the house. I felt sorry for not being able to help them, but if I missed this chance, I might have to wait indefinitely for the next ship. I shouldered my rucksack, which had already been packed, hurried back to the wharf, and got on board a very crowded motor-powered sailing boat. Standing on the deck, I enjoyed the refreshing sea breeze. I looked up to the sky and inhaled it to my heart's content. All the faces on board were beaming with the joy of home-coming.

Soon after the ship left the pier, I noticed a girl of about my age clad only in a slip, lying in the crowd of people. She seemed injured and un-able to walk. How embarrassing for her to be helplessly lying there in her undergarment, in full view of everyone. I heard she had been exposed to the atomic bomb at Mitsubishi Weaponry, where she had been drafted to work. She was so badly injured that she had had to be carried aboard by other passengers.

Remembering the true kindness I had received from A-san during my frantic escape from the disaster, I wanted to repay at least a fraction of his kindness through this girl. Fortunately I had an extra monpe and a blouse in my rucksack. I took them out quickly and handed them to her, saying, "If you don't mind wearing these, please go ahead and put them on." She just nodded, but her eyes, which had been expressionless, were shin-ing with tears. "How lucky you are to have survived this severe wound," I said to her. "Thank you, thank you," she repeated again and again in a weak, barely audible voice. She must have been very glad; however, the whiteness of her face remained impassive.

Under the boundless blue sky, the ship kept on sailing over the endless calm stretch of deep blue sea, leaving behind a long white wake. "The war is over, I am alive, and I am now returning home." I found myself saying the same thing again. With a smile on my face, I stood on the deck as if in a trance, enjoying the cold and refreshing sea breeze. If I had wings, I would fly high up in the sky; I would fly to my home as quickly as possible to see my parents, my grandmother and sisters.

A few hours must have passed; a countless number of islands began to appear in the dim distance. We were approaching the Goto Islands! Be-fore long, the ship was sailing almost majestically along the steep precipice of a rocky island. The peaceful droning of cicadas reached the deck of the ship. We soon arrived at Tomie, one of the major towns of Fukue Island, the largest of the Goto Islands. The girl with the white face got off there, helped by other passengers. She nodded a sad, smiling ap-preciation to me as she left the ship. May she get well soon, I prayed in my heart. What has become of her? Did she recover well enough to get married? Every time August 9 comes around I cannot help remembering her with these questions.

When the evening sun was about to set below the mountains, lighting the skies with a red glow, the ship finally arrived at Miiraku Port, which was on the other side of the island from Tomie. My house was four km away. After disembarking, I was resting near the port, when I was surprised to see my mother rushing breathlessly towards me. I had asked one of the passengers who got off at Tomie to inform my uncle who lived there that I would be arriving safely at Miiraku. It seemed my uncle had sent the message of my arrival to my mother. What thoughts had been going through her mind as she ran those four kilometres on a hot summer evening?

"Oh... you... safe... " The rest of the words were drowned by tears, which kept running down her cheeks. She just cried, as she held a bag containing rice balls in her arm. What would the pleasure of a mother be like who, nine long days after the atomic bombing, finally ascertains for herself the safety of her daughter?

I cried, too. Like an infant, I cried and cried. The moment I saw her, tears came gushing out and kept on running without stopping. My heart was crammed with emotions, and I cried as if to pour out all of them on my mother. The long agony I suffered, the loneliness, the sadness, and the joy of being alive...

And at long last, my hand got hold of a rice ball. It was not one made of pure white rice, but a large, round one mixed with barley. She must have made it with almost uncontrollable impatience to see me again. Leaning against a stone wall, I had a large bite of it, my tears flavouring it as they fell. The delicious salty taste spread over my palate, penetrating right to my heart. "This is so good!" I laughed, as tears still trickled down. Her eyes glistening with her own tears, my mother looked at the laughter on my tear-stained face and nodded contentedly. Though this was a brownish rice ball mixed with barley, not at all like the ones I had missed twice on previous occasions, it was far more precious. It contained the essence of the love and gentleness of my mother. It was the taste I had been missing so long, the taste of my mother, of my good old home town.

After a while, my uncle from Kishiue arrived with a cart pulled by a cow. My mother must have asked him for this. In those days buses and taxis were very scarce on this remote island. People, therefore, did not mind walking long distances of even more than 16 kilometres, and for the sick the cart pulled by a cow was the only vehicle available. I rode on the cart, which bumped its way over a rugged road, making a loud rattling sound, leaving behind clouds of sand dust.

The faint lights of my house came into sight. My two younger sisters were already dashing towards us, splashing the sand up behind them. They had been waiting impatiently for my arrival, looking out from the veranda for the first sign of our approach along the dusky road extending beyond the sandy beach.

"Mi-chan!" They called me by my old nickname, shouting excitedly.

At the gate stood my father, and with him, my grandmother, stretching her crooked spine as straight as possible as she leaned on her cane. "I'm so happy you're back safe. I couldn't be happier." Blinking her tear-filled old eyes, she looked like happiness itself. "I'm glad you're safe, I'm really glad. We have prepared a special dinner to celebrate your safe return," greeted my father. Joy was written all over his face, although he was ordinarily taciturn, seldom showing his emotions.

Just as he had said, a special dinner was waiting for me at the table, a big platter piled high with fresh sashimi (sliced raw fish) and all the other delicacies from both sea and land. Everything was so delicious. I could sense my stomach's astonishment at the sudden influx of all the good food of my home town.

I could hear the incessant sound of the waves washing back and forth on the shore. It was the soft whisper of my home town sea, which I had not heard for a year and a half. The wind, the trees, the grass, the white beach, the waves... everything greeted me gently, embraced me warmly.

Takuboku Ishikawa, a famous Japanese poet, wrote in one of his poems:

> What can need saying before the mountains in the old
> homeland?
> What can be so soothing, so consoling, as they?

Yes indeed, there is nothing like home. I just wanted to sleep day after day, in the sweet lullaby of the sea, surrounded by beautiful nature, and protected by the love of my whole family.

CLINGING TIGHTLY TO LIFE
Ten days had passed since my homecoming. Awakened by the cheery chirping of birds, I raised my head from my pillow to look at the white beach and blue sea which stretched from just beyond the veranda. The doors standing open to allow the cool sea breeze in at night seemed to symbolize the peacefulness of country life. I watched the sun rising from behind an island, its glittering light reflected by the morning sea, causing the white beach to shine like polished silver.

Not a sound could be heard in the house. My mother went out early every morning to search in the mountains for medicinal herbs. My physical condition had started to deteriorate about a week after I came home. I ran a fever, my body felt totally lethargic, I had no appetite, and nausea and diarrhea plagued me.

My two little sisters were fast asleep beside me as if it were the middle of the night. They were young, still in elementary school. I could hear my father turning over on his futon, sighing. He was surely awake. Although he spoke very little, I knew he was worrying about me. My heart could feel his anxiety.

We were a family of eight. I had an older brother, two older sisters, and two younger sisters. My brother, who had gone to the front, had sent us a postcard towards the end of last year, posted from Kanoya Air Base in Kagoshima Prefecture, but we had not heard from him since. (He returned safe late in the fall of 1945.)

My oldest sister was married and lived in a little village in Kamigoto. She was now very busy raising five children. Two of her brothers-in-law were killed in battle, and her youngest brother-in-law died in the A-bomb tragedy at Nagasaki. His body was never recovered. He was my age. Who could imagine the grief of a mother who had lost three sons in the war? But she was not alone; she was just one of the hundreds of thousands who were suffering the same grief all over the country. My other older sister had been drafted to work at an airfield at Kawatana, about 32 kilometres north of Nagasaki, and she had not returned home yet. My grandmother, who lived in seclusion on top of a hill, came down several times a day to check my condition, supporting her bent body with a cane. Sometimes she came with her cane in her right hand, while in her left dangled a pot containing a fish cooked with soy sauce. She knew that a fresh fish, cooked sweet and sour, by her, was my favourite food.

Mother, while of course deeply concerned about the well-being of my brother and sisters, devoted herself to looking after me. She gathered information on the treatment of radiation sickness. "There's some kind of strange poison in the bodies of those who were exposed to that bomb, they say. To get that poison out of your body you have to drink the decoction of various herbs," she told me.

Each morning, she faithfully collected the herbs: dokudami, gennoshoko, persimmon leaves, and more. She carefully boiled each of them over a mild fire for hours. Each blackish-brown decoction had its own strong odor and every one of them had a bitter taste. The decoction of dokudami had an especially bitter taste, and the foulest smell, and I had great difficulty drinking it. But my mother would look really relieved when I drank that, so I'd pinch my nose and gulp it down with a tremendous effort, just to see that expression on her face.

Her strong determination to make me well as soon as possible seemed to prompt her to try every cure available. "Without nutrition, you cannot cure any disease. Go ahead and drink it." She urged me to drink a fresh raw egg one morning. I closed my eyes and gave it a try, but the slimy object passing down my throat nauseated me, and I threw it up. Ever since then I have been unable to eat eggs unless they are cooked well.

Days passed with no signs of improvement in my condition. One day I found red spots appearing all over my body. "Mother, what do you think these red spots are?" I asked her, showing her my arm. "Must be flea bites, I think." "But aren't they too big and too many for flea bites?" She turned her face away without answering. Her sad hesitant look stopped me from asking any more about it. She had often gone out collecting information about A-bomb survivors, and must have known something about this symptom of red spots. She just could not bear to look at them appearing on her own daughter. Fortunately the red spots went away before long, but a slight fever and the lack of appetite persisted.

It was already September. I became impatient with the lack of improvement in my condition. How long would it be before I got well? Mother was busy as ever collecting various herbs from all different places, making decoctions for me every day. We had no doctors in our village and the herbs were the only treatment to which we could resort. As a result, my whole body began to smell of decoctions. Lying on my futon, I stretched my arms up and looked at them. They had always been thin as if from malnutrition, but I found them getting even thinner. I gently rubbed each of them, feeling pity for myself. I tried sitting up on my futon, or even standing on it, but my heart began thumping violently, and I had to lie down again in less than a minute. The war was over. I had survived it, and had shed my tears of relief. There were no more air raids; no longer did I work at a war factory, and I was here back home. Yet I was confined to bed, unable to move about. My heart was filled with self-pity and bitter sadness.

I had been confined to bed for days when a new, terrible symptom began. My hair began to fall out in surprising quantities. I did not want Mother to notice it, and did my best to hide it from her. "I'm not frightened at all. Nothing can frighten me. I crawled out of that hell on my own. I will never die. I will never lose this battle." I kept telling myself this, and never allowed myself to become disheartened.

The fateful summer was about to be over. Wind swept across the corn field behind the house, and faded dry leaves, which had been soft and fresh some time ago, rustled and fluttered about in the wind. I could feel the coming of autumn in the sound they made. From my futon I watched the sky, serenely emerald as it typically was in the fall. A feeling of bitter sadness welled up from within me, and tears coursed down my cheeks.

The second term of school should have started at the beginning of September, but I had heard nothing from them, perhaps due to the confusion after the war. The sound of the wind made me almost unbearably sad.

Towards the end of September, my fever finally began to come down and there were visible signs of recovery. I owed it to my mother's devoted care, and perhaps to her decoctions, and also to my own good fortune. I still had dizziness and palpitations when I tried walking, but I kept on trying hard to strengthen my weakened body by walking around the house, little by little. The unyielding will to get well works better than any medicine or treatment. I kept on walking, saying to myself, "I will get well, I will get well." I walked on the sandy beach and stood barefoot at the water's edge. The water came swiftly and wet my feet, then retreated to the sea, taking the sand from under my feet with a tickling sensation on the soles of my feet. I squatted down and picked up shells of different shapes and colours. They soothed my heart.

I was gradually getting stronger. One day I decided to visit S-san, one of my elementary school classmates who apparently was still lying in bed suffering from radiation sickness. I walked slowly about a kilometre on a road alongside the sea to her house. She was a student at Nagasaki's M Girls' High School, and at the time of the A-bomb explosion, was working at Ohashi Factory of Mitsubishi Weaponry, which was closer to the hypocentre than Morimachi Factory. She was said to have been one of the very few who had miraculously survived. I found her alone in her house, which was surrounded by trees rustling noisily in the strong wind. She was lying in her futon, her head completely covered by a scarf.

"You are lucky, Mi-chan. You have some hair left. I have not a single hair left on my head," she said enviously, looking at my thin hair. In a single impulsive movement, she took off the cloth covering her head. She was as bald as an egg, and looked like a Buddhist nun. No, a nun's head would have looked better, with a glossy complexion. The skin of her head looked gloomy and unhealthy, totally unlike the skin of a young girl of sixteen. I perceived in her mournful, stern look her grief at having been deprived entirely of her black hair, symbol of female beauty. I saw in her eyes a cursing condemnation of the inexcusable cruelty of the atomic bomb.

I had visited her, urged by an impulse of wanting to console and to also be consoled. As they say, misery loves company. But now I regretted coming. If I had had no hair left on my head like her, I could have been able to console her, but as it was, I made her feel even more miserable. "Oh, God, please restore her hair as it was before," I prayed silently from the bottom of my heart, and with heavy dragging footsteps, I left her house.

The wind was howling over the sea; it sounded like a wailing of the god of winds. The East China Sea, which is usually calm and serene, gets very rough and wild once a wind rises. The raging billows were now smashing against the dark rocks, breaking into white foaming splashes. "Blow, wind, as you will! Blow the clouds away, break the waves into pieces! I don't care if the earth screams. I will live, all the same. I will never be defeated!'' I shouted in my heart, as the relentless wind dishevelled my thinned hair.

I'll see you again when you have recovered, I had said to S-san when parting, but forty-five years have gone by without the fulfilment of that promise. We have, however, kept in touch with each other by occasional letters. She did pull through and, though not strong, she became healthy enough to get married and have two children.

Towards the end of 1983, a postcard arrived without the sender's name on it. It was a notice of moving, with a new address in Tokyo and a telephone number written on it. I was curious to know who the careless sender was, and dialed the number. To my great surprise, it was none other than S-san who answered the call. We talked for the first time in almost forty years. I was so moved at hearing her voice once more, that I could not hold back my tears. ''I thought I would die time and time again,'' said her weak voice. I sensed her anxiety and distress over the phone.

It is the anxiety shared by all the atomic bomb survivors. We are not freed from it until we die. Every day is lived in constant fear of another new radiation sickness. At the slightest sign of anything unusual in our physical condition, we get frightened, and fear that it may have something to do with the A-bomb radiation. It is my sincere wish that nobody else will ever suffer the fear we have been suffering, that we shall be the first and last people to know this constant anxiety.

Since that unexpected talk with S-san over the phone, I have been wanting to go to Tokyo and talk with her to my heart's content, but I have been unable to realize this wish.

My home town was a very small village in a remote corner of the island, yet the atomic bomb reached out its evil hand to many of our families, bringing indescribable misery to them. One of them was the family of Mr. M, a close friend and classmate of my brother. After graduating from Goto Middle School, he had become an officer of Nagasaki Prefectural Police and was working hard as a promising young officer. He was a pride to his family with a potentially great future, but the A-bomb destroyed everything. It annihilated even his dead body. I can never forget the mourning of his family, nor can I forget the youthful face of Mr. M.

Soon after my visit to S-san, I received a notice from my school, saying that school would open in October, one month later than usual. I did not feel strong enough to attend, so I decided to stay home one more month to build up my physical strength. My appetite increased remarkably and I began to eat a surprising amount of food. Although we had no white rice, we were never short of food. We had barley, sweet potatoes, vegetables, fresh fish, and more in abundance. And of course, we had plenty of pickled ume, which I ate at every meal.

These fresh foods and the extra month of rest helped me make a remarkable recovery, and I went back to my boarding home in Nagasaki at the end of October. Mrs. Hirai and Chi-chan greeted me warmly. Despite the heavy damage it had sustained, the house had already been repaired. Reconstruction work was well under way all around the city. People were rising up from despair and misery. Looking at them working busily, I was moved by their strength.

On the last day of October, I went to school for the first time in many months. Our school was in Nishiyama-cho, on the southeast side of Mt. Konpira. Since it stood near the edge of the mountain, it had been protected from serious damage. The four-story, cream-coloured building presented its usual calm appearance and quiet atmosphere. The green leaves of the phoenix trees planted by the front porch were as beautiful as ever, and the huge pine tree on the left of the front gate towered as high as it always had, with its long needles stirring in the breeze.

I was heading for my classroom, when I was taken aback by the sight of C-san, who had been sitting on my left when the A-bomb fell. She seemed to have noticed me first and had given a cry of surprise. "Oh, you're alive!" She must have thought that I had died under the debris. I wanted to ask her what it was like immediately after the explosion, but she walked away in an unfriendly manner, without saying anything else. This has always puzzled me.

In Nagasaki there were a number of Mitsubishi-affiliated war factories, to which third- and fourth-year students, and postgraduates, had been drafted to work. Although the exact number was not known, I was told that about three hundred students from our school died, including first- and second-year students who were exempt from factory work. I felt the ache in my heart increase as I remembered, one by one, the many familiar faces which were never to be seen again.

Even now I occasionally sing to myself the dirge which the surviving students sang, all in tears, at the memorial ceremony held at our school:

> Spring flowers, autumn tints yearly,
> come back again.
> Where have you gone, all dearly beloved?
> We cry and cry for you in vain.
> Deep is our sorrow for you, teachers and friends.
> May this mourning reach you in heaven.

Forty-five years have passed since I first tearfully sang this song, and I still cannot sing it without tears in my eyes. The old sorrow reappears in my mind as if it all had happened only yesterday.

I do not know whether it was mere good luck, or divine providence, or the protection of Buddha that I narrowly escaped death. But it is a life saved almost miraculously when tens of thousands were lost. It is a very special life, only one, and irreplaceable. I can never, never make light of it. It is of the utmost importance to me to continue living no matter what happens. With this conviction in mind, I have been living till now, making the most of every single day. And I will be living this way throughout my life.

POSTSCRIPT

"It's been almost forty years since that bomb... I just can't see why you waited so long," wrote a reader wonderingly in response to my first book, *The Epitaph in My Heart,* published in Japanese in 1984. It was a legitimate question. For all those years I had been wanting to write about my A-bomb experience, to bear witness to the devastation caused by one of the two nuclear bombings which were unprecedented in human history. I had thought it my duty to hand down my experience to coming generations. Yet, I had to wait that long. Why? The fact that I was just an ordinary housewife who was not at all accustomed to writing was certainly one reason, but not the main one. The main reason, I must confess, was fear—the fear of being known to the public as an A-bomb survivor. Concern for my two young daughters had prevented me from surmounting that fear. I had been unable to dispel an anxiety that if they should be known to be daughters of an A-bomb survivor, they might be handicapped in finding husbands, especially if they were to marry through our old Japanese system of arrangement. This fear and anxiety, I found later, was something shared by all my surviving school classmates. Indeed, most of the survivors have chosen to keep silent about their experience, fearing possible discrimination, and I remained just one of them until my two daughters got married.

Despite the long procrastination before actually setting down my A-bomb experience in writing, I never felt that the potential usefulness of such an account had diminished, for the nuclear threat has continued to exist. The nuclear nations have yet to learn the lesson from Hiroshima and Nagasaki.

It was not an easy task for me to write the story, because it involved not only technical difficulties arising from my amateurism, but also the emotional difficulty coming from having to relive the anguish of the most terrible experience of my life. Time and time again I had to put down my pen as I, overcome by heart-aching sorrow and irrepressible indignation, shed countless tears. But I continued on as if urged by the unheard voices of A-bomb victims. I kept telling myself it was my duty to speak out for them and for those who were still afflicted with various radiation aftereffects. My book came out in Japan on the thirty-ninth anniversary of the dropping of the Nagasaki atomic bomb.

Mitsue Kubo, 1986, seated left.

Looking back upon the past forty-five years, I consider myself lucky among A-bomb survivors. After graduating from high school in March, 1946, I returned home to the Goto Islands. I took a year's rest to regain my full strength and then started to teach at my old elementary school. I taught there for four years, during which time I met my present husband. We married in 1952 and have raised three children, two daughters, now both teachers and married to teachers, and a son still unmarried. (I will never feel true relief until he marries.)

Like all the other A-bomb survivors, I have been living in constant fear of developing some kind of radiation disease, but so far I have been lucky enough to have no major health problem. Recently, however, I have begun to experience occasional severe backache, especially when I am tense in front of a large audience. The pain becomes so acute that I can hardly breathe. It goes away when I sit still on a chair for a few minutes, but an anxiety hovers in my mind that if it were to become aggravated or happen more frequently, my backbone might shatter, because I hear A-bomb survivors have very brittle bones. But I do not let that worry me too much. I have always made it a point to take a positive attitude towards life. When

Mitsue Kubo speaking in 1986 at a meeting in Tokyo opposing nuclear war.

I think of the tens of thousands of A-bomb victims, I simply cannot make light of even a single day of my precious life.

I currently belong to the Confederation of A-bomb Sufferers Organizations at Nishinomiya and am actively involved in various peace activities. I have availed myself of as many opportunities as possible to share my A-bomb experience with other people, especially those who belong to the postwar generation. I have shared it with young children, too, at several elementary schools. I am always impressed with their earnest attitude when they listen to my speech. It is my sincere wish that through my humble activities I can contribute to the rousing of greater concern among more people over the issues of world peace and nuclear disarmament.

Dr. Dorothy M. Goresky

CHAPTER 3
Lanterns for Peace

DR. DOROTHY M. GORESKY

The six-year-old stood fascinated as light streaked across the desert sky.
"What's that?" he queried.
"It's a missile," answered his father.
His parents' conversation about missiles and the weapons they could bear whirled around the boy as the Nevada night-time sky continued to be

Dorothy M. Goresky received her B.A. degree from the University of Saskatchewan, and her M.D. degree from the University of Alberta. Her professional career was devoted to family practice of medicine, first in Saskatchewan, then at the Burnaby, B.C., Metropolitan Health Centre, and finally for 23 years at the University of British Columbia Student Health Service, as the first woman physician there. Her major interests were in non-organic illnesses, and in introducing and developing stress management classes for students, and also for the larger community.

Dr. Goresky was the Founding President of the B.C. Chapter of Canadian Physicians for the Prevention of Nuclear War (CPPNW) from 1982 to 1984, a member of the National Board of Directors of CPPNW from 1982 to 1988, and National President of CPPNW from 1984 to 1986. She was a Canadian delegate to the 1983 and 1987 International Congresses of International Physicians for the Prevention of Nuclear War (IPPNW).

Dorothy Goresky retired early in 1988 in order to devote more time to community activities, including teaching English as a Second Language, and to continuing activity with CPPNW. She is a former and present Board member of the Unitarian Church of Vancouver. She has four children and three grandchildren.

lit by the man-made objects. Then quietly and thoughtfully his words intervened. "Isn't it great that Grandma's doing something about it?"*

Early in the life of the North American Physicians' anti-nuclear movement, a similar story was related about primary school children. A teacher asked her class if they were worried there might be a nuclear war. All but one of the children replied that they were. Inquiry of this girl led to her responding that, "No, I'm not afraid because my Mommy and Daddy spend time every week working to see that it doesn't happen."

We cannot shield our children from knowledge of the threats which abound in the world today. We cannot prevent them hearing about the possible annihilation of all life on this planet by nuclear weapons. We *can* protect them from feelings of isolation, helplessness and from fear itself. We *can* provide them with the assurance that those adults who are most important in their lives care enough to do whatever they can to prevent such a catastrophe.

Today I am surrounded by the sights and sounds, the sunlight and shadow, the scents of the Saskatchewan Prairies. I am under the spell which they weave from the memories elicited from my childhood: the changes of seasons, each bearing its own special gifts and its own particular problems to be faced; the changes in weather, each adding to or detracting from anticipated harvests.

Thus Prairie-born and Prairie-bred, I grew with a deep recognition of our dependence on Mother Earth; with a deep sense of the interconnectedness of all life. That recognition is reaffirmed today by the intense job of oneness of the moment. But it was to take nearly half a century for that "seed of knowing" to mature into the fruit of action for peace.

I was 17 when my schoolmates went off to war, some not to return. I was 20 when the dropping of the bombs on Hiroshima and Nagasaki signalled that one need no longer wonder who else would fall victim to the clutches of war. I cannot recall precisely at what age—21, 23?—I first saw films of the devastation wrought upon those unfortunate cities. I *do* recall the false assumption I made at that time that nothing like that could ever possibly happen again, simply because those "in power" would feel the horror which I felt and therefore would be dedicated to ridding the world of all such possibilities.

For 35 years my time was occupied with medical training and practice, with marriage and the raising of four children. The warnings of friends in the sixties and seventies that something must be done about the stockpiles of nuclear weapons fell upon a yet-to-be-awakened mind. That awakening came one November night in 1980.

A group of young doctors returning from a Physicians for Social Re-

* Editor's note: "Grandma" is Dr. Goresky.

sponsibility (PSR) conference on "The Medical Consequences of Nuclear Weapons and Nuclear War" showed footage on the devastation of Hiroshima. This time when I saw that all there was left of the city were its burned-out, rubble-strewn streets and all there was to show that people had ever walked those streets were their shadows on the walls, it was like a physical blow. But even as I was experiencing an overwhelming sense of sadness, I recognized that it was not for people, for my children or for myself; it was for the Earth—the Earth which had nourished me as a child. I knew then, however small a contribution I could make, that I must become dedicated to its preservation. That night I joined with two other physicians to form the Steering Committee of what was to become one of the major chapters of Canadian Physicians for the Prevention of Nuclear War (CPPNW).

Early in CPPNW's life, many of its members recognized that associated with efforts to rid the world of the nuclear threat, there was an equally important task to be confronted. That task was to help bring about a paradigm shift—a change in basic thinking consistent with the building of a world in which life may continue on the planet, and consistent with working toward freedom and justice for all. Such a task has innumerable facets, not the least of which is learning about the ways of other societies in the world and how to resolve all types of conflicts nonviolently.

It is natural, then, for many centres in the countries affiliated with International Physicians for the Prevention of Nuclear War (IPPNW) to be attracted to the International Peace Lantern Exchange Project. This project was initiated by Wisconsin members of PSR, Dr. and Mrs. James Baumgaertner. They knew of the ancient Japanese custom in which candle-lit paper lanterns are floated on waterways as symbols of guiding ancestral souls back to the land of the dead. They knew how this ceremony had been adapted by the city of Hiroshima to honor the victims of the atomic bombing. Could it be used to create an awareness in children that common needs and hopes are held by people all over the world? Might such an awareness lead to creating bonds of goodwill and trust between children of "enemy nations"?

From this background grew the project for school children to draw pictures of what they considered essential in their lives and to write messages about their desires for peace. The papers which the children produce become shades for these lanterns. Shades exchanged between countries, assembled with candles on bases, become part of a lantern ceremony associated with the commemoration of Hiroshima and Nagasaki.

There are several major reasons for such an undertaking. The first is that it provides entry to discussing with children one or more of the many aspects of peace building. Secondly, the lanterns are a means for establishing communication between children internationally. Perhaps more importantly, by expressing in pictures and words their own ideas about peace, it provides children with the vital experience of discovering that it is possible for each individual to participate in peacemaking. The culmination of this project is the production of a particularly meaningful and beautiful ceremony to commemorate Hiroshima and Nagasaki, and a means through which people may dedicate themselves to prevent the recurrence of such a tragedy.

Students' and teachers' responses leave little doubt that well-thought-out presentations make invaluable contributions to building value systems consistent with world peace and justice. The content of these presentations will depend upon the grade level, and obtaining student participation is crucial.

Participation is achieved particularly well in primary grades by asking who has ever been to see a doctor and for what reasons. Hands fly up in great competition to share experiences. Inevitably students talk about getting a needle so they "won't get sick with bad diseases." The stage is then set to explain why it is particularly important to prevent those illnesses for which we have no treatment, and to lead into explaining why it is that doctors find it important to be actively concerned about preventing nuclear war. Our multicultural society provides a natural setting for launching discussions about differences between people and the goal of settling disagreements amicably without verbal or physical violence. One child talks about the strange food his friend brings for lunches and another about how "funny it is" that some people don't celebrate Christmas. A third child remarks that some wear clothes very different from hers. It is a short step from here to talk about how disagreements arise between people even of the same family and how it might be possible to settle disputes non-violently. The responses given by these students when invited to tell the things over which they have disagreements with their siblings may seem rather inconsequential in the context of international conflicts. Laughter, but also a great deal of affirmative nodding, greets statements such as: "My brother and I fight over what T.V. program we should watch;" "I hit Joe yesterday because he broke my favorite coloured crayon and he didn't even ask if he could use it;" "Betty makes me upset when she teases me because I don't know how to tie my shoes;" and "It made me mad when Marnie ran out to jump on the swing when she heard me say I was going to." Perhaps, just perhaps, by learning to respect the different customs and ideas of others and to reach friendly resolutions to such childhood conflicts, these children may develop an ability to resolve larger conflicts in a manner much superior to that generally achieved by the adults of today.

In an era when violence abounds around the globe at all levels of society, where violence dominates adult and children's entertainment, it is imperative to present children with practical, workable alternatives. Many schools do introduce such techniques to their students. The lantern project provides a powerful reinforcement of these teachings and allows children to comprehend the connection between interpersonal and international peacemaking. Similar approaches are valuable for *all* age levels.

Senior grades are receptive, in addition, to factual information. There are innumerable topics from which to choose when speaking to senior grades about the nuclear threat. Inquiry from the teacher about current class topics will usually help in making a choice. Plans to present pictures or verbal details of the medical consequences of a nuclear war must obviously be cleared with the teacher and requires forewarning the students as well as restricted accounts and great sensitivity. One may choose to speak about the current number of weapons, their various types and capabilities, and which new ones are being developed. Military policies and strategies and their relationship to treaties already in place, on hold, or to be negotiated are excellent topics for Socials classes. Information on Canada's complicity in the arms race and the record of her voting at United Nations' Disarmament Sessions should be made available to every high school student. Perhaps the most effective and timely approach is to relate world-wide military expenditures to current expenditures for health and education.

As with the general public, students are staggered to discover how just fractional amounts of world-wide military spending, if used in other ways, could provide such enormous benefits. A yearly publication by Ruth Leger Sivard is an excellent resource for such figures. The 1989 figure for world-wide military expenditure was 1 trillion dollars. That translates into 100 students being able to spend eleven thousand dollars every day for the next 100 years and still having a balance left over. It also means that an amount equivalent to only 5 hours of that arms race being spent over a period of 10 years was all that was needed to wipe out the once dreaded disease, smallpox. The United States, alone, now *saves* $130 million a year by no longer having to vaccinate its population against smallpox. It will take less than two hours of that arms race to eradicate polio, a disease which in the first year of my medical practice accounted for several deaths in my own patient load and left many crippled for life. The world population at present suffers from 100 million new cases of malaria every year with deaths reaching the 1 million figure. It would take only 4½ hours of the arms race to eliminate this disease. It is even more astonishing to learn what steps might be taken to control other diseases. Fifty per cent of the peoples of the world drink disease-contaminated water. That contamination causes 80 per cent of all illnesses among half of the people in the world. It would take the equivalent of only 180 days' worth of current military spending to provide permanent, safe water supplies for everyone in the world. Statistics such as these provide students with a basis on which to build their own conclusions as to how they would wish to see the world's resources used and distributed. (See first reference to chapter by Professor Tom Perry, which provides many of these details.)

Words are very poor vehicles by which to communicate the last numbers mentioned above or the numbers of nuclear weapons which abound today and the strength of their fire power. One husband and wife team used a kettle drum into which they dropped the pellets needed for illustrating past and present nuclear fire-power. It was remarkably effective. It also achieved the not easily attained humorous relief for such a subject, as students scurried around the classroom to retrieve the bouncing pellets! Another physician took the trouble to edit our video to include photos of the planet as taken by the astronauts and their reflections on those experiences.

Much was achieved in both years during which the project was undertaken (1989 and 1990). Twenty-four physician members of the BC Chapter of CPPNW, otherwise not actively involved in the organization, spoke to over 3000 students in 40 schools. With rare exceptions these doctors reported enthusiastically on their school visits and, as indicated, many came up with interesting additions or ideas for future presentations. Students in special programs, who cut the paper for shades, made bases and drilled candles, experienced an all too rarely achieved sense of accomplishment and contribution to a major project. Our load was remarkably decreased and it was with justifiable pride that these students had their photos taken with samples of the paper and wooden bases on which they had worked so hard. Finally, the public event each year turned out to be an unusually beautiful ceremony.

Much thought was given to that event and what was to precede it. Two large tents were set up on park grounds adjacent to the tidal waters of False Creek. Carefully selected joyous music delivered at a moderate volume invited people to join in assembling the lantern shades and candles on their wooden bases under the protection of one of the tents. The other tent held commemorative buttons and shirts as well as tables at which additional lantern shades could be made on site. At 8:00 p.m. the formal program began.

A brief account of the background and meaning of the project was followed by greetings from civic authorities. Moving performances were then given of songs especially composed for the occasion by a folk singer. The first year a Japanese Women's choir also sang. On the second occasion, a young people's dance troop which had recently toured in the Soviet Union, gifted us first with words from one of their members, followed by two beautiful dances. At this point members from Veterans Against Nuclear Arms (VANA) gathered to mark a route from the park site to the water's edge by forming two lines with flourescent ribbon.

The lighting of the candles in Vancouver has a very special significance. Across a bridge from the site of the ceremony is a Peace Park in which there is a continuously-burning flame. CPPNW held a ceremony in October 1989 at this site, during which a tree was planted to mark the occasion and charcoal, which had been ignited from the Hiroshima Peace Flame, was united with the Vancouver flame. This flame became the source for lighting the peace lanterns.

An unexpected hush fell over the gathering each year as young and old proceeded to collect a lantern and have the candles lit. The first year the procession was led by the playing of a Buddhist drum; the second by the sound of a Japanese flute. The solemn beauty of this procession making its way to the water was as impressive as the wonder and sense of magical harmony inspired by the lanterns as they became launched on the outgoing tide. The brilliance of one of Vancouver's most magnificent sunsets became reflected in the lights of the multicolored lanterns, each bearing a child's message for peace.

This account must not end here. The personal recollections of Mitsue Kubo whose moving account appears in Chapter 2 of this book were made available to me. There are no more suitable words than hers to express the immorality existing which led to the dropping of the atomic bombs on Hiroshima and Nagasaki and the immorality of present nuclear stockpiles with unabated research into ever newer weapons technology. Mrs. Kubo states that "The bomb is the worst demon in human history" and she speaks of "the inexcusable cruelty of the atomic bomb," that "War reduces us to animals," and that "Deterrence is a treacherous balance which might collapse into an abysmal calamity at any moment." A responding chord is struck when she speaks of her "communion with nature in (her) childhood," and of the "tickling sensation on the soles of (her) feet" as she stood upon the beach and the "sea (took) sand from under (her) feet." With all the recent changes in Eastern Europe and in the cold war, it is far too easy to be lulled into inaction against the nuclear threat. Mitsue Kubo reminds us that, "The horror (of the Hiroshima/ Nagasaki experience) *must not be forgotten.* To forget would be at our own peril." See her Chapter 2 in this book.

What role can we play in the search for peace with justice? The Lantern Project is an effective approach for imparting to the general public and especially to young people information relevant to a world in need. It can help children realize that all of the earth's people have the same basic needs and desires, and to discover how important it is to learn how to settle differences non-violently. Can we rediscover or discover with our

Author Dorothy Goresky helping children complete their floating peace lanterns.

Making peace lanterns.

Launching peace lanterns in English Bay, Vancouver, at dusk.

children and grandchildren how to be truly rooted to the earth? When did we last take off our shoes to walk on the sand and feel our soles being "tickled"? How often do our children go barefoot? After a rain is there any mud in our yards or back lanes in which our children may experience the sensuousness of stamping up-and-down, up-and-down, barefooted in that mud until they have worked their way knee-deep?!! When did we last take time for our souls to be truly touched by the beauty of the sunrise or sunset? How regularly do we reach into the heart of Mother Earth to find where true wisdom lies? Readers will find suggestions for educating Canadian children to become peacemakers in Chapter 11 by Dr. Joanna Santa Barbara.

How dedicated are we to preserving the Earth for ourselves and future generations? The questions are ours to answer. The tasks are ours to perform. The time is now.

Professor Thomas L. Perry

CHAPTER 4

The Social Ruin and Continuing War Danger Caused by the Arms Race

PROFESSOR THOMAS L. PERRY, M.D.

THE THREAT OF DEVASTATING NUCLEAR OR CONVENTIONAL WAR IS STILL WITH US

In 1990 the nations of the world are spending U.S. $1000 billion preparing for war. This enormous sum of public monies accounts for 5.6% of the world's gross national product (GNP) and employs about 26 million people in the armed forces alone.[1] A trillion dollars is hard for most of us to comprehend; but the obscenity of this expenditure may be easier to understand when translated into the world's spending U.S. $1.9 million each minute preparing for war.

An estimated 57,000 nuclear weapons are stockpiled worldwide, and their total explosive power amounts to about 1000 times the total explosive power used in all wars since gun-powder was invented six centuries ago. Despite the welcome Intermediate Nuclear Forces (INF) agreement between the United States and the Soviet Union in December 1987, the number of nuclear weapons in the arsenals of the superpowers has not decreased. Nuclear warheads have been removed from intermediate range delivery vehicles (rockets) by the Americans and the Soviets in Europe, but there is substantial evidence that the warheads themselves have simply been reused, especially by placing them in new vehicles on submarines and naval surface vessels. The testing of nuclear weapons by the United States, the Soviet Union, France and the United Kingdom has continued through the first half of 1990. It is widely agreed that the *only* reason for continued nuclear weapons testing is to perfect ever more accurate and dangerous weapons, ones which are most certain to cause the

For biographical note about Professor Perry, see Chapter 1, page 9.

greatest amount of destruction to precisely located targets in the territory of a potential enemy. Nuclear weapons do not need to be exploded to ascertain whether or not their shelf life has expired.

Meanwhile, there is still intense pressure by certain nations to develop their own nuclear weapons technology. Six nations possess nuclear weapons ready to use in their arsenals: the United States, the Soviet Union (the two between them have 98% of the world's total), France, China, the United Kingdom, and Israel. In addition three other countries (South Africa, India, and Pakistan) have nuclear weapons capability, that is, they are states judged to have now the essentials for building nuclear weapons. Seven other countries (Brazil, Argentina, Libya, Iraq, Iran, and North and South Korea) are considered to be "emerging nuclear powers," that is, states with interests or facilities that might in the years ahead lead to nuclear weapons. This lateral proliferation of nuclear weapons technology is very worrying and is undoubtedly stimulated by continued nuclear weapons testing by the established nuclear weapons powers, and by continued opposition to the conclusion of a comprehensive nuclear weapons test ban treaty by the United States, the United Kingdom, and France.

Despite many initiatives by the Soviet Union to reduce both nuclear and conventional armaments, despite the profound political changes which have occurred in the Soviet Union and the Eastern European countries, and despite the welcome lessening of tension between the United States and the Soviet Union that has taken place in the last three years, the danger of a global nuclear war is far from over. Canadians who have worried about a nuclear holocaust throughout most of the 1980s have very little reason to forget their fears and let their guard drop now.

Especially sobering is the rapid pace of militarization in the Third World. More and more independent developing countries are ruled by military governments. By 1988, 64 of 113 of these countries, or 57%, had military governments.[1] By 1987, Third World countries accounted for 17% of global arms expenditures,[1] and developing countries now absorb about 82% of the world's arms transfers.[2] People in the developing countries have paid a terrible toll in war casualties as a result of this increasing militarization. Since the end of World War II in 1945, 127 wars have been waged, virtually all of them in the Third World. The casualties have totalled 20,000,000 people killed, and more than twice that number injured, the majority of them civilians.[1] The loss of life due to warfare was especially severe in Vietnam and during the eight-year war between Iraq and Iran.

The degree of increasing militarization has been highest in the Middle East. By 1987, 46% of all arms transfers destined for developing countries were being shipped to the Middle East.[2] The United States, the Soviet Union, the United Kingdom, France, and West Germany have all competed greedily to sell arms to Iraq, a nation ranking sixth in the world for the size of its armed forces in proportion to its population, and a nation spending 32% of its gross national product on military purposes.[1] In fact, West German companies have recently built nerve and mustard gas factories in Iraq, as well as factories for advanced conventional weapons, including the infamous 150-metre-long giant cannon. Rather than shipping finished weapons to Baghdad, the German companies have concentrated on exporting seemingly harmless goods or machinery that could easily be used to make weapons.[3] Should we be surprised that Iraq invaded and seized oil-rich Kuwait on 2 August 1990, and that the whole world now dreads the outbreak of a major war in the Persian Gulf?

DEVASTATION BEFORE DESTRUCTION: THE HARMFUL EFFECTS OF MILITARISM IN THE THIRD WORLD

Increased militarization and deepening underdevelopment go hand in hand in the Third World. Lives are being lost, and life itself is brutalized. People are hungry, and ill, and unemployed because resources that could be used to tackle these problems are being wasted to support armies and to purchase arms from the developed nations, and then to pay burdensome interest on the debts owing from earlier arms purchases.[4]

It is important for those of us living relatively comfortable and safe lives in a rich, developed country like Canada to understand what life is really like for ordinary people living in Third World countries. Of the world's 1990 population of 5.2 billion, about 1.2 billion of us live in the developed countries, and 4.0 billion live in the developing countries. Some statistics should make it easier to comprehend what life is like for those four billion human beings. Statistics have been described as "people with the tears washed off";[5] and Epp-Tiessen has movingly described how "statistics do not tell of the despair experienced by a mother who must watch her child die of hunger, the weariness of the farmer whose meager crop brings less income each year, and the lost hope of the unemployed and uneducated".[4] In considering the figures given below, readers need to leave their imaginations sensitized.

Table 1 compares some parameters important for judging the quality of life between the developed countries and the developing countries. The contrast in individual income (gross national product per capita), in literacy, and in health standards (measured most accurately by infant mortality rates and life expectancy) between the richest 20% of our world and all the rest is dramatic. In Table 2, I list figures for the same parameters in three particularly poor Third World countries, one in Latin America, one in South Asia, and one in sub-Saharan Africa. Note the enormous differences for these countries from the figures given for the developed countries in Table 1. These figures are for 1987,[1] but those for 1990

TABLE 1

QUALITY OF LIFE, 1987—WORLD AS A WHOLE

World Population: (1987 = 5.0 billion)	Developed Countries (Richest 20%)	Developing Countries (Poorest 80%)
GNP per capita	US $11,392	US $731
Public expenditure on education (% of GNP)	5.2%	3.7%
Public expenditure on health (% of GNP)	4.6%	1.6%
Literacy (% of female/ male population)	98/99%	51/72%
School age population in school	69%	51%
Life expectancy at birth	74 years	62 years
Infant mortality (deaths under 1 year per 1000 births)	14	79
Population with access to safe water supply	97%	54%

Data from Ref. 1

and 1991 are unlikely to be much better. They do demonstrate that life for a huge fraction of our fellow human beings is brutalized and hopeless.

WASTE OF RESOURCES ON MILITARISM
Table 3 gives some key figures to illustrate the enormous squandering of public funds that goes on to promote militarism and to prepare for war. Most of the figures are for 1986 or 1987, the latest year for which accurate statistics are available. For 1990, the expenditures for military purposes are likely similar, except for the Soviet Union, which has reduced military spending in line with the unilateral reduction of its large forces in

TABLE 2

QUALITY OF LIFE, 1987—SOME POOR COUNTRIES

	Haiti	*Bangladesh*	*Mozambique*
GNP per capita	US $369	US $164	US $272
Public expenditure on education (% of GNP)	0.011%	0.024%	?
Public expenditure on health (% of GNP)	0.008%	0.006%	0.018%
Literacy (women)	35%	22%	22%
School age population in school	47%	31%	28%
Life expectancy at birth	54 years	50 years	45 years
Infant mortality (deaths under 1 year per 1000 births)	117	119	141
Population with access to safe water supply	35%	40%	13%

Data from Ref. 1

Europe, and in an effort to correct major problems in its civilian economy. The figures make it clear that both the two superpowers, as well as the developing countries, are guilty of enormous wastage of public funds in preparing for war. Contrast the US $143 billion spent by Third World countries preparing for war, and the US $45 billion of arms exports (75% purchased by developing countries), with skimpy amounts spent by developing countries for education and health care. And what a disgrace it is that six times as much public funds are devoted to weapons-related research by scientists and engineers as to health research!

Canada's expenditures in 1990–1991 for military purposes are shockingly high, even if substantially lower than those of the United States and the Soviet Union. And it is worth noting that our defence budget of over Canadian $12 billion remains that high even after the Canadian govern-

71

TABLE 3

ANNUAL PUBLIC EXPENDITURES

World military expenditures (1990)	US $1000 billion (This equals US $1.9 million per minute.)
United States military expenditures (1986)	US $281 billion
Soviet Union military expenditures (1986)	US $271 billion
Third World military expenditures (1986)	US $143 billion
Canada's defence expenditure (1990–1991)	Canadian $12.36 billion
Arms exports by developed countries (1987)	US $45 billion
World expenditures on weapons-related research (1987)	US $100 billion
Public financing of health research (1987)	US $17 billion

Data from Ref.1, except for Canada.[6]

ment has abandoned its foolish plan to purchase a fleet of nuclear-powered submarines. In 1986, with a considerably lower defence budget than at present, Canada still ranked 12th among 142 countries in its military expenditures.[1]

Figure 1 shows the increasing disparity between military expenditures by the developed countries and the minute amounts they spend on economic aid to Third World countries. Figure 2 illustrates the divergence between military and economic growth in the developing countries between 1960 and 1987. Money used for production or purchase of armaments is money that is not available to immunize children against disease, to provide people with clean drinking water, or to assist local industry and help small farmers. At present, developing countries owe the developed countries about US $1000 billion in foreign debts. About 25% of this debt burden results from arms imports. Efforts to keep up with interest payments on foreign debts greatly curtail expenditures for socially useful purposes in Third World countries. In addition, the need to service foreign debts causes more and more land in poor countries to be used to produce crops for export (such as sugar, tea, tobacco, soybeans and cotton) rather than to produce food stuffs required by the local population. The net result of militarization of Third World countries is almost always increased hunger, less health care and education, and frequently replacement of relatively democratic governments by authoritarian and repressive regimes.

SOME ALTERNATE HEALTH USES FOR MONEY NOW WASTED ON MILITARISM
An excellent example of what can be accomplished in health protection when people and governments have the will to do so is the complete eradication, throughout the world, of smallpox. When the World Health Organization (WHO) proposed in 1967 a campaign to eradicate smallpox, 10 to 15 million new cases of smallpox were occurring annually in 31 endemic countries, and 2 million people died of smallpox each year. Several factors made smallpox a favorable target for eradication, including the lack of known animal carriers of the virus, the life-long immunity of persons recovering from the disease, and the availability of an effective heat-stable vaccine. The WHO strategy involved the vaccination of large numbers of people, chiefly in developing countries, and a 10-year goal was set for complete eradication of the disease, with universal governmental support. The last case of smallpox was diagnosed in 1977 and since then the world has been free of the disease. The total cost of the WHO's 10-year campaign was US $200 million, which is the equivalent of less than two hours of current world military expenditures. The outlay of US $200 million has been estimated to have resulted worldwide in annual savings for health care of US $1500 million![9]

Of course, there is no *guarantee* that if one country, or a group of countries, reduces military expenditures by a substantial fraction, the savings in funds will be spent for a socially useful purpose such as the prevention of disease, or the provision of better education or food supplies. However, a beginning has to be made somewhere, and it is up to ordinary citizens to press their governments for morally acceptable expenditures of public funds both at home and abroad. In an effort to demonstrate what is *possible* with conversion of military expenditures to socially useful expenditures, I present Table 4 which gives examples of what *could* be done to improve people's health in Third World countries. Let me emphasize again that these positive steps would require a political revolt of the public in wealthy donor countries against foolish armaments

FIGURE 1

FOREIGN ECONOMIC AID AND MILITARY EXPENDITURES BY
DEVELOPED COUNTRIES

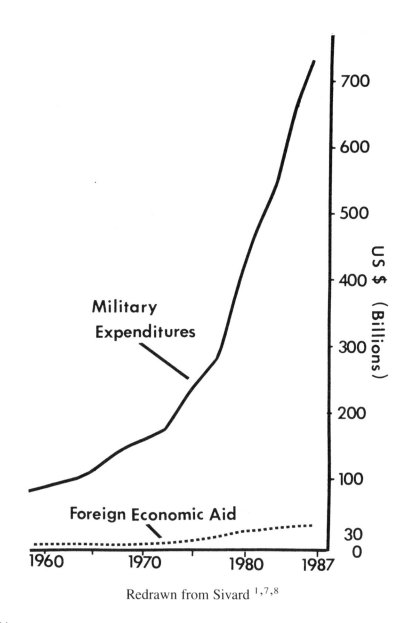

Redrawn from Sivard [1,7,8]

Thomas L. Perry

FIGURE 2

MILITARY VERSUS ECONOMIC GROWTH IN DEVELOPING
COUNTRIES

Dollar figures are 1986 US dollars, indexed to 1960 = $100

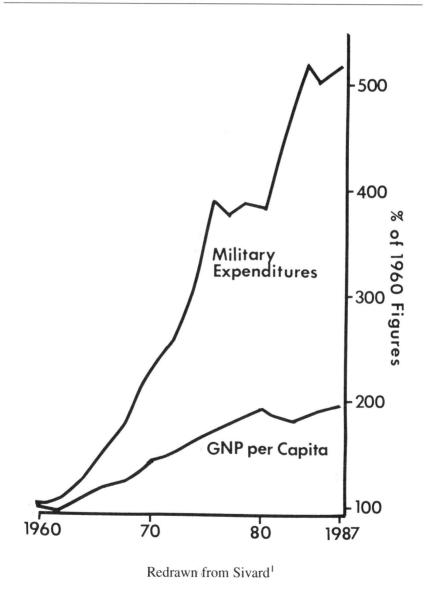

Redrawn from Sivard[1]

75

TABLE 4

POTENTIAL HEALTH BENEFITS FROM FUNDS
NOW WASTED ON THE MILITARY

Third World population at risk	Number of persons	Cost to prevent (US $/year)	Fraction of annual arms spending which must be sacrificed
People lacking safe water supply	1.60 billion	50 billion*	18 days*
People lacking adequate sanitation	2.78 billion		
People chronically malnourished	950 million	50 billion†	18 days†
Children dying of dehydration, preventable by oral rehydration	3.5 million	3.5 million	2 minutes
Children dying of 6 diseases preventable by immunization	4.0 million	40 million	21 minutes
People with iodine deficiency disorders, preventable by iodized oil injection	200 million	1 billion	12 hours
Children dying of measles: preventable by eradication of measles	0.9 million	$500 million	6 hours

* Annual cost for 10 years.
† Annual cost for 20 years.

expenditures, governmental determination in recipient developing countries to solve health problems, and firm treaty agreements between donor and recipient nations.

In the Third World, huge numbers of people lack safe and adequate water supplies, and an even greater number lack safe sanitation facilities.[1] The result is that some 1.6 billion people are forced to drink water contaminated with human feces, and a billion more must eat food potentially contaminated by flies with access to human feces. For these people, approximately 80% of the illnesses they now suffer are intestinal infections, sometimes relatively mild, but often severe such as typhoid fever or cholera. Eighty per cent of their illnesses are preventable, by construction of permanent safe water supplies and proper waste disposal facilities. The WHO has estimated the cost of such a program to be about US $500 billion. In Table 4, the cost is listed as US $50 billion a year for 10 years, or giving up 18 days of the world's military expenditures each year for 10 years. Table 4 shows that almost a billion people in the developing countries are chronically malnourished, and many millions actually starve to death. The WHO estimates that giving up 18 days of world military expenditures annually for 20 years would yield enough money to provide essential food and health care for this huge group of hungry people permanently.

Table 4 also gives some examples of the benefits that could come from much more modest cuts in military spending. About 3.5 million infants and small children die in Third World countries each year from dehydration brought on by the vomiting and diarrhea of intestinal infections. Often all that is necessary to save their lives is giving them oral rehydration therapy, a fluid containing a balanced salt and sugar solution, which the mother can give in the home setting, at a cost of US $1 per child treated.[1] About 4 million children still die each year in the developing countries from one of six diseases readily preventable by immunization (diphtheria, tetanus, whooping cough, measles, poliomyelitis, and tuberculosis). The cost of preventing these 4 million deaths by a comprehensive immunization program has been estimated at US $10 per child,[1] or the equivalent of what the world wastes every 21 minutes on armaments. One can see that if even Canada devoted a fraction of its military budget (equal to US $10.5 billion annually) to solving Third World health problems, there would no longer be children dying from dehydration and from diseases preventable by immunization.

Table 4 points out that 200 million people on our planet are affected by iodine deficiency disorders, as a result of their living in geographic areas with insufficient iodine content in the soil. Eight hundred million people live in iodine-deficient regions. The 200 million clinically affected suffer impaired physical growth and mental development, and as adults are apathetic and lacking in energy. Iodine deficiency disorders are easily prevented, and are treatable if not too long established, by addition of iodized salt to the diet, or by an annual injection of iodized oil.[1,10] Sacrificing 12 hours of the world's annual military expenditures would provide the funds needed each year to treat these 200 million people.

Measles now causes 900,000 deaths a year, chiefly in children aged one to four years and living in the poor countries of the world. I have pointed out above that these deaths can be prevented by a routine immunization program, which includes measles vaccine. A more ambitious program would be the permanent eradication of measles from our planet, just as was done with smallpox. The prospects for wiping out measles for ever are good because there is no animal reservoir for measles virus, there is no chronic carrier state in humans who have contracted measles, and the live measles vaccine is now cheap and relatively heat-stable.[11] All that is required is a coordinated campaign in all countries of the world to vaccinate 90% or more of all children reaching the age of 12 to 15 months. Once again the costs would be a drop in the bucket of world annual military expenditures—six hours worth!

There are many further examples of health scourges affecting people living in the Third World that could be helped by infusions of funding from developed countries, combined with firm political decisions in recipient countries *not* to spend funds on importing arms or building up local armies. Malaria is probably the most important of these. Approximately one billion people live in countries where malaria is endemic. There are 100 million new cases of malaria each year, with more than a million deaths per year. Successful treatment of malaria is steadily becoming more difficult due to the emergence of *Plasmodium falciparum* infections that are resistant to the usually effective anti-malarial drugs. An urgently needed priority is the development of an effective anti-malarial vaccine, a task requiring substantial funding of medical scientists in many countries.[12]

Schistosomiasis, a parasitic worm infestation, now affects 200 to 300 million people in Africa, Latin America, China and Southeast Asia, and causes chronic ill health lasting for years. Recent scientific research suggests that developing a vaccine may be feasible, and meanwhile use of a new anti-schistosomiasis drug, praziquantel (costing US $2 per person treated), together with development of proper sewage systems, makes wiping out this great disease problem practical.[13] Onchocerciasis is another parasitic worm infestation which affects the health of 85 million persons living in endemic areas, particularly West Africa. Eighteen million of these people are infected, and onchocerciasis causes blindness or severe visual loss in one or two million of them. The worm infestation can be prevented by mass treatment with ivermectin, a new safe and effective drug.[14] In some parts of the world, notably India, Africa and Indonesia, infants suffer a chronic dietary deficiency of vitamin A, and this nutritional deficiency renders them particularly likely to die from from intestinal and respiratory infections which well-nourished infants normally survive. The mortality rates of these illnesses can be dramatically reduced by mass distribution to infants and young children of vitamin A supplements, at an annual cost of about US $2 per recipient.[15,16]

UNDERFUNDED HEALTH PROBLEMS FACING THE ENTIRE WORLD

Conversion of wasteful military expenditures to socially useful ones is badly needed in the developed countries as well as in the Third World. Probably the worst single health problem facing the entire world now is the pandemic of human immunodeficiency virus type 1 (HIV-1), an infection that started in the mid to late 1970s. HIV infection causes the acquired immunodeficiency syndrome (AIDS), a universally fatal disease that deprives young people especially of years of useful and enjoyable life. As of July 1, 1990, a cumulative total of about 250,000 cases of AIDS had occurred, and the WHO estimates that between 5 and 10 million persons are now infected with HIV-1 worldwide.[17] In the developed countries, transmission of the virus has so far occurred primarily as a result of sexual activity between homosexual and bisexual men, and as a result of intravenous drug abuse with contaminated needles and syringes. In sub-Saharan Africa, Latin America and the Carribean, transmission of HIV-1 is primarily heterosexual between men and women, especially via prostitutes, and from mother to fetus during pregnancy. AIDS has now become the leading cause of death for women aged 20 to 40 in major cities in the Americas, Western Europe, and sub-Saharan Africa.[18] In Abidjan, Ivory Coast, and in other cities in sub-Saharan Africa, AIDS is now the most common cause of death. Reliable forecasts are that during the early 1990s deaths from AIDS could equal or exceed the expected number of deaths from all other causes in many sub-Saharan African cities. Life expectancy at birth is likely to fall by as much as six years. And several million uninfected children will be orphaned because a large proportion of HIV-infected mothers will have died of AIDS. Chances for better economic conditions and better health care will be ruined in many Third World countries because of the loss of young and middle-aged men and women.

AIDS is wreaking almost as great havoc in some North American cities, notably New York, San Francisco and Vancouver. Although the drug now used to treat most AIDS patients, zidovudine, can slow down the progress of the disease, it does not eliminate the HIV-1 virus infection,

79

and all AIDS patients undergo a prolonged wasting illness inevitably leading to death. There is a great need to develop more effective drugs than zidovudine, and especially to develop an effective vaccine against HIV-1. Throwing money at a health problem does not always guarantee progress, because some scientific problems are much harder to solve than others. But the WHO's Global Programme on AIDS is now facing severe donor fatigue, with pledges of money from governments of developed countries running 30% below the US $100 million needed for 1991.[19] Reference to Table 4 reminds us that what the WHO asks for AIDS prevention is still less than what the world wastes in under an hour on military preparations.

Unsolved health problems that are common in Canada and other developed countries include unsatisfactory care for chronic mental illness, especially schizophrenia, and the medical profession's inability to cope with the growing number of people with Alzheimer's disease. Approximately one out of every 100 persons develops schizophrenia, and for most of them the disorder lasts from the second decade of life until old age. With proper and continued doses of antipsychotic drugs, and good psychiatric care, schizophrenic patients can lead adequate although not full and happy lives, either in long-term mental hospitals or in sheltered homes outside hospital. But in many North American large cities, properly supervised homes for the chronically mentally ill are not available, due to lack of mental health funding. At least half of the homeless adults who live under bridges, in railway stations, or in cardboard boxes over heating vents, in our big cities, have schizophrenia. Why can't we use some of the wasted "defence" dollars to provide them comfortable homes?

Alzheimer's disease is the most common dementing illness, and may soon be the fourth leading cause of death in the United States and Canada. It severely affects about 1.6 million North Americans now; and as the population ages, this number is predicted to increase fivefold during the next half century.[20] There is no effective drug for treating Alzheimer's disease at present, and enormous suffering is caused, especially for the relatives of a spouse or parent who progressively loses memory, the ability to think, and the capacity to care for self. Once again, spending more money on medical research looking for the cause of Alzheimer's disease, or for an effective way of treating it or preventing it, does not guarantee success. But how much more sensible to spend money on this research than on devising ever more deadly nuclear or chemical weapons!

WHAT CAN CANADIANS DO?

I have given some details above regarding the dismal situation faced by most of the world's population as a result of the huge wastage of money (and of skilled people) in preparing for wars—wars which will compound human misery, and which conceivably could obliterate most of us. One can ask, what can Canada do as a middle power to correct the situation, and why should individual Canadians exert themselves in this direction? It is easy to see why Canadians should be working for a comprehensive nuclear weapons test ban, and then for the complete abolition of all nuclear weapons from the arsenals of the nuclear powers, and to prevent lateral spread of nuclear weapons to other states. If we fail to accomplish this task, we continue to risk having all 26 million Canadians killed in a global nuclear war. And for those relaxed readers who think this is no longer a possibility, what with dramatic and welcome lessening of hostilities between the United States and the Soviet Union, it is worth imagining what might happen in the crisis precipitated by Iraq's invasion of Kuwait. As of late October 1990, more than 250,000 American soldiers, together with battle tanks and military aircraft, are stationed in Saudi Arabia, clearly ready for battle with opposing Iraqi troops. The Persian Gulf is crisscrossed with western naval vessels. And hostile statements by President Bush and Saddam Hussein bristle on our television screens nightly. What happens if accidentally, or on purpose, fighting starts in the Gulf and on the Arabian Peninsula? What happens if the Iraqis then make deadly use of their long range chemical weapons against the American troops in the desert? What then if the United States retaliates by attacking Baghdad with a few nuclear weapons? Who can feel secure that nuclear explosions would then be limited to Iraq?

Hopefully the conflict in the Persian Gulf will be settled by economic embargoes and diplomacy, without a terrible war ensuing. Why then should Canadians concern themselves during the 1990s with efforts to reduce military spending? It seems to me that there are two answers. The first is that as human beings we have a moral responsibility to be deeply concerned for the welfare of human beings whom we have never seen, and whose languages we do not understand. I strongly recommend to readers of this chapter that they obtain and use the booklet *World Military and Social Expenditures,* produced almost annually by Ruth Leger Sivard.[1] The next edition should be available in 1991, and will provide many more details than I have summarized in this chapter.

A second reason why Canada should do something, even though our country alone can solve only a part of the problem, is that allowing injustice and a miserable standard of living to persist in the developing countries encourages planning for devastating local wars. Is it reasonable to expect the 80% of human beings living in these countries to remain satisfied with using only 20% of the world's energy, while the 20% of us who live in the developed world consume 80% of all energy used? Do we really expect the poor in Sao Paulo or Soweto to remain passive forever when they can readily see how we live in the world's rich countries? Continuing ill health, illiteracy, and injustice in the Third World are bound to provoke violent reactions, and sooner or later these will lead to wars which involve us. Canadians who want to continue leading their relatively peaceful and privileged lives would be well advised to move rapidly to correct poverty and injustice in Third World countries. This will require money, and that money can and should come from major cuts in Canada's "defence" expenditures.

WHAT MUST CANADA DO?

1) Clearly the government of Canada ought to reduce its military expenditures substantially, certainly to less than half their present $12.36 billion level. This will require skillful economic conversion to provide jobs for the workers displaced from arms and military-related industries, as well as for the men and women discharged from our armed forces. It is inconceivable that sensible governmental planning, carried out together with business and trade union leaders and economists, cannot find ways of creating useful and satisfying employment for every person displaced from war-related jobs. For instance, using a mere 5% of Canada's current defence budget would have been sufficient to prevent the cancellation of VIA Rail's transcontinental passenger trains. Use of a larger proportion of our current military expenditures could provide for long-term and much more rapid railroad transportation across Canada for both passengers and freight. This surely is a desirable goal as fossil fuels are progressively depleted, and the carbon dioxide content of the atmosphere is steadily increased, leading to profound harmful environmental changes associated with the greenhouse effect.

Some apologists for the arms race argue that military spending creates jobs and decreases unemployment. But numerous studies have concluded that investment in socially useful areas creates more jobs than does military spending, not only for skilled workers, scientists and engineers, but especially for less skilled workers. For instance, a US Department of Labor study in 1976 showed that $1 billion of military expenditure at that time created 76,000 jobs, yet $1 billion spent for civilian programs created 100,000 jobs.[21] A 1985 study by the Canadian Union of Public Employees produced even more striking results. Spending by the Department of National Defence in fiscal 1984 created an estimated 147,000 jobs in 181 industries. But had the same amount of money been spent by Canadian consumers on housing, food, clothing, education and other needs, the outcome would have been 258,000 jobs—or 111,000 more![22]

Phony claims to be preventing unemployment must not be permitted to get Canadian politicians off the hook. Canada's military expenditures should be reduced by at least one half. Part of the savings should be spent on badly needed corrections of deficiencies in Canada which can improve the quality of life for those of us in this country. And the rest—a generous fraction—should be given as economic aid to one or more developing countries. The United Nations has called on all developed countries to devote, by the year 1995, at least 0.7% of their GNP to aid to Third World countries. So far, only four countries—Denmark, Norway, Sweden, and the Netherlands—annually meet that goal, and Canada has not come close to it yet. In 1984, the latest year for which statistics are available, we gave 0.5% of our GNP in economic aid to developing countries,[23] and much of that money compelled recipient countries to purchase Canadian goods, often to their own disadvantage. Our economic aid to the Third World should be generous, and I would put only one firm condition on recipient countries. These countries should be requested to reduce their military expenses virtually to zero, and they should under no circumstances produce arms for sale to other countries.

2) Canada should immediately stop exporting arms to other countries, developed or developing. The latest available figures (for 1987) indicate that the developed countries exported US $45 billion in arms, the great majority to developing countries.[1] These arms exports, as discussed earlier, make possible some dreadful little wars between Third World nations, and only consolidate the poverty, injustice, and repression common in these countries. A dramatic example of the harmful effects of arms exports is the current threat of a major war in the Persian Gulf. Five countries, the Soviet Union, the United States, the United Kingdom, France, and the Federal Republic of Germany, have during the last decade been pouring arms into Iraq, and making dirty profits from the sales. Should they now be surprised that a well-armed Iraq invades Kuwait and challenges foreign control of the rich oil fields in the Gulf?

Since 1981 Canada has been exporting one to two billion dollars annually in weapons sales. About three-quarters of these sales have been to the United States, with the remainder split between Europe and the Third World.[24] But most of the details of the international arms trade, and Canada's involvement in it, are closed to public scrutiny, even to members of Parliament. Military sales are not like other sales. They are ultimately the sale of war-making capacity, and Canadians have the right to know whose war-making capacity we are supporting. At a minimum, all the facts should be made available to the public. I suspect that a majority of voters would then support an end to government subsidies to Canadian arms manufacturers, and a ban on all weapons exports.

One of the contributors to this book has pointedly described a major obstacle to our achieving a substantial cut in Canada's military expenditures, or a ban on weapon exports from Canada. He writes, "Particularly in the U.S.A., but also in Canada and no doubt in the U.S.S.R. and many other countries, there is a large number of people whose careers and prosperity depend upon the arms trade, and upon armaments research and development. The scientists in that field have it so good—almost unlimited research funds for any project they can make sound half-way reasonable. . . ." "The firms with government contracts have it so good— the higher their costs the greater their profits. The big point is that *all these people will be determined enemies* of every move to reduce military spending, and there are a huge number of them."[25] It will be up to the readers of this book, and the other countless Canadians who value peace and justice, to block the selfishness of these "determined enemies" by political action in the 1990s.

3) The Government of Canada should immediately revise its lacklustre, foot-dragging support of a Comprehensive Nuclear Weapons Test Ban. In the United Nations, Canada normally supports those resolutions which do not call for meaningful action on stopping nuclear tests. But in each of the last six years (1984–1989), Canada has abstained in votes in the United Nations which called for actual comprehensive test ban negotiations. In practice, this has meant that Canada has refused to call for any major steps unless the United States, the United Kingdom and France have already announced their support for them. Amongst other failures, Canada has not supported the convening of an amendment conference (now scheduled for January 1991) to turn the 1963 Partial Test Ban Treaty into a Comprehensive Test Ban Treaty. Success in negotiating the latter would not only stop all work by the nuclear powers to develop more accurate and deadly nuclear weapons, but would be a key to strengthening the 1968 Nuclear Non-Proliferation Treaty. A total test ban is the minimum price that the nuclear powers must pay to assure that lateral proliferation of nuclear weapons capability to near-nuclear states such as Argentina, Brazil, India, Pakistan and South Africa does not occur.

4) Canada should cease permitting low-level bomber training flights of NATO warplanes over Labrador, or of American warplanes over British Columbia. Testing of the American stealth cruise missile over northwestern Canada should be cancelled. These exercises are designed to prepare for offensive nuclear weapons strikes against the Soviet Union, a nation which is clearly not Canada's enemy.

5) Participation of Canadian troops, warplanes, and naval vessels in military conflicts overseas should be strictly at the request of the United Nations, and controlled by that body. Although the current economic blockade of Iraq has been approved by the United Nations Security Council, it is very questionable whether the military build-up in the Persian Gulf has

been authorized by the Security Council. It appears, as of October 1990, that the enormous build-up of troops, warplanes and tanks in Saudi Arabia, and of naval vessels in the Persian Gulf, is an operation organized by the United States, rather than by the United Nations. It seems high time that Canada's foreign policy and military commitments were designed in Canada, and not imposed from Washington, D.C.

Once again, it will be up to peace-minded Canadians in the 1990s to find effective political ways of changing Canadian Government policy to include the five steps outlined above.

References and Notes

1. Ruth Leger Sivard, *World Military and Social Expenditures 1989* (World Priorities, Box 25140, Washington, D.C 20007, USA). Briefly referred to as Sivard, *WMSE 1989,* to distinguish from earlier *WMSE* editions.

2. US Arms Control and Disarmament Agency, *World Military Expenditures and Arms Transfers 1988* (Washington, D.C.: US Government Printing Office, 1989).

3. Steven Dickman, "Illegal exports: pass the gas masks, please." *Nature 347:* 504, 1990.

4. Esther Epp-Tiessen, *Missiles and Malnutrition: The Links between Militarization and Underdevelopment,* Project Ploughshares Working Paper 90-2, 1990 (Project Ploughshares, Conrad Grebel College, Waterloo, Ontario N2L 3G6).

5. Victor W. Sidel, "Destruction before detonation: The impact of the arms race on health and health care." *Lancet 2:* 1287–1289, 1985.

6. Bill Robinson, "The 1990–1991 military budget: Where does the money go?" *Ploughshares Monitor 11 No.2:* 4–7, 1990.

7. Sivard, *WMSE 1983.*

8. Sivard, *WMSE 1985.*

9. Anonymous, "Lessons from the smallpox eradication campaign." *Lancet 2:* 980, 1987.

10. Basil S. Hetzel, "The biological effects of iodine deficiency and their public health significance." *Neuro Toxicology 8:* 363–368, 1987.

11. D. R. Hopkins et al., "The case for global measles eradication." *Lancet 1:* 1396–1398, 1982.

12. G. Kolata, "The search for a malaria vaccine." *Science 226:* 679–682, 1984.

13. G. Kolata, "Avoiding the schistosome's tricks." *Science 227:* 285–287, 1985.

14. H. R. Taylor et al., "Impact of mass treatment of onchocerciasis with ivermectin on the transmission of infection." *Science 250:* 116–118, 1990.

15. L. Rahmathullah et al., "Reduced mortality among children in southern India receiving a small weekly dose of vitamin A." *New England Journal of Medicine 323:* 929–935, 1990.

16. G. T. Keusch, "Vitamin A supplements: too good not to be true." *New England Journal of Medicine 323:* 985–986, 1990.

17. J. M. Mann and J.Chin, "AIDS: A global perspective." *New England Journal of Medicine 319:* 302–303, 1988.

18. James Chin, "Current and future dimensions of the HIV/AIDS pandemic in women and children." *Lancet 336:* 221–224, 1990.

19. P. Aldhous, "AIDS programme faces donor fatigue." *Nature 346:* 595, 1990.

20. T. L. Thompson II et al., "Lack of efficacy of hydergine in patients with Alzheimer's disease." *New England Journal of Medicine 323:* 445–448, 1990.

21. United Nations Group of Consultant Experts, "Economic and social consequences of the arms race," in Pradip K. Ghosh, ed., *Disarmament and Development: A Global Perspective,* Greenwood Press, Westport, Connecticut 1984, p.94.

22. *The Facts,* January–February 1986, p.8.

23. Sivard, *WMSE 1987–1988.*

24. Anonymous, "Full disclosure of Canadian arms exports," *Ploughshares Monitor 11, No. 2:* 27, 1990.

25. Alan F. Phillips, personal communication.

CHAPTER 5

Canada's Military After the Cold War

C.G. "GIFF" GIFFORD, D.F.C.

When Tom Perry asked me to write on Canadian defence policy now, I took it on, recognizing that it is a difficult task. Veterans Against Nuclear Arms (VANA) has for years urged an alternative to Canada's NATO plus NORAD approach. The guidelines for the alternative are clear, but nailing it down to ships, aircraft, personnel, and costs has been a hard challenge—a task in which we have not yet succeeded.

At the same time, most people in the peace movement believe a peace dividend is due—that the budget of the Department of National Defence could be cut in half, for example. We have responded that it is too soon to know about that. We do need new global arrangements to guarantee all nations' security, including our own, and to eliminate the possiblity of nuclear war. These new arrangements will cost something. What will Canada's share be? What is required to keep watch on our new 200-mile coastal economic zone, for fishing and environmental and other concerns? What surveillance of our great land mass is absolutely essential to our security, at a time when funds are sorely needed to stop acid rain and the deterioration of the ozone layer?

In what follows, I attempt to take VANA's ideas a step further, but the chapter is suggestive rather than a precise formula.

The Target: Is to eliminate forever the possibility of the greatest of environmental disasters, a nuclear war, by the year 2000, making the 1990s the decade of peacemaking. This includes getting acceptance by all states to settle their disputes by negotiation, and if that fails, by reference to the International Court of Justice as the last resort. It means making the United Nations the centre of policing to prevent war, and of "fire bri-

C.G. "Giff" Gifford, D.F.C.

gade" action to snuff out smoldering wars. It also means the abolition of nuclear and other weapons of mass destruction, of the capability for invasion, and of the major offensive weapons—tanks, bombers, medium and long range (strategic) missiles, submarines, and long range artillery.

These objectives seemed like wild dreams only five years ago. The rapidity of change since then, the beginning momentum of arms reduction measures, and the lessons of the Iraq invasion of Kuwait make them practical goals. After these goals have been achieved, policing the peace will still require vigilance and constant effort, but less than during the present transition period.

THE CONTEXT OF MILITARY ACTIVITY

We in the peace movement have long called for dialogue instead of confrontation between the Soviets and NATO, and between the USSR and the USA. We have wanted nuclear weapons to be cut back towards eventual elimination. We have wanted the use of the United Nations instead of big-power militarism to solve international conflicts. And lo and behold, beginning with Soviet President Gorbachev's launching of "Perestroika" (restructuring) in 1985, it seems to be happening. After 45 years of often angry confrontation and threat between East and West, and a nuclear arms race of stupendous proportions, very important first steps have been taken to reverse the process.

Cuthbert G. "Giff" Gifford was born in Montreal in 1918, before the guns fell silent in World War I.

A graduate of the class of '39 at McGill University, he enlisted in the RCAF in 1941, and served as an air navigator in Lancaster bombers of the Pathfinder Force of Bomber Command, participating in 49 raids over Europe. He was decorated with the Distinguished Flying Cross. His later career was in social work, and included teaching and administrative work at McGill University, the University of Manitoba, and Dalhousie University.

As a citizen, he became active in the movement to end H-Bomb tests in the atmosphere in the late 1950s.

In 1982, with three other Air Force veterans, he founded Veterans Against Nuclear Arms, and was its national chairman for eight years, stepping down with the title "Founding Chairman" in 1990.

He has published articles on social work and on peace and other social concerns. In 1990, he authored a book about the history of, and the present challenges facing the Canadian seniors' movement, titled Canada's Fighting Seniors, *James Lorimer & Co., Toronto.*

He has four children and eight grandchildren.

IS THE COLD WAR REALLY OVER?

Yes, the cold war is over. Suspicions linger. The weapons have not yet disappeared. The navies of the U.S. and the USSR, especially the former, at the time of writing, still act as though it were 1983 instead of 1990. That is, the U.S. Navy continues to strengthen its position in the Norwegian Sea and on the coast of Norway (to the distress of the Norwegians) and continues preparations for its "Maritime Strategy" of attempting to attack Soviet nuclear missile submarines in their home waters in a crisis.

But, the Warsaw Treaty Organization is finished as a military alliance. The forces of Poland, Czechoslovakia, and Hungary are now under national command and are no longer participating in joint exercises with Soviet Forces. These countries are all reducing their forces unilaterally by at least one third. The Soviets are withdrawing all their troops from these countries. East Germany, the former spearhead of the Warsaw Pact, has been annexed by West Germany. West Germany is even paying the upkeep of the Soviet Forces stationed there, until they all go home over the next five years.

Germany is reducing its own forces to just over half their present size. The U.S., Britain, and France have all announced reductions of their forces stationed in Germany. NATO has given up the idea of strengthening its nuclear weapons on German soil. The Soviet Union and all the Warsaw Pact countries now have direct liaison with NATO in Brussels.

More than this, the Gorbachev and Bush administrations are dialoguing and sometimes cooperating, in Angola, Afghanistan, Kampuchea. There is even a beginning recognition that it is contrary to both Soviet and Western interests to keep on supplying Third World countries with missile technology and chemical and nuclear weapons capability.[1]

World militarism has not been defeated, new nuclear weapons are still being produced, not all the cold warriors have given up their foolish ways, and some of the recent improvements could be lost if the peace movement ceases being vigilant and determined. But so far as the cold war itself is concerned, we are in a stage when patterns of cooperation are replacing the old military competition between East and West. This new, more hopeful situation is shown especially in the improved effectiveness of the Security Council of the United Nations.

Military Force in the Post–Cold War World, Underlying Factors:

a) The good news:

i) *The U.S. is the last of the global dominators.* The world's growing economic powers are very unlikely to turn their strength into military ambitions for world domination or a global military competition. Japan and the new Germany might be able to create the means, but it is hard to imagine their elites submitting their economic well-being to the hazards of war. Both have much more to gain from a disarmed international system.

China would have to choose between a shaky attempt at global expansionism and improved economic well-being for its people. In none of these three countries, unlike Germany in the 1930s, is there an ideology which would inspire the citizens to support global military adventures.

Some Islamic movements might have the ideology, but how could they marshall the means? How could they achieve unity to mount the necessary effort, when they are driven, like other religious populations, by divisions among themselves? And how could they mobilize the industrial strength without the help of Europe or the United States or Japan?

Brazil? Or other Latin American countries? Again, the ideology is lacking, let alone the industrial base or the size of population for military domination of large neighbours.

Imperialism used to be associated with glory and patriotic pride. Now it carries a bad name everywhere. Also, it has become too expensive a luxury. The U.S., as Mr. Bush's pleas for help to finance the U.S. military build-up in Saudi Arabia show, is learning the lesson which the old empires—Britain, France, Portugal, the Netherlands, Spain—learned, that the political and financial costs of global military power are unsupportable.

The underlying factors make the old alliance system obsolete, and make the United Nations the only practical tool for eliminating war.

ii) *Military secrecy is being replaced by military transparency.* Creating the military strength for starting a war could not be achieved secretly. While the capacity of national leaders to blind themselves to realities which they do not wish to see is probably unlimited, it has become impossible to blind the citizens so completely. The popular organizations in the churches, the peace movement, the environmental movement, the human rights movement, the movement for Third World development, the labour movement, and the senior citizens' movement provide a guarantee that such a tendency would lead to an outcry within the countries concerned.

iii) *Their own citizens would resist.* All potential dominators have important publics in their own countries with an aversion to militarism. (In China this may currently be suppressed, but without question it is there.) In no industrial country would major war be greeted today as it was in Europe in 1914, with public outpourings of nationalistic enthusiasm. Any industrial megapower launching a military attempt at global domination would have loud and rebellious resistance from important sections of its population.

iv) *New thinking on military strategy,* which is going on in the 35-nation Confidence and Security Building talks in Vienna, focuses on strengthening defensive forces and weakening offensive capabilities. Already measures to reduce the capability for surprise attack, such as the removal of bridging equipment and the moving of tanks back more than a day's travel from a frontier, are being introduced. This orientation of forces to be strong in defence and weak in offence has implications for the future forces to be designed for United Nations service.

v) *There is no likelihood of Canada or the U.S. being invaded.* The only military danger to our territory continues to be that of an intercontinental exchange of nuclear weapons, the solution to which is nuclear and conventional disarmament and the replacement of war by negotiation and recourse to the world court.

vi) *The United Nations Security Council* is beginning to operate as it was intended 45 years ago. The five permanent members are achieving beginning cooperation to promote peace. This is the most important new development for the long term.

b) The bad news (three interwoven processes):

i) *The military/technological residue of the cold war continues to be a danger.* Thousands of weapons, use of even one of which would constitute a horrendous disaster, continue to be deployed, and accident or miscalculation could lead to unparalled suffering. The lavish provision of nuclear killing power by the Soviet Union and the USA, followed by Britain and France, far beyond any rational military justification, continues to cost billions to maintain, and to pose serious environmental threats. This will be so until their nuclear arsenals have been reduced to about 2 per cent of their present size. (China's estimated 190 nuclear weapons do not go beyond "minimal deterrence".)

Currently, Strategic Air Command B-52 bombers armed with cruise missiles with their 200 kiloton warheads are still on ground alert; the Soviets are still producing seven nuclear powered submarines each year (a cutback of two per year); both the US and the USSR have Intercontinental Ballistic Missile (ICBM) submarines on station with missiles targeted on hundreds of sites in each country; and still in each country production lines of nuclear warheads continue to grind out their lethal freight.

ii) *Territorial anomalies left behind by history, ethnic and tribal inherited animosities, and the residue of past injustices (Irish, Armenian, Palestinian, and many others), along with increasing competition for resources, are all expressing themselves in actual or potential military duels* between nations (Iran/Iraq; Israel and her Arab opponents; Turkey/ Greece; Romania/Hungary; Libya/Chad; India/Pakistan; Iraq/Kuwait/ Saudi Arabia; South Africa and the "Frontline States", to name a few). Among the armed forces of such countries, there are altogether 250 submarines. Israel, India, and South Africa have or are close to having nuclear weapons. Brazil, Argentina, Iraq, Pakistan and one or two others are developing the capability to have nuclear weapons. One hundred and two countries now have cruise missiles. The cold war between the Soviet Union and the western nations may be over, but many countries feel threatened by their neighbours, or have old scores or new ambitions which they hope to settle by force of arms.

iii) *The industrial arms race continues its characteristic patterns.* For 150 years it has been fostering preparation for war and war itself, for profit. Now, in the environment of possible war in the Middle East, billions of dollars worth of new weapons are being provided by industrial states to Saudi Arabia, Iran, Israel, and Egypt. The pattern which made Iraq able to invade Kuwait is being repeated with its neighbours.

In the 1860s and 70s, the arms race was dominated by Krupp of Germany, Schneider of France, and Armstrong-Vickers of England, and these companies both competed and cooperated with each other.[2] Such firms used extensive bribery of officials, and of newspaper reporters to plant war scare stories in their press in order to frighten parliaments and public into authorizing lavish military expenditures.[3] They sometimes helped to arm their governments' enemies, and then used the opponents' possession of the improved technology which they had supplied to press their own governments for yet further increases in military expenditures. Books like *The Arms Bazaar* by Anthony Sampson show that these same practices are used today by Lockheed, General Dynamics, Litton, and other arms suppliers. Recent news reports of German firms helping Libya and Iraq to work towards chemical and nuclear weapons capability[4] show how firms like these promote their wares secretly on the international market, in violation of the laws of their own countries. Israel, Brazil and China have joined the game of strengthening their arms industries by exporting weapons around the world.

The history of companies such as Krupp and Lockheed show that they are in a symbiotic relationship with their governments, and that government departments and some politicians are so interwoven with them that even the most blatant examples of cheating their own governments result in only symbolic penalties.

Canada has subsidized both foreign and local enterprises of these types, such as Litton Industries and Pratt and Whitney, which are involved in export of arms to future warmakers in the Third World.

This is bad news because of the power, persistence, deviousness and criminality of these enterprises. However, the high-tech nature of their research and production and the visibility of the delivery vehicles for their most dangerous products (usually missiles), make surveillance, control, and elimination, once the political will has been achieved, a feasible proposition. Citizens' groups have an important job in keeping watch on and exposing such enterprises.

From Balance of Power to a Common Security System: Our planet is in an in-between period between the old pattern of seeking security through (unstable) military alliances, and a pattern of negotiated settlements to long-standing military conflicts, peacekeeping forces to maintain truces, the "fire-brigade" use of military blockage against potential aggression, and economic sanctions and blockade to end aggression and threats to peace—in other words a system based on security through common rules and protection for all against war.

Canada is fortunate that none of the regions of which it is a part have military competitions and potential conflagrations among their members, once the old U.S./Soviet competition is finally laid to rest. North and South Korea in the north Pacific could be an exception, but even there there are signs of reduction of tension and first steps towards a modus vivendi.

Fire brigade methods leave underlying issues unsettled, but say to the belligerent(s) that military attempts to resolve conflicts are no longer acceptable, and that other methods are required now. This new pattern is currently being applied regarding Iraq's invasion of Kuwait, though obscured by the fact that the military initiative has come from the U.S., rather than from the U.N. And yet the U.S. administration is *possibly* realizing that if it takes military action beyond the blockade authorized by the Security Council, it will risk a bloody enterprise which will end being condemned not only by many Arab countries, but by many of its European allies and its own people. In addition, it would grievously injure the world economy by devastating the Gulf oil fields. This is a forerunner of the probability that the Security Council will expand its "fire brigade" role by activating the U.N. Military Committee for the first time. This would allow for a U.N. headquarters staff to undergird military activity to snuff out or quarantine local duels.

Duels between persons were outlawed scores of years ago. In other words, it became accepted that the community could take away the right of consenting adults to try to kill each other. So now with nations. The refugee problems created for neighbours, the suffering caused for vast numbers of innocent civilians, the widespread environmental hazards beyond the borders of the dueling states, and in the case of Iraq/Kuwait, the dangers to the global economy, are all sufficient cause for the world community to ban the settlement of disputes by military means. The industrial countries have both the military and the economic means (through sanctions and blockade) to enforce this. Elimination of the greatest portion of the arms trade, with vigorous inspection, will be an important part of this. Ultimately, though, such measures can only eliminate the most disastrous aspects of war. Only a universal recognition that attempting to settle conflicts by military means is contrary to *every* nation's interests will lead to the total elimination of war.

We have learned from Chernobyl, from acid rain, etc., that the consequences of industrial and military misbehaviour affect persons and nations far removed from the scene of the event. A nuclear attack on Baghdad (or in the future by Baghdad) would spread radioactive fallout on unintended as well as intended victims—friends as well as foes. This is why all in the international community have an interest in seeing that such weapons are not used, and this means seeing that military action itself is replaced by diplomatic and political means of resolving disputes between nations.

WHAT KINDS OF FORCES WILL THE UNITED NATIONS NEED FOR THESE TASKS?

Highly mobile forces equipped with precision "smart" weapons for use against tanks, aircraft, missiles and infantry attacks of an aggressor; naval vessels, usually of small, fast corvette types, also equipped with "smart" weapons for use against evading ships or aircraft or submarines; jamming equipment and decoys for use against guidance systems of missiles. The range of capabilities cannot be fully described without consultation with experienced planners of U.N. peacekeeping activities, and potential partners in expanded international policing and military roles.

What must emerge are a kind of international fire department and an international police department with the following tasks:

1. To snuff out beginning military conflagrations.

2. To offer police protection (international border defence forces) to nations which feel threatened by lawless behaviour of other states.

3. To create a worldwide alarm system, by which planetary citizens can alert the "fire department" when they see the danger or actuality of military conflagration.

4. To eliminate the manufacture, selling and distribution of offensive weapons and mass destruction warheads, especially to areas of potential conflagration like the Middle East or the India/Pakistan arena.

5. To establish regulations which make research, development, and possession of weapons of mass destruction and their delivery systems illegal.
6. To find and punish violators of these regulations.

Some of the required regulations are already established—the illegality in international law of intervention in the affairs of other states, of aggression, of use of weapons of mass destruction, of use of poison gas. Other regulations have yet to be established. Although the *use* of weapons of mass destruction is illegal, *research, development and production* of such weapons are not, for example.

The present discussions in Europe of making national armed forces strong in defence and weak in offence have implications for what kinds of weapons production should have international sanction and which should not. Long range artillery, heavy bombers, missiles with ranges beyond a defensive front all should become illegal. Similarly, military submarines cannot be considered defensive, while anti-submarine weapons can be. A major political/diplomatic task for the 1990s is to establish a regime of elimination of production of unequivocally offensive weapons like tanks and cruise missiles.

A key part of this will be a seagoing policing mechanism to monitor and control the arms trade, as well as an industrial mechanism to ensure that firms cease and do not renew the production of such weapons. The citizens—whistle blowers within industries and governments, and residents of communities where parts of the weapons process may take place—will be a vital element in this, but technically knowledgeable people in our armed forces will be important to work hand in hand with the citizens in the suffocation of the residual arms production part of the economy.

This emerging United Nations capability will rely, as peacekeeping does now, on participation by units from U.N. member states. The international "fire department" will require a rapid response system in which the branches of Canada's military forces will have a role. What the shape and size of that role should be depends on the kinds of forces required, and the share in them which other countries will undertake. At present it is only the U.S. which possesses such a global rapid response capability, but few nations are willing to accept a global "Pax Americana". Only international forces coordinated through the U.N. on behalf of the world community can be acceptable to the member states. In addition, many components of the U.S. arsenal are irrelevant to and excessive for any kind of internationally approved rapid response policing. The international community as expressed in the U.N. is likely to be ready to quarantine conflicts or to block aggressors, but not to sponsor the kinds of mass destruction and nuclear terror weapons which the U.S. arsenal currently contains. The same can be said of the arsenals of all the nuclear powers.

This approach will only work permanently when the permanent members of the U.N. Security Council and the other major industrialized countries agree always to submit themselves to the International Court of Justice, and never to resort to arms, for final settlement of their conflicts with other countries. A beginning has been made on this—the Soviet Union has said that it will do this, if the other permanent members of the Security Council will do the same.

A NUMBER OF MILITARY BELIEFS MUST BE REPLACED.

i) A hundred years ago, Bismarck told the German parliament that *"increased armaments were the best guarantee of peace."*[5] The century since has shown that this "peace through strength" faith is a recipe for arms races, which until now have always led to war.

ii) The idea, still expressed by leading Canadian military officers, that *the military profession's first* raison d'être *is to "win wars."* This concept has been obsolete since 1945. Weapons have become so destructive that the losses for all participants, especially civilians, have been far greater than the gains.

The *raison d'être* of the military profession now is to block aggression and achieve stalemate, to create the conditions for negotiated or adjudicated non-violent solutions, even if the stalemate goes on for years. This changed military goal is frustrating for those trained in the belief that their highest aspiration is glorious victory on the field of battle.

iii) The belief that *investment in military industry is a good economic and employment strategy.* The overall economic health of those countries where investment in militarism has been low, compared to that of the U.S. and the USSR where it has been high, is conclusive proof that investment in militarism carries a heavy cost in civilian opportunities foregone.

IMPLICATIONS FOR CANADA'S MILITARY POLICIES:

a) *It is time to switch Canada's allegiance in military matters from NATO and NORAD to the United Nations.* Since 1949, Canada's decisions in military matters have been determined by its membership in these two alliances. For at least a little while, NATO still has some useful political and diplomatic functions, but its military tasks are melting away. With Germany cutting its armed forces from over 500,000 to 302,000, and the U.S., Britain, and other NATO members making cutbacks in the scores of thousands, the need for Canada's symbolic 8,000 person contribution in Europe has dropped to zero.

We have a vital stake in how the new security order in Europe works out, because we want it to be effective in keeping peace there permanently, and we want it to be a model for permanent security arrangements elsewhere. Therefore, like Iceland, France and Spain, we should keep our seat at the NATO Council without military participation.

NORAD has the purpose of "defending us" from Soviet bombers and cruise missiles. This has always been an impossible task, especially since any cruise missile attack would be part of a larger intercontinental missile attack, against which no defence exists. With the end of the cold war, such an attack has become more than ever unbelievable, and the North Warning System should be abandoned. Space surveillance will be sufficient for discovering isolated unauthorized intrusions into our air space.

b) *It is time to develop regional arms control/disarmament/security zones around our borders.* These would be building blocks towards a world-wide United Nations international security system, but would not have to wait for such U.N. development. In the Arctic, the North Pacific, and the North Atlantic we need naval and air disarmament down to policing level. The sea and air spaces in the region should be jointly policed by the regional powers to ensure that arms control and disarmament agreements are being adhered to, to eliminate the arms trade in the air and waters of the region, to stop drug and arms smuggling, and to prevent economic and environmental violations of international treaties and national economic zones. These regional operations will assure the nations bordering them that threatening military activities have become a thing of the past. Participation in this regional policing will require both air and sea participation of Canada's military forces, at a policing level. Perhaps civilian aircraft can contribute to this by being fitted with automatic equipment giving surveillance information over the territory traversed by their normal routes.

These regional security arrangements must replace unilateral U.S. air, sea, and undersea strategic patrolling, and require the internationalizing of satellite surveillance as the quickest and most comprehensive way of monitoring air and sea activity. The most desirable development would be if the U.S. and the USSR were to turn over their existing satellite surveillance systems to the United Nations, with operational costs shared among all nations. If the U.S. and USSR are unwilling to do this, then a separate United Nations satellite system as proposed by France should be developed. The first approach would be the most economical for all concerned, including the U.S. and USSR. Costs would be involved for Canada (see Table 2), but these costs would be shared with Japan, China,

Taiwan, Korea and the countries of Europe, and therefore would not be excessive considering the military, economic and environmental advantages.

The main political tasks are to get the big powers to accept for themselves the jurisdiction of the World Court and to make real their United Nations commitment not to intervene in other nations; to accelerate the various disarmament negotiations; and to reform the United Nations to enhance its capability for blocking aggressive behaviour. It is certain now that the economies of all nations are so intertwined that sanctions and blockades organized by the U.N. can successfully block aggressors.

For the creation of a standing, or at least ready, U.N. seagoing police force, a definition of the need is required, along with an indication of what forces other middle powers are ready to contribute. A rational division of labour on the basis of kinds of forces countries have and geographical (regional) allocation of responsibilities, will need to be sorted out.

PRINCIPLES FOR A CANADIAN MILITARY POLICY FOR THE 1990s:

1. The cornerstone is *preparation to participate with others in the developing U.N. international "fire brigade" and police force,* to quench or put on hold military conflagrations, and to offer police protection to nations requesting it. This is an expansion of Canada's traditional U.N. peacekeeping role.

2. *Monitoring, in cooperation with policing units from regional partners, of disarmament agreements,* of shut-downs of most parts of the arms trade, and of approved military activities of the nations.

3. *Suppression, with regional partners, of the drug trade, environmental misbehaviour, and fishing and other economic violations.*

4. *Participation, with others, in international disaster relief efforts.*

5. *Close cooperation with citizens' organizations* in scrutinizing military, arms trade, and drug smuggling activities in Canada and other countries.

6. *Preparedness only for clear threats, not for hypothetical possibilities.* Enormous resources, needed to cope with environmental and other problems, can be wasted on expensive military preparations against highly improbable threats. For example, money is needed *now* to fight the greenhouse effect and damage to the ozone layer. The possibility that Soviet and US submarines will threaten the sea lanes of communication, or that the 250 submarines owned by about a dozen Third World countries will threaten world peace is negligible, and in the latter case, the members of the U.N. Security Council are well supplied with anti-submarine warfare capabilities. Should Canada continue to put into anti-submarine warfare

Table 1

Canadian Defence Budget 1990–91—Estimated Costs

(Cost shown in millions of dollars)

Unit	Personnel Persons	Salaries	Operations/ Maintenance	Equipment Expenses	Total
Navy	18,000	$ 783	$ 500	$1,181	$ 2,464
Army	24,400	1,065	461	394	1,920
Air	28,500	1,239	1,291	447	2,977
Europe	7,900	417	451	408	1,276
Communication	4,600	233	87	109	429
Personnel[a]	19,700	867	280	162	
		381[b]			1,690
Matériel[c]	11,600	547	250	86	883
Policy/Management[d]	5,000	321	133	32	
(Grants)			236[e]		722
Total	119,700[f]	$5,853	$3,689	$2,819	$12,361
Less revenues, mainly rent paid by personnel:					357
Final Total					$12,004

a) Personnel includes medical and dental services, military colleges, the chaplaincy, military education and training, physical fitness, education for dependents, benefits, etc.
b) Supplementary retirement pensions allocation.
c) Matériel includes research and development; maintenance; property management; supply, procurement and storage of equipment, etc.
d) Policy Direction and Management Services include development of defence policy; financial, management and legal services; emergency planning; Canadian contributions to NATO.
e) The largest portion of the grants item ($205 million) is for contributions to NATO's military budgets and infrastructure. Other grants include funds for university military studies, contributions to non-profit strategic studies centres and several "defence associations", to the Civil Air Search and Rescue Association, to the Defence Industrial Research Program, and other miscellaneous items.
f) Total personnel comprise about 86,800 military, in addition to 33,000 civilian personnel.

measures resources which could go to working on the greenhouse effect problem? Abandonment of an anti-submarine warfare role would release several scores of millions of dollars.

7. *End all weapons research and development.* There are more than enough weapons for every conceivable purpose in this world. Further investment in research and development is a self-destructive waste. There may be room for continued research in technology for disarmament verification.

Will These Changes Produce a "Peace Dividend"?

Let's look at present costs, and what the new assignments might mean in dollars.

Budgeted Costs of Canada's military in 1990–91[6]

Over all, $12,005,000,000, plus up to $200,000,000 in the Defence Industry Productivity (D.I.P.) Program.

United Nations peacekeeping in six different operations involves participation of about 1,000 of Mobile Command's (Army) personnel currently. In addition, "Mobile Command continues to maintain one infantry battalion and supporting elements (perhaps about another 1,000 uniformed men and women—Author) for other peacekeeping operations as may be required."[7] Air Transport Group of Air Command has provided supply transport for United Nations Peacekeeping operations, as well as transport in relation to natural disasters (e.g., the Armenian earthquake). Canada's contributions to United Nations peacekeeping were limited in the 1987 Defence White Paper to not more than 2,000 military personnel at any one time. It is not identified as a separate budget item in the estimates. At present it is "small potatoes" in Canada's military arrangements.

The changed roles that I have described require well-trained but lightly equipped military forces—a small-ship navy, for example, well-supplied with corvette-type vessels (see capital equipment list in Table 2). The frigates now being constructed would not be useless, but in general are over-armed for the Navy's main sea surveillance and control tasks. On U.N. "fire brigade" assignments they might be up against "enemy" naval vessels or submarines, but normally they would be dealing with civilian ships and fishing vessels which might be involved in illegally transporting arms and/or drugs, or violating Canada's 200-mile economic zone.

Our approximately 130 CF-18 fighter aircraft, designed and equipped to strike targets behind the now defunct Iron Curtain, also would not be

Table 2

Current Weapons Purchase Commitments

Purely offensive are marked "o"; purely defensive are marked "d"; mixed are marked "m". Those marked "d" and "m" presumably could fit into a common security approach. Costs shown in millions of dollars.

	Item	Estimated Total Cost	Already Spent	1990/91 Expense	Future Cost
d	Towed Array Sonar	$ 124	$ 32	$ 12	$ 80
m	Frigates	9,792	4,662	675	4,455
m	Destroyer Update	1,356	933	63	360
m	Heavy Vehicles	396	217	140	39
m	Light Vehicles	201	0	25	176
m	CF-18s (138)	4,928	4,784	61	83
m	CF-18 Fuel Tanks	70	11	14	45
d	Arctic Surveillance Aircraft (3)	257	3	7	247
d	Low Level Air Defence	1,138	561	303	274
m	Small Arms	353	235	25	93
m	Tactical Communications	50	1	11	38
m	NORAD	857	414	112	331
m	Tactical Command, Control, Communications	96	21	8	67
d	Sonobuoys	61	1	18	42
m	Night Vision Goggles	49	22	13	14
d	Helicopter-Towed Array System	40	0	0	40
o	CF-18 Missiles	334	294	7	33
m	Torpedoes	220	199	4	17
m	Replace Ammunition	787	0	259	528
m	Miscellaneous Ammunition	167	0	47	120
	Totals			1,804	7,082

useless. They might be called upon for "fire brigade" duty as in the Iraq crisis, and to intercept rare unauthorized intruders into Canadian air space, but they are over-armed and too fast for policing roles. What *will* be needed are transport planes to move troops and their equipment quickly to crisis or disaster areas, and planes well-suited to surveillance assignments. CF-18's are designed as destroyers. Airborne drug or arms smugglers will be subject to being forced down and dealt with by police on the ground, rather than being shot down.

The heavy tanks of our forces in Europe *will* be useless—too heavy to transport and use in the "fire brigade" situation. For police protection of threatened nations and for disaster intervention and peacekeeping, what is needed are motorized transport, helicopters, and possibly light armored vehicles. The "fire brigade" situation of confronting an aggressor calls for mobile forces equipped with highly accurate "smart weapons" for destroying or disabling tanks, aircraft, infantry, and missile sites. These might be needed as back-up for the police protection role.

The Low Level Air Defense Project (LLAD) is intended to provide anti-aircraft defence for Canada's two air bases and the Canadian Mechanized Brigade in Germany, and for the Canadian AirSea Transportable (CAST) Brigade held in readiness in Canada to be deployed overseas in a crisis. While LLAD will continue to have value for a situation like Iraq/Kuwait, with the removal of our forces from Europe, surely the original planned size of the LLAD can be reduced.

One criterion for judging the suitability of equipment, as distinct from personnel, is whether it is by nature purely offensive and therefore threatening and should be dropped, or purely defensive and therefore non-threatening, or is it both?

A second criterion: Is the role which the weapons support focussed on a present, visible threat or on an unlikely one, which is of secondary importance compared to visible environmental threats?

Table 2 lists the weapons purchases to which the Department of National Defence is currently committed, which are not yet fully paid for

What could be saved from the above? What should be added?
(Millions of dollars)

Cancel last six frigates	$4,000
Cancel completion of early warning system (NORAD)	300
Cut back on artillery and eliminate tank ammunition	300
Cancel remaining LLAD	250
Stop adding small arms	80
Cut back on ammunition	100
Cut back CF-18 missiles	38
Total capital savings (over several years)	$5,068
Less new capital spending: 20 Corvettes	2,000
Less U.N. Satellite Monitering Agency Contribution	500
Net Capital Savings	$2,568

and therefore have future costs. One part of a peace dividend could come from cancellation of those which don't fit the requirements of common security.

(Abandoning the anti-submarine focus would permit cancellation of at least another $170 million of the above capital acquisitions.) These are examples of the kind of thinking which a Government committed to a common security approach might use. Investigation would show other potential savings. For instance, are the three Arctic surveillance aircraft worth it at $80 million dollars each, even though they are purely defensive?

Annual contributions and operations:

Withdrawal and transfer of forces from Europe, once the transfer itself was paid for, would produce some saving. Elimination of heavy tanks now with our forces in Europe will reduce operations and maintenance costs. (No new capital expenditures for tanks are planned.) Surely savings on operations, maintenance and travel would be at least $300 million.

Cancel grants to NATO military budgets and infrastructure—$275 million. Cancel Defence Industry Productivity Program and Defense Industrial Research Program—up to $200 million.

Annual savings beginning in 1991:   *$775* million

Offset by contributions to future U.N. military budgets and infrastructure, which might be as much as they have been to NATO: $275 million annually.[8]

Net annual saving: *$500* million

After definition of U.N. standing force needs, and a survey of U.N. members' ability to contribute, numbers of personnel and kinds of equipment needed for Canada's contribution could be identified. Certainly mobile land forces are needed for both peacekeeping and protective policing assignments. CF-18 fighters may be needed for "fire brigade" roles. Some other countries are well supplied with minesweepers. Does Canada need any for potential U.N. service? Do we need a handful for the possiblity that someone might sometime mine our harbours, or is that a risk we should take in order to save resources for visible environmental problems? Again, these are examples of the thinking to be done.

Personnel:

Recruiting should be put on hold until the new roles and requirements of

Canada's military are clarified. However, with the falling away of the offensive tasks of the Army and Air Force for NATO, and the ending of the fears for the sea lines of communication for the Navy, which were all part of the cold war, it should be possible to reduce the numbers in the Army and the Air Force. Within an Army of more than 20,000 uniformed persons, it should be possible to expand the personnel prepared for United Nations peacekeeping and for international disaster assistance far beyond the 2,000 person limit set in 1987. The Navy may need the same or greater numbers as at present, as seagoing policing of the oceans becomes a reality under the authority given to the United Nations by the yet-to-be-implemented Law of the Sea. Thus, personnel saving should yield a peace dividend too, but it is more difficult to define until the new emphasis in the armed forces has been settled.

It is logical that a strong Canadian contribution to a U.N.-based global policing and "fire-brigade" program will cost less than our current alliance-based forces. There will not be the need for high-tech offensive forces, and there will be many more partners with whom to share the load.

A final question:
The spokespersons for our Department of National Defence have clung to the past like limpets. As recently as August 1990, a Canadian naval representative expressed the hope that the Soviets will keep on producing nuclear submarines "because they are my threat": this at a time when we have no more to fear from Soviet submarines than from those of France or the U.S. Are our leading officials capable of accepting international policing, and, in crises, producing military stalemates rather than winning wars, as our military job? Does this new approach require more than ordinary change at the top? Is the break with tradition (except the peacekeeping tradition) so great that we should cease to think of them as military at all, and call them something else, as Costa Rica has done?

Let us not fool ourselves. Achieving such changes will require relentless citizen effort.*

* Editor's note: It certainly will require relentless effort! Michael Wilson, the Minister of Finance, in his budget speech of 26 February 1991, announced an increase in defence expenditures of at least $600,000,000 for the next fiscal year, presumably to cover Canada's incremental costs incurred in the Persian Gulf War. This would bring Canada's "defence" expenditures to more than $13 billion annually.

References and Notes

1. A couple of years ago, NATO and the Russians agreed that an Argentinian plan for a high-tech "Condor 2" missile was very dangerous. They embargoed the necessary parts, and Argentina was forced to drop its missile plan. Dr. Jamie Shea, "Is NATO still neces-

sary?", *Nato Watch,* Vol. VI, No. 2, Summer 1990, p. 15.

2. Manchester, William, *The Arms of Krupp,* Little Brown, Boston, 1968, p. 92.

3. Manchester, Chapter 11.

4. "West German jailed for part in chemical warfare plant," *Ottawa Citizen,* June 28, 1990; "Shipment Seized," *Globe and Mail,* August 22, 1990; "West German Firms under investigation," *Globe and Mail,* August 24, 1990. In the last case, "Nearly 60 West German companies" were being investigated! The West German government was urging industry to "police itself to purge such trade."

5. Manchester, p. 148.

6. Figures are drawn chiefly from *Budget Estimates, 1990–91, Department of National Defence,* Department of Supply and Services, Ottawa, 1990. Those for the Defence Industry Productivity Program are based on the 1990–91 estimates for the Department of Industry and Commerce.

7. 1990–91 National Defence Budget Estimates, p.38.

8. Canada's 1990–91 contributions to the civilian and scientific side of NATO are $6.281 million and $1.540 million respectively. When these are added to the $275 million military contribution to NATO's central costs, *the total to NATO's central costs in 1990–91,* apart from maintaining our forces in Europe, *is $282.821* million. The contribution to the U.N. itself is $33.444 million, and to the U.N.'s five major affiliated agencies, a total of $41.482 million. Contribution to the central costs of three U.N. peacekeeping operations total $13.152 million. *The total to United Nations central costs in 1990–91 is $88.078 million.* Based on 1990–91 Budget Estimates, Department of External Affairs, pp. 2–42, figure 20.

CHAPTER 6
Canadian Foreign Policy in the 1990s

PROFESSOR MICHAEL D. WALLACE

INDEPENDENCE AND NATIONALISM IN THE 1990s

As citizens of a medium-sized nation living in the long shadow of the dominant global power, seized by no territorial ambitions, and possessing no ideological or evangelistic creed to proselytize in the external world, Canadians have seldom regarded foreign policy as the most pressing item on the national political agenda. They often seem to regard their foreign policy as little more than a *pro forma* ritual of statehood like royal visits or the opening of Parliament. Years may go by without a foreign policy issue becoming a serious matter of political contention and debate. The skills and virtues Canadians bring to public life—a knack for negotiation and bargaining, an instinct for civility, an eye for the middle ground—are often fully employed in papering the fissures of our own sprawling, fractious disunity.

Yet there have always been those among us far-sighted enough to understand and appreciate Canada's potential in the realm of foreign affairs. Under the stewardship of Lester Pearson, Canada acquired an enduring reputation as a disinterested peacemaker, an upholder of international law and of civilized conduct in international relations, an advocate of human rights, and a champion of economic development in the Third World. Although many would argue that the Pearsonian mantle can no longer cloak the inaction and reticence of recent governments in the international arena, the fact remains that Canada's stock is still high within the comity of nations.

Not entirely without reason, many Canadians felt a sense of helplessness during the height of the Cold War. With its passing, the scope for independent Canadian action and initiative has grown enormously. So too

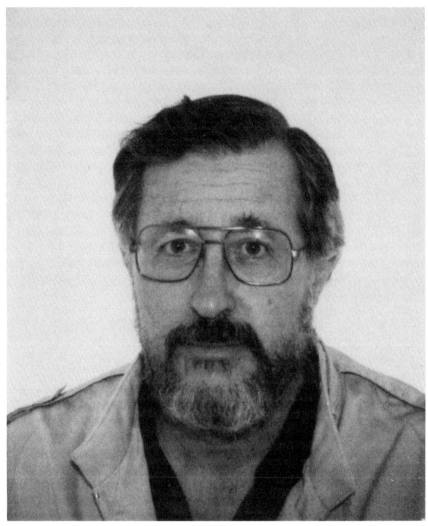

Professor Michael D. Wallace

has the urgency for action. The simultaneous proliferation of regional conflicts and weapons of mass destruction among the protagonists, an ever-expanding environmental agenda, the running sore of the Third World debt crisis, and the emergence of three continental blocks dominating global trade all pose unprecedented challenges to Canadian goals and values. On the positive side, the new global problematique provides a unique opportunity for Canada to re-establish its influence of old. We cannot do so, however, unless we make sure that both the ends and the means of Canadian foreign policy are in accord with the new realities.

Fortunately, we need not undertake this task *de novo*. In late 1985 and early 1986, a Special Joint Committee of the Senate and the House of Commons undertook a thoroughgoing public examination of Canada's international relations. Travelling across the nation and receiving submissions from thousands of individuals and groups from all walks of life and representing every sector of the community, the Committee produced a final document[1] which represents a remarkably insightful summary of the problems and prospects for Canadian action in the international arena in mid-decade. Since that time, of course, the world has become a vastly different place. But the 1986 Report nevertheless represents an excellent launching pad for our reevaluation.

The Report sets out what it refers to as "seven major directions for Canadian foreign policy," which, taken as goals in the broadest sense, are hard to fault. Listed somewhat tersely, they are: 1) work to strengthen the United Nations system, 2) develop a distinctly Canadian security policy, 3) expand opportunities for multilateral trade, 4) expand and improve development assistance, 5) promote human rights, 6) extend Canadian sovereignty in the Arctic, and 7) improve the management of Canada-U.S. relations.

In six of the seven categories, the events of the past five years have created more opportunities for middle-power action and initiative, and

Michael Wallace was born in Montreal and educated at McGill, the University of Michigan, and the École des Hautes Études Internationales in Geneva. He is Professor of Political Science at the University of British Columbia, specializing in International Relations. He is the author of several books and numerous articles on the causes of war, the arms race, the risks of accidental nuclear war, and arms control. He is principal investigator in charge of a research project funded by the Social Sciences and Humanities Research Council of Canada which studies the behavior of leaders in crises, wars and negotiations.

Professor Wallace is a Vice President of the United Nations Association of Canada, and a member of the Board of Directors of Science for Peace.

relatively straightforward analysis yields innovative policy proposals. The all-pervasive problem of Canadian-American relations is, as always, the exception. Since it inevitably affects every area of Canadian foreign policy, it is logical and necessary to deal with this topic at the outset.

THE FUTURE OF CANADA–U.S. RELATIONS

Since our earliest days of nationhood, relations with the great republic to the south have represented a Scylla and Charybdis between which Canadian policy-makers carefully steer. On the one hand, we must somehow get along with our enormous and often difficult neighbour. On the other, our own distinct national goals and interests, and on occasion our very existence and identity as a nation sometimes requires that we pursue distinct policies in many areas, even—and there's the rub—when these create annoyance or even consternation south of the line. This duality is all the more elemental in that it reflects a deep polarization in the Canadian psyche: the mixture of attraction and aversion that characterizes Canadian attitudes towards the United States, so fundamentally different from the unalloyed fear and loathing that most small states feel towards powerful neighbours. It is only to be expected, then, that from time to time Canadian foreign policy has found itself in opposition to U.S. policy on a variety of matters. What is important to understand, however, is that this opposition at its height has never been as serious or as fundamental as it has been portrayed, nor—despite what the more cantankerous American policy-makers profess to believe—is it really typical of the broad sweep of Canadian policy-making. Nor has it ever really affected normal economic and other day-to-day relations with the U.S. Indeed, Canadian foreign policy may be more justly accused of unabashed sycophancy than knee-jerk anti-Americanism.

In recent times, Canada-U.S. opposition reached its height during the Vietnam War. For the first time in decades, Canada voiced strong, public opposition to a central tenet of U.S. policy, beginning with Lester Pearson's speech at William and Mary College in 1965, in which he rejected the use of outside military force to settle the Vietnamese conflict. Not only did Pearson refuse Canadian military involvement, his government's policies made Canada a haven for American draft resisters and (eventually) military deserters.

Yet the clash was less fundamental than it seemed. In most other areas—issues involving Europe, the Middle East, and, most critical of all, the equipping of the Canadian forces assigned to NATO and NORAD with tactical nuclear weapons—our policies were directly in line with American wishes. Although officially a sanctuary for U.S. draft resisters, Canadian security and law enforcement authorities cooperated with their American counterparts in surveillance activities, including not only the

110

American refugees themselves but also their Canadian support organizations and even antiwar groups operating in Canada. Ironically, then, even though official Canadian policy was antiwar, unofficial antiwar activity was regarded as subversive! And for all that, at no time did Canadian opposition to the war exceed that articulated within the U.S. political process itself.

Nor were Canada-U.S. economic relations in any way affected by this official rift. 1965 also saw the signing of the auto pact, representing the virtual fusion of the two nations' largest industry. Indeed, Canada derived considerable economic benefit from the war, finding markets for every military need, from artillery shells at one end of the process, to body bags at the other.

Since that era it is hard to detect any major disagreement between the two states on foreign policy issues, despite the ultrahawkish Cold War stance of the Reagan administration. Canada agreed to allow testing of American air-launched cruise missiles in Canadian airspace despite the government's advocacy of a testing ban in the United Nations. Canada supported the deployment of the destabilizing Pershing II missiles in Europe, and the U.S. invasions of Grenada, Lebanon, and Panama. Since taking its seat on the United Nations Security Council in 1989, Canada has avoided any independent initiative—be it in the Middle East, Southeast Asia, or Latin America—that might conflict with U.S. policy. Only on relations with South Africa could it be said that Canada possessed a distinct policy, and even here the issue was one of emphasis rather then direction. Worst of all, perhaps, the 1989 trade deal has forced Canada ever more firmly onto the U.S. economic orbit and limited even still further such little manoeuvering room that we had in the economic realm.

More than ten years of unwillingness to take independent stands has left Canada directionless and has begun to erode our influence in world councils. If the Vietnam experience is any guide, asserting our independence will not create any serious or lasting harm to our interests or to U.S.-Canada relations, and it is an essential prerequisite to success in pursuing the other six "directions" identified in the 1986 Report. Beginning with this premise, let us turn to these six policy areas *ad seriatim* and explore what Canada could and should try to achieve.

STRENGTHENING THE U.N. SYSTEM
The end of the Cold War has begun to reverse the long decline of the United Nations peace and security role. From Cambodia to Namibia, Palestine to Kashmir, the United Nations has an ever-increasing role in negotiating, keeping, and even enforcing the peace. Unfortunately, Canada has played a passive rather than active part in this process, and such action as the government has taken has not been helpful. Canada's response

to the Iraqi invasion of Kuwait—the most serious security challenge faced by the U.N. in over a decade—has been to join the U.S. in independent military action rather than to encourage and participate in collective enforcement through the U.N. While the initial announcement in August committing Canadian forces to the Gulf can be explained as an understandable reaction to a very serious breach of the peace, the announcement in October that Canadian forces might act against Iraq even without authorization by a specific resolution of the U.N Security Council cannot be taken lightly. Since the impact of our action on the overall military balance is derisory, choosing this course merely has the effect of signalling that, for Canada, supporting American policy takes priority over our commitment to building a collective, international consensus capable of responding forcefully to breaches of the peace.

Canada's role in many of the other U.N. agencies has been considerably better. We did not join Britain and the U.S. in their petulant walk out from UNESCO, and, in contrast to many other rich states and the U.S. in particular, we have been generous and prompt in paying our U.N. dues. Nevertheless, Canada is often found on the side of that group of predominantly Western nations who seek to curtail the important U.N. programs in the name of "fiscal responsibility," and who seek to use the World Bank and other multilateral financial agencies to impose Chicago-school monetarism on the broken backs of Third World economies.

It is unfortunate that this unprecedented half-heartedness toward the U.N. comes at the very moment when the political conditions exist—for the first time in forty years—to make the system work as it was intended. It is time for Canada as a nation to renew our commitment to the United Nations system as the embodiment of global collective action, and to express this commitment in word and in deed.

A NEW SECURITY POLICY

The 1986 Report's recommendation for a new and distinctively Canadian security policy mutated into the disastrous 1987 White Paper on Defence.[2] At the very moment when glasnost and the signing of the INF Treaty were heralding the end of the Cold War, the Department of Defence was trumpeting hawkish homilies such as, "The principal direct threat to Canada is a nuclear attack on North America by the Soviet Union."

The cold war tone of the White Paper, combined with the ill-considered proposal to purchase nuclear attack submarines, aroused widespread opposition and dissipated a parturient consensus on a post-cold war security policy. In the process, fundamental questions concerning the appropriate roles to be played by our armed forces, and the procurements necessary to equip them for these roles, were left unanswered.

The decision to deploy the forces in Oka and the Persian Gulf—taken without Parliamentary debate or approval—poses these questions anew with unprecedented intensity. With the end of the Cold War, the role for Canadian forces in Europe will soon be obsolete. This leaves three traditional roles remaining: 1) aid to the civil power, 2) maintenance of sovereignty and continental defence, and 3) peacekeeping under the flag of the U.N.

To begin with, the vague and all-encompassing power of both federal and provincial jurisdictions to call upon the armed forces for assistance at their sole discretion raises disturbing political and constitutional issues that run well outside the purview of this chapter. It is enough to point out that in 1970 and again in 1990, this power was used to turn the forces into an adjunct of the police in circumstances involving political controversy, and without any reference to elected legislatures. Moreover, in both cases this occurred because the regular law enforcement agencies had manifested gross incompetence. Although no one can deny that civil authorities may need the assistance of the armed forces to deal with natural disasters and the like, the current legislative and constitutional regime governing aid to the civil power cries out for reform.

A far more detailed discussion of the other roles for the Forces—protection of sovereignty and peacekeeping—along with details of a proposed force structure is available in C. G. Gifford's chapter in this volume. Here I shall only summarize the political and military requirements these roles mandate. To begin with, it is axiomatic that the Forces should be used to assert Canadian sovereignty; the only question is how. The nuclear submarine controversy distracted debate from the very real issues posed by the need to replace much of the Forces' aging equipment.

On the Atlantic and Pacific coasts, protecting sovereignty requires multipurpose frigates and long-range surveillance aircraft, and must be backed up by a considerably enhanced Coast Guard patrol and air-sea rescue capability. Existing deployment programs are attempting to meet some of these needs, but they have been delayed by short-sighted budget politics and a politically-driven and incompetent procurement process. As our expensive European commitments end, some resources should be used to rationalize and expedite these deployments.

The Arctic poses the most formidable challenge to the assertion of Canadian sovereignty. This is due not only to the hostile physical environment, but even more to the continued refusal of the U.S. formally to recognize Canadian sovereignty over the Arctic Archipelago. Canada's response should be both military and political. First, the Canadian government should give formal notice to the U.S. that further renewal of the NORAD treaty will be contingent upon U.S. recognition of Canadian sovereignty over the Archipelago. Second, until this is forthcoming, Canada should end all joint operations and base agreements with the U.S. north of the 60th parallel. Third, Canada should increase substantially the air and ground forces based in the Arctic. Finally, the government should build and deploy not one but several heavy-ice-capable icebreakers in its Arctic territorial seas.

Turning to the third remaining role for our armed forces, little needs to be done to enhance their peacemaking ability. An enhanced airlift capability could be of assistance in some circumstances. Additional ships of the *Protecteur/Provider* class would provide independent logistical support at relatively little cost.

TRADE: MULTILATERALISM VS. "THE DEAL"

In the last two decades Canada's traditional efforts to expand global trade have run up against the emerging dominance of three trading "superblocs": Japan, the European Community and the U.S. In a departure from our usual policy of eschewing blocs in favour of multi-lateralism, we have opted for a lopsided and destructive affiliation with the U.S. bloc. Abandoning our own tariff barriers, we have given a veto over our economic development, social programs, and entertainment in-dustry to an American-dominated body, without obtaining in return con-cessions in such crucial areas as agricultural subsidies. The trade deal has thus ensured the destruction of our noncompetitive sectors without any benefits for our competitive ones. The Canadian government should give notice that it intends to withdraw from the deal, and begin vigorous ef-forts to avert a trade war and promote multilateral trade. In doing so, we should recognize that among our natural allies in this effort are many na-tions in the Third World, whose primary producers and infant industries have more in common with their Canadian counterparts than do the hy-perdeveloped economies of Germany and Japan.

EXPANDING DEVELOPMENT ASSISTANCE

This strategy of trade cooperation with the Third World dovetails with a renewed strategy of development assistance. From the outset, it should be emphasized that the right sort of help to the world's impoverished econo-mies is neither totally altruistic nor narrowly self-beneficial; we are not "throwing money away," nor should we tie our aid to narrow, short-run economic advantages for Canada. We should view it as part of our en-lightened self-interest; restoring economic health to these nations will not only open up many new trading opportunities for Canada, but will en-hance our security by reducing the economically-driven violence and dis-order that pervade the Third World.

The major criticism to be levelled at Canada's current foreign aid effort is its small size. Over a decade ago, Canada was one of many developed nations who agreed to set a goal of 1 per cent of GNP as a target for foreign development assistance. In fiscal 1988–1989, Canada's disbursements were only .47 of 1 per cent of GNP, which percentage ranked a shameful 13th among the 20 Organization of Economic Cooperation and Development nations.[3] As if that were not bad enough, the government chopped nearly 25 per cent from that amount for 1989–1990. By contrast, Sweden and Denmark disbursed .88 of 1 per cent of GNP, the Netherlands .98 of 1 per cent, and Norway no less than 1.09 of 1 per cent, more than double the proportion donated by Canada!

Of course, there is more to effective development assistance than money; the assistance must also reach those who most need and benefit from the help. CIDA (Canadian International Development Agency) officials work hard to ensure that money is not wasted on site, but there is more to it than that. Many countries accepting Canadian development assistance also spend exorbitant amounts of money on the military, wasting their own precious development resources. One may well ask why Canada should be providing assistance to states that spend a great deal more of their GNP per capita on the military than Canada does itself, and whose military spending is growing by leaps and bounds. India, Pakistan, Indonesia, Thailand and the Philippines (to note only the most conspicuous cases), fall in this category and collectively account for no less than 255 million dollars of Canadian aid annually, nearly 15 per cent of the total. Perhaps Canada should reallocate its assistance to those nations who do not waste their own resources to such a great extent.

PROMOTING HUMAN RIGHTS
Canada has without question been a world leader in the promotion of human rights in the international community. Of particular note has been the Canadian diplomatic effort to promote economic sanctions against the South African regime in opposition to its apartheid policies. Without question, Canada's efforts are in part responsible for many of the positive changes that have taken place in that country. In some other parts of the world, Canada has played a less conspicuous role in promoting human rights, but our actions have at least been helpful, if not as forthcoming as many Canadians would have wished. In Central America, Canadian efforts in Guatemala and El Salvador have been directed behind the scenes to promote respect for human rights. Although this has precluded public condemnation of the frequently atrocious human rights violations that abound in these and other Central American states, most would argue that our role has at least been helpful.

In other cases, however, the Canadian government has allowed human rights to take a back seat to political expediency, pressure from its allies, and even narrow economic self-interest. Although, unfortunately, many cases can be cited, three examples stand out.

First, Canada has by and large ignored the flagrant human rights violations that have occurred and continue to occur in Israeli-occupied Palestine. While rightly urging peaceful solutions to the Arab-Israeli conflict, the government—undoubtedly in response to political pressure—has been far less forceful in asserting the obvious truth that peaceful solutions cannot be achieved by denying some of the parties their political, legal and civil rights. During Canada's recent two-year tenure as a non-permanent member of the Security Council, Canada voted with the American delegation almost automatically each time this issue arose.

Canada's policy on Cambodia—Kampuchea, and indeed its policy toward the entire Southeast Asian region, has shown the same slavish copying of American positions. Canada's support for the genocidal Pol Pot gang over the existing Cambodian government is rooted in cold war real politik, and could very easily help recreate the brutal "killing fields" of the 1970s. Our refusal to provide economic assistance to the governments of Cambodia or Vietnam is explicable only as timidity in the face of the persistent American wrath toward Vietnam for winning the war.

Finally, our willingness to allow economic expediency to overshadow our concern for human rights is shamefully illustrated in the sale of a CANDU nuclear reactor to the Ceaucescu government of Romania. Even while the sale was being negotiated, the horrifying truth about grotesque abuses of human rights—appalling even by the lesser standards of authoritarian regimes—was circulating widely among diplomats and human rights advocates. Worse yet, when construction was begun on the reactor, it became clear that much of the work was being done by slave labour. Despite this, the Canadian government said nothing in public, and, as far as we know, nothing in private to the Romanian government.

CONCLUSION

Compared to some nations, and particularly to the great powers, the ideals and principles that form the basis of the traditional Canadian foreign policy consensus need relatively little transformation to bring them into line with post-Cold War reality. The orientation toward conflict resolution, internationalism, and sustainable economic development, that has characterized our policy consensus since the Pearson era, is more apposite than ever as we move toward the 21st century. What is urgently required, however, is a political leadership (both in government and in opposition) that is willing to lead the Canadian people to struggle and sacrifice for those ideals and principles.

Michael D. Wallace

References

1. Independence and Internationalism: Report of the Special Joint Committee of the Senate and of the House of Commons on Canada's International Relations, Canadian Government Publishing Centre, Ottawa, June, 1986.
2. Challenge and Commitment: A Defence Policy for Canada, Minister of Supply and Services, Ottawa, June, 1987.
3. Canadian International Development Agency Annual Report 1988–1989, Ministry of Supply and Services Canada, 1990, p.117.

Professor James G. Foulks, Ph.D., M.D.

CHAPTER 7

Arms Control: Promises and Reality

PROFESSOR JAMES G. FOULKS, Ph.D., M.D.

INTRODUCTION

As the 1980s drew to a close, the prospects for moving toward a peaceful world seemed promising. The need to learn to think in a new way for which the Einstein-Russell Manifesto had appealed in 1955 appeared at last to have penetrated the awareness of the world's leaders. President Reagan and General Secretary Gorbachev had embraced in Red Square and both had acknowledged that a nuclear war could not be won and must never be fought. A treaty to eliminate a part of the nuclear weapons based in Europe had been signed. With the fall of the Berlin Wall, the figurative barriers between East and West also had collapsed and politicians generally conceded that the cold war had drawn to a close. In various parts of the world, a number of dictatorial regimes had been replaced with incipient democracies. Hopes were high that steady and rapid progress toward more extensive disarmament was possible and that a "new world

James G. Foulks is Professor Emeritus of Pharmacology and Therapeutics in the Faculty of Medicine at the University of British Columbia, and is a past president of the Canadian Association of University Teachers. He is a member of Canadian Physicians for the Prevention of Nuclear War, and has served on the national executive of Science for Peace. He is presently a vice president of End the Arms Race, a Vancouver coalition of community organizations which oppose war and advocate disarmament. He was co-editor of the 1986 publication "End the Arms Race—Fund Human Needs," the proceedings of the Vancouver Centennial Symposium on Peace and Disarmament, and he played a major part in organizing this Centennial Symposium.

119

order'' might be in the offing. This chapter will attempt to chart the background and assess whatever progress has been achieved thus far in efforts to restrain the arms race which has absorbed such a huge and wasteful share of the world's human, material and technological resources ever since the end of the Second World War.

EUROPEAN THEATRE DISARMAMENT AGREEMENTS

Intermediate and Short Range Nuclear Weapons

During 1987, the Soviet Union indicated that it was now prepared to accept a proposal previously made by the United States for a "double zero option" to deal with intermediate nuclear forces in Europe. In December of that year, President Reagan and General Gorbachev signed an agreement to eliminate all (some 1300 to 1400) Soviet and U.S. ground-based intermediate range (500 to 5,000 kilometre) nuclear-armed Pershing and SS-20 ballistic missiles. This intermediate nuclear forces (INF) treaty marked an historic milestone in the ongoing campaign for disarmament. It provided the most extensive and rigorous verification procedures yet successfully negotiated. It was the first agreement which will lead to an actual reduction in the deployment of an entire class of nuclear weapons systems (the earlier SALT treaties had placed rather high ceilings on the continued accumulation of long-ranged nuclear weapons but did not provide for the destruction of any already in existence).

The importance of the INF treaty lies in the fact that it will abolish an entire class of particularly destabilizing missile systems—ones which were capable of striking the Soviet heartland from West Germany. Their deployment had forced European nations toward an automated launch-on-warning strategy because of the pin-point accuracy and extremely short flight-times of these missiles. The INF treaty had also gained significance in the precedent it established in demonstrating that verifiable nuclear disarmament agreements including on-site inspections were feasible. A special verification commission was established to deal with questions of compliance.

Nevertheless, the INF treaty had serious limitations. It did not call for the destruction of the nuclear warheads or the missiles' computerized guidance systems which can now be removed and adapted for transfer to other types of delivery vehicles. The United States has been reported to be transferring its W-84 and W-85 warheads from the Pershing and ground-launched cruise missiles covered by the INF treaty into advanced models of its B-61 bomb for installation on air and sea-launched cruise missiles which could then be returned to Europe in this new guise. Moreover the number of weapons involved comprises only a very small proportion (2 to 4 per cent) of the nuclear arsenals.

Approximately 5,000 tactical battlefield nuclear weapons (artillery shells as well as short range missiles) remain based in western Europe, and military analysts generally believe that an even larger number of short range nuclear missiles are deployed in eastern Europe. It is apparent that these quantities exceed by orders of magnitude what could plausibly be used in war before the battlefield itself dissolves into chaos. Hardline militarists, especially in the U.K., have expressed fear that the acceptance of the INF treaty presaged the "denuclearization" of Europe and its "decoupling" from the United States. Nevertheless, the need for an early start to negotiations and a sharp reduction in these weapons leading to their ultimate elimination (the "triple zero" option) is highly desirable. Europe should follow Latin America and some other regions of the world in declaring its intention to become a zone free of nuclear weapons.

Immediately following ratification of the INF treaty there were apprehensions that its spirit would be negated by compensatory measures. For example plans were made to modernize some 700 shorter-range land-based (LANCE) nuclear missile systems based in Germany by increasing their accuracy and power and extending their reach to the very limits allowed by the INF treaty, although this proposal has been resisted by Chancellor Kohl as well as by many members of the United States Congress. Moreover, plans were made for NATO to dramatically expand its airborne and sea-launched cruise missiles by adding to the 700 to 800 weapons of this type already deployed in order to bolster its strategy of flexible response, restoring its capacity to strike the Soviet homeland from European sites. This followed the pattern of response after the SALT treaties were signed, when cruise missiles were first introduced in order to compensate for this treaty's restrictions on intercontinental ballistic missiles. However, the change which transformed Eastern Europe in 1989, leading to the reunification of Germany in 1990, has rendered some of these plans moot. For instance, it became politically impractical to deploy new ground-based nuclear weapons with ranges under five hundred kilometres at locations which would allow them to strike only at the emerging democracies to the east. In the spring of 1990, the United States and its NATO allies announced that plans to modernize short-range nuclear weapons in Europe were being scrapped and that consideration would be given to the withdrawal of hundreds of nuclear artillery shells from this region. Soon thereafter, the Soviet Union announced its intention to withdraw 1,500 nuclear warheads on short-range delivery vehicles from central Europe within the year. These announcements have raised hopes that if an agreement could be reached with respect to the mutual balanced reduction of conventional forces in Europe, it might be possible to eliminate all short-range nuclear weapons from the European theatre, leaving the problem of air and sea-launched cruise missiles in that region to be dealt with in the negotiations with respect to strategic nuclear weapons including those deployed by the United Kingdom and France.

CONVENTIONAL FORCES IN EUROPE

Throughout the decades of the 1970s and the 1980s, representatives of the North Atlantic Treaty Organization (NATO) and the Warsaw Pact met periodically in Vienna for the announced purpose of negotiating "mutual and balanced force reductions in conventional arms in Europe," but little progress was made and these discussions were discontinued in 1988. These talks had been beset by quarrels as to how various components were to be classified and counted and as to the accuracy of the information being provided. Each side pointed to those types of weaponry in which its adversary was said to enjoy numerical advantage. Western analysts, often adopting worst case scenarios, expressed apprehension that the Warsaw Pact possessed overwhelming superiority in conventional weapons which posed the danger of a surprise attack on Western Europe, a threat which could only be deterred by the counter-threat to respond with nuclear weapons. This policy was expressed in NATO's "flexible response" doctrine and its refusal to renounce the first use of nuclear weapons. Critics of this view stressed those respects in which NATO's advantage in the quality of its weapons and the superior training and reliability of its personnel were felt to counterbalance any quantitative edge assigned to the Warsaw Pact forces. They concluded that neither side could launch an attack with conventional forces and have any confidence in its success. Moreover, American military leaders admitted that they would be unwilling to exchange places with their Soviet counterpart. Nevertheless both sides assumed a military stance in Europe as if each might be called upon to repel an attack from its adversary by mounting a massive counter-offensive, postures which only served to fuel and reinforce their reciprocal fears, even in the absence of any rational motivation or evident intention for either to initiate hostilities between the large forces which were confronting one another in Central Europe.

This bottleneck was broken in March 1989 when President Gorbachev made it clear that the Soviet Union was not prepared to use its armed forces to prevent political change and renewal in eastern Europe and announced the intention to carry out unilaterally a substantial phased reduction of Soviet armed forces in central Europe and, within a few years, their complete removal. He also expressed a willingness to redress any military imbalance or asymmetries between the alliances. He indicated that the Soviet Union would take steps to eliminate the capability to initiate large-scale offensive actions and to make it clear that in the future its armed forces would possess only a strictly defensive character. Negotiations were soon resumed and by the summer of 1990 general agreement was reached.

The "most complex arms control treaty in history" was signed by the 22 NATO and Warsaw Pact countries at a summit in Paris in the fall of that year. The treaty mandated substantial phased reductions in the conventional forces stationed in Europe from the Atlantic Ocean to the Ural Mountains. The general principle adopted was that for each category of military force, the side with the smaller number would reduce by an agreed percentage (for example by 15 per cent) and the other side would reduce its counterpart force to the same absolute level, thereby achieving numerical parity across the board. The limits set were 20,000 each for tanks and for artillery, and 30,000 each for armed personnel carriers. For tanks, artillery pieces and motorized infantry vehicles this required the Warsaw Pact to reduce its forces by 30,000 to 40,000 items in each category, whereas the NATO allies had to relinquish only 1,000 to 2,000 of each type. A further stipulation was that limits were to be set for the quantities of these forces which could be stationed outside of the Soviet Union (in eastern Europe) and outside of European NATO (in West Germany) to much lower levels (3,200 tanks, 6,000 armed troop carriers and 1,700 artillery pieces) for each side. Overall personnel strength in Europe was to be limited to 270,000 for each alliance, which would lead to the removal of approximately 300,000 Warsaw Pact troops and some 30,000 NATO troops. American reluctance to include aircraft within the framework of this treaty was overcome when it was presented with the opportunity to secure such deep cuts in Soviet land forces, and agreement eventually was reached which would lead to a 15 per cent reduction in NATO ground-based aircraft and attack helicopters and parity with the Warsaw Pact.

The successful conclusion of this treaty undoubtedly was facilitated by the far-reaching changes taking place in the political structure of the countries of Eastern Europe and the Soviet withdrawal of its opposition to a unified Germany within NATO, together with the withering away of any perception that the Soviet Union might conceivably attack the NATO allies. Both sides foresee that this agreement constitutes only an initial phase in process which should lead to further reductions in the conventional forces in Europe during the coming decade (perhaps by 25 to 50 per cent). The realization of this prospect undoubtedly will depend upon satisfaction of the treaty's verification provisions. These are complicated by the difference in the geographical situation of the two major powers. The areas involved include the bulk of the heavily populated and industrialized part of the Soviet Union itself, where approximately 70 per cent of its total ground and air forces are stationed, but excludes the territory of the United States, where 90 per cent of its combat aircraft and 70 per cent of its tanks normally are based. The recent crisis in the Middle East demonstrates the rapidity with which these forces can be mobilized and transported over large distances, and mitigates to some extent the argument that Soviet proximity to Europe should preclude its accomplishing force reductions by transfer beyond the Urals.

The conference on confidence and security building measures and disarmament in Europe has approved steps to reduce the dangers of armed conflict through misunderstanding or miscalculation arising from military exercises. In its 1986 Stockholm Agreement, the Soviet Union agreed to the inspection of these activities on its own territory. Equally important is the transition to a new military doctrine which both sides now appear to be prepared to accept in principle, and which the Soviet Union and its allies have indicated that they are willing to begin to implement unilaterally. This doctrine has been variously described as "non-offensive defence," "defensive dominance," "reasonable sufficiency," "mutual inability to attack," and "non-provocative sufficient defence." It was initially advanced at a series of Pugwash Conferences during the 1980s. It proposes that NATO and the Warsaw Pact should restructure the composition and deployment of their military forces, especially those which have been confronting one another in Central Europe, restricting their density, mobility, range, and deep-strike capacity so that their offensive potential is degraded to such an extent that neither side would be capable of embarking upon large-scale offensive operations or of launching an unexpected assault or counter-attack against its opponent with any reasonable prospect of success. Instead each would dispose its forces solely for defensive purposes in amounts adequate only to repel any conceivable surprise attack. Thus the defence would be made superior to the offence on a regional basis. The entire September 1988 issue of the Bulletin of the Atomic Scientists was devoted to this topic.

STRATEGIC ARMS LIMITATIONS (SALT) AND REDUCTION (START) TREATIES

Strategic weapons are those which are armed with nuclear warheads and by virtue of their range or proximity are capable of striking targets on the territory of another nuclear power. They include intercontinental ballistic missiles (ICBMs), submarine-launched ballistic missiles (SLBMs) and long-range aircraft (medium and heavy bombers). Their restriction has been the paramount concern in arms control and disarmament negotiations between the nuclear superpowers. Some progress has been made, but much remains to be accomplished. In May 1972, the United States and the Soviet Union signed the Anti-Ballistic Missile (ABM) treaty, which restricted each superpower to a single site to be defended by a ground-based system for defence against ballistic missiles. The Soviet Union chose Moscow; the United States chose missile silo sites in its midwestern region. This treaty banned the development, testing or deployment of anti-ballistic missile systems or components in space.

The major impetus for this agreement came from American experts who correctly concluded that the widespread deployment of missile defences would fuel an open-ended escalation of the race to deploy compensatory strategic offensive nuclear systems in order to overwhelm these defences. In 1972, the SALT I treaty also was adopted. In it the United States and the Soviet Union agreed that for a five-year period, while further negotiations were taking place, each side would limit its strategic offensive weapons to those already deployed or under construction, without however specifying numerical limits on bombers or on missiles equipped with a number of multiple independently targetable re-entry vehicles (MIRVs) for nuclear warheads, and it disregarded any asymmetries in the composition of their strategic arsenals.

In 1974, an interim agreement was signed at Vladivostock which established a mutual limit on the overall number of strategic nuclear weapons delivery vehicles at 2,400, a ceiling above the number then deployed. In June 1979, the SALT II agreement was signed. This treaty reduced the ceiling on intercontinental ballistic missiles, submarine-launched ballistic missiles, and long-range bombers to a total of 2,250, and fixed a sublimit on MIRVed vehicles to 1,320 (including 120 U.S. bombers equipped to carry air-launched cruise missiles [ALCMs]). In addition, the Soviet Union accepted a sub-limit of 820 on its MIRVed ICBMs, with a further limit of 308 for its heavier (SS-18) version, and also agreed that the range of its "Backfire" bomber would be restricted so as to remove it as a strategic offensive threat.

The SALT treaties suffered from serious limitations. In placing upper limits on the quantity of vehicles for the delivery of nuclear warheads, the ceilings were set so high that they had little effect on the actual numbers and types of nuclear weapons systems deployed. They did not prevent the continued expansion of the nuclear stockpiles. The numbers of nuclear warheads in the combined strategic arsenals of the United States and the U.S.S.R. grew from about 10,000 before SALT I to about 25,000 while the SALT treaties were being negotiated and signed, and to more than 30,000 since then as MIRVing of these vehicles has progressed. The sea-launched ballistic missiles (SLCMs) on a single Trident submarine can deliver 240 nuclear warheads. The SALT treaties placed no restrictions on the replacement of old weapons with new ones as modernization and technological improvements increased the accuracy with which weapons could be directed to their targets, developments generally viewed as destabilizing. They placed no limitations on the strategic nuclear weapons systems of the other three members of the United Nations Security Council. The number of warheads which the other three nuclear powers possess consist of approximately 300 each deployed by China and the United Kingdom and more than 600 by France. Israel is also widely believed to have as many as 100 nuclear weapons and missiles to deliver them over large distances. Finally the SALT II treaty was never ratified by the United States Senate, although both sides continued to abide by its terms until 1987, when the U.S. breached its ceiling while adding to its fleet of Trident submarines.

Following a five-year hiatus, strategic arms negotiations were resumed in 1985. The new START talks were intended to reduce rather than merely limit further increases in these weapons systems. After prolonged and extensive discussions, general agreement on the major substantive issues was announced in May 1990, and at that time it was indicated that a completed START treaty was expected to be ready for signing at a summit meeting scheduled for mid-February 1991.* A disappointing feature of this announcement was the report that the reductions in the nuclear arsenals projected at the first summit between President Reagan and Secretary Gorbachev in Iceland had been scaled down. The original plans called for a 50 per cent reduction, with a ceiling of 6,000 nuclear warheads on 1,600 strategic delivery vehicles. Sublimits provided for 4,900 of these 6,000 warheads to be allocated to ICBMs and the remaining 1,100 to bomber aircraft. Instead, in its final form, it was decided that reduction in strategic arsenals during this initial phase would only be by about one-third, except for the heavy Soviet SS-18 ICBMs which are to be cut by one-half, both in number and in throw weight. An important obstacle was overcome by the agreement to restrict the range of the Soviet "Backfire" bomber and to classify all cruise missiles with a range greater than 1,600 kilometres as strategic, whether launched from the ground, from airplanes, submarines or naval vessels. An exception was made for a new American high-tech cruise missile dubbed "tacit rainbow" which, like some 3,000–4,000 other U.S. short-range sea-launched cruise missiles (SLCMs), is being armed with conventional rather than nuclear warheads.

The SLCMs have been a particularly difficult sticking point during START negotiations because of the refusal of the United States to allow inspection of its naval vessels in order to distinguish between missiles carrying nuclear or conventional warheads. This was an extension of the

* Editor's note: Unfortunately it has just been reported, January 28, 1991, that the superpower meeting between President Bush and President Gorbachev scheduled for February 1991 to complete signing of the new START agreement has been postponed indefinitely.

U.S. Navy's rather inane policy of refusing to acknowledge ("neither confirm nor deny") whether or not particular naval vessels carried nuclear arms. Inasmuch as retired high-ranking naval officers have declared that virtually all nuclear-capable vessels do in fact carry these weapons on a continuous basis, this policy appeared to be designed to thwart those who wished to protest the visits of these ships to unreceptive ports rather than for legitimate security purposes. This obstacle was overcome when it was agreed to made a "politically binding" declaration outside of the treaty that neither side would deploy more than 880 nuclear-armed SLCMs. The generosity of this limit is reflected in the fact that in 1989 the U.S. planned to produce and deploy only 758 nuclear-armed SLCMs, and this figure was later reduced by budgetary constraint to 442 (of which 300 were already in service). At that time, no Soviet nuclear-armed SLCMs were known to be deployed. The status of this special agreement outside of the treaty of course meant that it was not subject to the stringent verification procedures which were to be applied to the weapons systems constrained under the treaty itself. The verification procedures included in the START treaty will be more complex than any others yet attempted. In addition to a number of technological innovations, they provide for extensive data exchange with respect to the location and nature of all places involved in relevant nuclear weapons production from start to finish, for continuous perimeter and portal monitoring of relevant weapons production facilities, and short notice mandatory on-site inspections of any facilities where covert unauthorized production might be suspected.

Another major dispute had arisen from the American Strategic Defense Initiative (SDI) which had been announced by President Reagan in 1983 with much fanfare as an effort intended to provide an effective shield which would prevent strategic nuclear warheads from reaching their targets and hence render nuclear weapons "impotent and obsolete." Knowledgeable scientists and many former military officials generally regarded this scheme as a pipe-dream which was not technologically attainable within the foreseeable future. Moreover, they viewed it as a destabilizing proposal which would interfere with efforts to achieve arms reduction agreements, by reversing the retarding effect on offensive strategic nuclear weapons systems which the ABM treaty had provided. In fact, the SDI proponents in the Reagan administration had offered a revised "broadened" interpretation of the ABM treaty by exploiting loopholes and ambiguities in its language so as to permit testing and potential deployment of the space-based defences which previously had been thought to be forbidden. This issue was stressed by the Soviets who insisted on the conventional interpretation of the ABM treaty according to the clear intent of its framers. They had warned that the ABM treaty could be abrogated if these terms were to be violated and had insisted that abandonment of SDI and acceptance of the validity of the traditional interpretation of the ABM treaty be included in any START agreement. This stumbling block was finally removed by adoption of a Soviet proposal that this disagreement be set aside with an acknowledgement that either signatory could withdraw from the proposed START treaty if the usual understanding of the ABM treaty was transgressed by its partner. Ironically, by eliminating one-third of the Soviet offensive strategic weapons, the START agreement would do far more than SDI to reduce the threat nuclear weapons have posed to the United States and at much less cost.

Unfortunately, the proposed START treaty suffers from some of the same shortcomings noted with respect to the SALT treaties. The treaty will not constrain the arsenals or weapons systems of the other three major nuclear powers, although the United States agreed to restrict the sales of certain of its nuclear weapons to the United Kingdom. The treaty establishes many important precedents in the sphere of the verification of disarmament agreements, but the actual reductions it will mandate are far too modest to appreciably alter the massive overkill capacity now represented by the more than 50,000 nuclear warheads which have accumulated as the nuclear arms race escalated over the previous decades. The nuclear stockpiles will remain massive, larger still than they were ten years ago when SALT II was completed, and many of the weapons to be eliminated are due for retirement on grounds of obsolescence in any event. The treaty does not place serious constraints on the pace of further modernization and enhanced lethality of these weapons systems or on the deployment of mobile missiles. Just as the INF treaty for Europe left aside the question of land-based battlefield nuclear weapons, the proposed START treaty fails to address the question of non-strategic nuclear weapons at sea. Both Ambassador Paul Nitze, a former U.S. Navy secretary and long-time arms control advisor and negotiator, and retired Admiral Eugene J. Carroll, former commander of the carrier-strike force of the U.S. Sixth Fleet, and later Deputy Chief of Naval Operations for Plans, Policy and Operations in the Pentagon, have advocated the removal of all 5,500 tactical nuclear weapons from U.S. and Soviet warships, the maritime equivalent of the zero option. This is particularly important because naval nuclear weapons, unlike all others, are without electronic locks (permissive action links) designed to prevent unauthorized use. Admiral Carroll has referred to these weapons as the most likely triggers for a nuclear war, because of the risk of starting a nuclear exchange by accident or miscalculation, a possibility which has been accentuated by the aggressive and provocative "forward maritime strategy" adopted by the U.S. Navy in the 1980s, which envisioned the early offensive use of nuclear weapons in the northern ocean areas in the event of a military conflict between the nuclear powers.

Altogether there are approximately 16,000 nuclear weapons at sea, about two-thirds on NATO vessels and one-third on Soviet warships. They comprise nearly one-third of the world's total nuclear stockpile. Nearly half of these are tactical or anti-submarine weapons which have not yet been covered by any arms control negotiations. The U.S., which has clear naval superiority over any potential adversary, has been loath to consider any measures for naval arms control whether nuclear or conventional. According to U.S. Secretary of State James Baker, this reluctance is justified because the U.S. is surrounded on both sides by major oceans and depends on its navy to maintain its lines of communication and supply with its allies in Asia and Europe. Therefore, in spite of the START agreement, the large nuclear arsenals continuing to exist mean that, for the foreseeable future, the world will remain in the grip of an unchanged balance of nuclear terror with the threat of an accidental or unintentional use, like a sword of Damocles suspended by a slender thread, hanging over our heads.

OTHER WEAPONS OF MASS DESTRUCTION

Biological Warfare

The deliberate infection of populations with disease-causing microorganisms is a possibility which creates horror and revulsion. Organisms which possessed the desired properties were produced and means for their dispersal were designed and evaluated during the Second World War, and these studies continued for a decade or two thereafter. Because of the virulence of some of these agents and their nondiscriminatory characteristics, their potential use entailed a threat that such agents might not only decimate the civilian populations of enemy countries, but also might well spread to the populations of the nations responsible for their introduction. Because of these considerations, the need to discourage biological warfare has been generally recognized. In 1972, the United States and the Soviet Union accepted the United Nations General Assembly's Biological Weapons Convention (BWC) and agreed not to produce offensive biological weapons and to confine research with these organisms to measures of defence against them. However, a number of countries, particularly in the Middle East, have signed but not ratified this convention. It established a system of data reporting, and the General Assembly of the United Nations has unanimously authorized the Secretary General to conduct on-site investigations of allegations of the actual military use of such weapons. However, verification procedures have not thus far been feasible, and the possibility that other countries with irresponsible leadership might be tempted to try to develop a biological warfare capacity cannot be excluded.

CHEMICAL WARFARE

Chemical weapons of several kinds were manufactured and used during the First World War, producing many casualties. Mustard gas, a blistering agent, has continued to be a mainstay of this type of agent in spite of a 1925 protocol banning its use. This pact had 130 adherents but no enforcement mechanism. During the Second World War, highly potent neurotoxins were developed, and these now comprise the most important class of chemical warfare agents. They can be used on the battlefield in artillery shells or against longer range targets by air-launched rockets. In recent years the United States has been converting much of its stockpile of military nerve poisons to binary form. These vehicles contain two separate non-toxic ingredients which are converted to the toxic agent by automated admixture after they have been launched. Hence they are safer to store and handle.

Most nations have paid lip service to the aim of a world-wide ban on the production and stock-piling of chemical warfare agents. Multinational negotiations toward this objective have been carried out at Geneva for the past twenty years and at a recent conference in Paris, but thus far without a practical outcome. Since the facilities for producing these chemicals can also be used for the manufacture of other useful products, the task of assuring compliance with a ban is formidable, requiring mandatory "challenge inspections." A related difficulty arises from the fact that the relevant ingredients and technologies are in private hands with commercial interests in a number of industrialized countries, who have resisted restrictions on their operations. This has resulted in the widespread sale of the means to produce chemical warfare agents to perhaps as many as 20 Third World countries, especially to Arab nations, even in contravention of legal restrictions on export by the countries of origin. In a world where nuclear weapons have become a status symbol of military power, chemical weapons have been referred to as the "poor man's atom bomb," providing an alternative weapon of mass destruction to be used as a counter-deterrent to those who have or aspire to obtain nuclear weapons. Nevertheless, the U.S. and the Soviet Union have been the major producers of chemical weapons, and a bilateral treaty between them has been widely considered as an essential example which is prerequisite to an effort to achieve a wider multinational treaty leading to a global ban. In May of 1990 the Soviet Union and the U.S. announced that they had reached an agreement on a bilateral pact to end their production of chemical warfare agents and progressively, albeit gradually, reduce their stocks of these materials, and to forego further production of binary chemical weapons. The Soviet Union has reported that it possesses 50,000 tons of chemical warfare agents, and the U.S. about half that amount. (France has about 500 tons, which it has planned to increase to 1,000 to 2,000 tons.) The present agreement calls for these stocks to be reduced to 5,000 tons each in the near term and to 500 tons each over an eight-year period. Further reductions to zero would hinge on success in achieving a verifiable worldwide ban. The major criticism of this agreement is that setting an interim ceiling as high as 500 tons, without a firm commitment to proceed to a total ban unless universal adherence is secured, renders the achievement of this essential goal rather uncertain.

Banning Nuclear Weapons Tests

Negotiations for an agreed end to nuclear weapons testing were undertaken by the U.S. and the U.S.S.R. when the Cuban missile crisis in 1962 convinced them that something had to be done to reduce the likelihood of nuclear war. They failed to achieve this objective when they could not find an acceptable compromise between U.S. insistence on eight annual on-site inspections of suspicious events, and Soviet unwillingness to permit more than three. However, prompted by virtually universal concern over the hazard to health created by the worldwide fall-out of long-lived radioactive debris, they were joined by the U.K. in a treaty in which they agreed not to carry out nuclear weapons explosions in the atmosphere, on the seabed or in outer space. The preamble of the Partial Test Ban Treaty (PTBT) of 1963 includes a commitment to seek a complete ban and a promise to achieve an end to the nuclear arms race at the earliest possible date. This pact was soon ratified and has been signed by 113 additional countries. France and China did not join this pact and both continued occasional atmospheric testing of nuclear weapons for a number of years. Nevertheless both have gradually come to honour its provisions. Meanwhile, the testing of nuclear weapons at underground sites has continued unabated.

According to the Center for Defense Information, a non-governmental American think-tank based in Washington, D.C., "the first, most important, most effective action that can be taken to avert nuclear was is the termination for all time of nuclear weapons explosions." Emphasis has been placed on this measure because it offers a simple and straightforward way of stopping the technological arms race, which is characterized by a continued effort to gain some military edge over one's perceived opponent by producing more lethal and often destabilizing weapons devices. The International Physicians for the Prevention of Nuclear War, recipient of the 1985 Nobel Peace Prize, has referred to a comprehensive test ban as the litmus test of how seriously the super-powers regard efforts to put an end to the nuclear arms race, pointing out that this measure would not affect the stability of the military balance and could not offer any special advantage or disadvantage to either side. In 1985 the heads of government of Sweden, Greece, India, Mexico, Argentina, and Tanzania issued their "Five-Continent Appeal" which included a call for a CTBT and they renewed this appeal in their 1988 "Stockholm Declaration." The United States Congress has also urged the early adoption of a comprehensive nuclear test ban by a vote of 77 to 22 in the Senate and 268 to 148 in the House of Representatives. In response to these various appeals, the Soviet Government undertook a unilateral moratorium on nuclear weapons testing which lasted for about eighteen months, from the 1985 anniversary of Hiroshima (August 6th) until February 1987. Their invitation for the United States to join them in suspending tests and in proceeding to negotiate a permanent ban went unheeded, and the United States has often cast a lonely negative vote, along with one or two of its closest allies, against numerous (some 70) United Nations General Assembly resolutions calling for a permanent comprehensive nuclear weapons test ban treaty. U.S. opposition to a comprehensive test ban is widely believed to be attributable to a reluctance on the part of American militarists to give up the process of weapons innovation. The claims that tests are needed to check the reliability of stockpiled weapons is given little credence by knowledgeable experts. However, the major stated American justification for resistance to a ban on underground nuclear tests is the alleged difficulty of assuring verifiable compliance.

Progress in seismic verification techniques led in 1974 to a threshold test-ban treaty, limiting underground nuclear weapons tests to a maximum of 150 kilotons (ten times the magnitude of the bomb which levelled Hiroshima). However, the military significance of this restriction has been negligible. There is little reason to believe that it has slowed the nuclear arms race or retarded the rate of nuclear weapons testing underground. Between 1977 and 1980, the U.S., the U.K., and the U.S.S.R. negotiators finally prepared a draft treaty to end underground weapons explosions for a trial period of three years and to test the validity of verification procedures including on-site inspections. However, renewed international tensions led the Reagan administration to abandon these negotiations just when they appeared to be on the verge of success. Since that time, the efficacy of seismic instrumentation has been amply demonstrated and the technical capabilities needed to police a comprehensive test-ban down to explosions of very small size (1 to 3 kilotons) are now available and have been for some time. For example, in recent years the New York-based National Resources Defense Council and the Soviet Academy of Sciences have arranged an informal (non-governmental) exchange whereby scientist have brought their equipment to one another's test sites (Semipalatinsk and Nevada) and shown that they are entirely adequate for this purpose. Present seismic devices can readily detect explosions decoupled from surrounding rock and distinguish them from natural earthquake tremors at distances at great as 600 kilometres from test sites.

Information made available in recent years has led to a wider appreciation of the dangers to the health of those who live near the sites where underground nuclear tests are carried out, as well as those who live adjacent to the facilities where nuclear materials are processed and bombs fabricated or stored, or to the sites where the radioactive residue from nuclear weapons factories and nuclear power plants are being stored. These environmental concerns have increased public pressure by the local inhabitants for measures to remove these hazards. As a result of the objections expressed by their own aroused citizens, underground nuclear explosions at Semipalatinsk, one of the two Soviet sites for testing nuclear weapons, have been suspended for more than a year, and a single nuclear explosion in the fall of 1990 at the other Soviet test site at Novaya Zemlya, an island in the Arctic, received widespread criticism within the Soviet Union as well as international protests from Nordic governments and from Greenpeace. Protests have also taken place at the Nevada test-site in the United States.

The demand for a comprehensive test ban is motivated by a perceived need to prevent "vertical proliferation" of nuclear weapons by curbing the military appetite of the five nuclear powers for continued technological innovation and expansion of their nuclear arsenals. It has been complemented by the desire of the five (original) members of the nuclear club to prevent "horizontal proliferation," the potential expansion of the number of countries possessing nuclear weapons or the capacity to produce them. This was the objective sought by the 1968 "non-proliferation treaty" (NPT) which obligated the three initiating nuclear powers (U.S., U.S.S.R. and U.K.) not to provide the materials or technological information necessary for the development and production of nuclear weapons to other countries. It committed non-nuclear nations not to attempt to produce fissile material or to acquire nuclear weapons, and to open any non-military nuclear facilities they might develop to inspection by the International Atomic Energy Agency in order to ensure compliance. The latter provision has been criticized as discriminatory because this agency, which had been set up by the nuclear powers in 1957, was not authorized to subject their own activities to similar restraints and inspections. One price which the non-nuclear states exacted for their participation was the stipulation that the three major members of the nuclear club provide assistance to them in developing the peaceful uses of nuclear energy. However, another essential ingredient of their bargain was carefully spelled out in Article VI of the treaty. It recalled the 1963 commitment of the

133

three nuclear powers to seek an end to all nuclear testing and required that they "undertake to pursue negotiations in good faith on effective measures relating to the cessation of the nuclear arms race at an early date and to nuclear disarmament."

The non-proliferation treaty came into effect in 1970 for a term of 25 years and has now been joined by 138 non-nuclear states. Unfortunately, two major nuclear powers, France and China, have not accepted its provisions, and non-nuclear states who have failed to join include several who are thought to have nuclear weapons or the potential capacity to acquire them, including Israel, South Africa, India, Pakistan, Argentina and Brazil. The NPT contained a provision for periodic review of its implementation at conferences of its adherents to be held at five-year intervals. At each of the four conferences held thus far, the non-nuclear states have complained, often bitterly, at their disappointment and frustration that the nuclear powers are not fulfilling their obligations under the treaty, particularly with respect to Article VI. Because of Mexico's insistence that the signatories adopt a commitment for the completion of a comprehensive test-ban by 1995 and the U.S. refusal to accept this stipulation, the recent 1990 review conference for the first time failed to reach a consensus on a final declaration. Clearly this implies that the NPT is threatened with considerable difficulty when it comes up for renewal or extension at the end of its term in 1995.

Mexico also has been the leader of a group of non-aligned countries who have pursued another avenue in the quest for a comprehensive test ban by implementing a provision of the 1963 partial test-ban treaty. This clause provides that at the request of one-third of the signatories of the PTBT, a conference must be held to consider amendments to this treaty where a majority vote would be able to convert it into a comprehensive ban. Seventy nations have joined this initiative and the conference is being held in mid-January 1991 as this article is being written. However its outcome can be predicted. On the one hand, at the 1985 United Nations General Assembly, a resolution "to undertake urgent negotiations to convert the PTBT to a CTBT" was adopted by a vote of 121 to 3, with 24 abstentions. However the PTBT also stipulates that any amendment requires the consent of all three nuclear signatories, and the United States has served notice that it is not prepared at this time to accept the proposed amendments. The U.S. has indicated its preference for a gradual stage-by-stage reduction in the number and size of allowed nuclear explosions, rather than an immediate complete ban, reflecting continued resistance by the U.S. Defense Department to restraints on nuclear weapons testing.

The Soviet Union has remained a firm advocate of a mutual moratorium and a permanent ban on underground nuclear tests, and improved international relations as well as continued public pressures have led to renewed negotiations on this topic. Apparently with some reluctance, the Soviet Union has acceded to the U.S. gradualist approach as better than no agreement, with the hope that this will soon lead to further steps toward a complete ban. In December 1989, tentative agreement was reached that the U.S. would at long last ratify the 1974 threshold test-ban treaty, taking advantage of improved verification procedures. Verification provisions will consist of intrusive procedures including on-site or in-country geological inspection as well as seismic and hydrodynamic techniques according to the size of the explosions. These protocols are expected to be included in the agreements to be signed at a summit meeting planned for February 1991.* Sustained public pressures of increased intensity in the United States and the U.K. apparently will be required to create the political will necessary to proceed to a comprehensive testban in the foreseeable future. France and China have recently indicated their willingness to sign a comprehensive testban if universal adherence to it is assured.

PROSPECTS FOR DISARMAMENT IN THE 1990s: THE PERSIAN GULF WAR

As the new decade began, the evident end of the Cold War produced optimistic expectations that the arms race might at last be reversed. Achievements to date have been meagre insofar as meaningful reductions in the world's nuclear arsenals are concerned (more than 50,000 nuclear weapons still populate these stockpiles in 1990). Nevertheless, hopes were high that a corner had been turned and preliminary steps taken which might pave the way for a turn away from militarism, ones which could help to create an atmosphere in which the nations might once more, as they had when the United Nations was formed, place efforts to move toward general and complete disarmament back on the world's agenda. These hopes were dashed and optimistic expectations received a rude and nasty jolt in August when Iraq occupied and annexed Kuwait. There was near unanimity in the world community that such military aggression could no longer be tolerated. A consensus quickly emerged within the United Nations Security Council, where a number of resolutions were adopted to require Iraq's withdrawal, initially through the application of economic sanctions enforced by an embargo, and subsequently by whatever other means might be necessary to accomplish this objective. A massive build-up of American military forces in the region was supplemented by token additions from several European and Arab allies and financial contributions from some other nations including Germany and

* Editor's note: This summit meeting between Presidents Bush and Gorbachev has unfortunately now been postponed.

Japan. In mid-January 1991, the deadline for Iraq's acquiescence expired and hostilities began with a dramatic all-out assault on military targets near Baghdad and at other locations in Iraq. Iraq responded with missile attacks against Saudi Arabia and its arch-enemy, Israel. A catastrophic conflagration appears imminent at the time of this writing, but the likely intensity and duration of the struggle remains an open question. A major cause of concern is the assumed presence of nuclear weapons on naval ships in the area and the fear that sizeable quantities of environmental pollution with radioactive materials might ensue if some of these vessels were struck by Iraqi missiles. The deliberate or accidental use of any nuclear weapons in this conflict seems unlikely, but their very presence in the hands of belligerents in the region makes this a fearful possibility. Other environmental concerns have been aroused by the possibility of large spills of petroleum into the Persian Gulf, or the atmospheric consequences of fires being set to many of the oil wells in the region.

The past failure of the United Nations to apply force in order to seek implementation of its resolutions expressing opposition to international aggressions raised troublesome objections to the double standards implied by this new, more belligerent course of action. The deep divisions displayed by the debates which took place in the U.S. Congress and the Canadian Parliament have reflected a widespread desire that the economic sanctions should have been given a longer opportunity to accomplish their objective without the resort to war. It is clear that humanity yearns for some way to resolve crises of this sort by political rather than military means.

In view of the armed struggle now being waged in the Middle East, it is ironic that during its long war with Iran in the 1980s, Iraq received technological know-how and generous supplies of arms from both eastern and western industrialized nations. Its arms suppliers included China, Czechoslovakia, and Brazil, as well as the United States and the Soviet Union. Although Iraq received substantial help from the Soviet Union, the key technologies and most dangerous weapons were supplied by the West. These included Mirage fighter planes and Exocet guided missiles from France, critical technologies for its chemical weapons as well as for its nuclear program from Germany, the United States and the U.K., and the ingredients for its chemical warfare agents as well as helicopters and machine guns from the United States. The blame for equipping Iraq for its aggression against Kuwait must be widely shared. However Iraq is not alone in its appetite for sophisticated weaponry. At least seven other Middle Eastern countries also now deploy ballistic missiles, and this is only one small facet of the consequences which flow from the international trade in armaments between the industrialized countries and those of the Third World. This trade amounts to many billions of dollars annually. For example, between 1975 and 1985 the United States sold or gave away 150 billion dollars in weapons and military services to other countries. The Soviet Union and its allies also have played substantial albeit smaller roles in this traffic (perhaps half that of the West). The annual value of the international arms trade as a whole rose from 25 billion dollars to 35 billion dollars between 1977 and 1986.

Although political and ideological considerations undoubtedly have played their part, the world arms trade has been conducted primarily for commercial reasons: the desperate need of the socialist countries for hard currency with which to acquire supplies and advanced technology from the West; the thirst for profits by western arms manufacturers; and the desire of western governments to cover their budgetary deficits (which are largely due to military expenditures) by dumping their outmoded weapons on Third World markets. Unfortunately, this process also has served to perpetuate some Third World dictatorships, to impoverish their countries, and to contribute to regional conflicts which all too frequently have erupted into bloody armed conflict in such trouble spots as Cambodia, Afghanistan, Angola, Mozambique and Ethiopia, as well as in Central America and the Middle East.

The United Nations has adopted many praiseworthy non-binding resolutions advocating restrictions on the international arms trade. It is high time that the permanent members of the United Nations Security Council, who are also the five largest suppliers of arms to the developing nations, begin to take practical concrete steps to curtail this traffic. Instead of participating in the arms trade, they should use the resources which are now being wasted in this way to help the poor countries overcome the economic, political and social maladies which lie at the root of the regional conflicts and which fuel their appetite for conventional arms. This aid can take the form of relief from crushing burdens of debt as well as the transfer of technology and expertise to the countries most in need. But a willingness on the part of the major powers to reduce their own military arsenals, together with regional arrangements to ensure the common security of their constituent nations, will be necessary to persuade smaller countries that they can safely follow this example. A non-proliferation treaty with respect to conventional weapons is urgently needed.

Realization of the goal of a reciprocal pattern of "defensive dominance" in Europe (as well as in other regions of the world) will require further deep cuts in all forms of armaments and the development of greater degrees of international cooperation and trust in the political sphere. These steps would need to be reinforced by extensive and intrusive verification procedures, and supplemented by confidence and security-building measures, including advance notice of military exercise and avoidance of provocative actions (such as aerial manoeuvres near or across national boundaries, trailing submarines in the open seas, or engaging in intrusive naval manoeuvres in sensitive waters). These understandings would need to include provision for rapid communication between opposing command centres, and the speedy exchange of information whenever circumstances arise which might lead to misunderstandings or tragic mistakes, such as those which in the past have led to the interception and shooting down of innocent civilian aircraft. Agreement to destroy redundant armaments and equipment rather than redeploying them to more remote sites would greatly strengthen these arrangements. Reducing hostility, limiting military rivalry, and eliminating conflict and confrontation, especially in circumstances likely to lead to crises, can in time allow progress toward the eventual goal of establishing a durable and predictable framework of stable and secure demilitarized international relations. At a Paris Summit in November 1990, the 34 members of the Conference on Security and Cooperation in Europe endorsed the new East-West security treaties and established the European Conflict Prevention Centre. This conference can play an important part in the process of building confidence and trust in this region, and can help to extend its principles into the political and social spheres.

The major nuclear powers should work to continue to build an atmosphere of mutual trust and confidence in place of the outmoded strategy of mutual assured destruction. Progress along these lines should make it possible to place the question of substantial reductions in naval forces on the disarmament agenda. Many experts now recognize that competing for military superiority over a powerful foe, or even the quest for a high level of military parity, leads not to security but to insecurity. Stable security requires mutual security. Counter-force strategies should be abandoned. Targeting the potential adversary's weapons and communications systems implies a policy of pre-emptive first-strike, and therefore is highly destabilizing. It should be replaced by a declaration disavowing the first use of nuclear weapons, as China and the Soviet Union already have done. It is becoming increasingly clear that security cannot be obtained by placing primacy upon military means. The doctrine of deterrence which has been the cornerstone of superpower military policy is illogical. One cannot argue that nuclear weapons prevent war, and at the same time oppose the spread of nuclear weapons to other countries who may also aspire to "prevent war" in this way. Moreover, this strategy is morally bankrupt because one cannot justify the mass slaughter of innocent civilians in any circumstances, even in retaliation. The threat to do so lacks credibility and should be discarded. MIRVed missiles weaken stability, and their reduction and elimination should become a priority in disarmament negotiations. The effort to create space-based defences against ballistic missiles can only lead to an escalation in offensive weapons and should be jettisoned. Future arms agreements should insist on the elimination of nuclear warheads, as well as the vehicles which carry them, and should provide for the disposition of their fissile components. Antisatellite weapons also should be banned to ensure the uninterrupted integrity of surveillance systems which make a vital contribution to confident and reliable means for verifying compliance with arms control agreements, as well as providing insurance against the undetected mobilization of offensive forces for a surprise attack. As the newly approved intrusive verification procedures gain acceptance through experience, and their feasibility becomes well established, it should become possible to apply these techniques on a world-wide basis to eliminate the threat of chemical and biological warfare.

Other measures which should be placed on the disarmament agenda include an agreed program of progressive and substantial budgetary reductions in military expenditures on the part of all industrialized countries, especially those who now produce the bulk of the world's arms, and conversion of their military industries to the production of the goods and services the world's people desperately need. Military expenditures in the world have now risen to exceed the astronomical sum of one trillion dollars annually. Only by redirecting their resources and achieving a great deal of international cooperation will it become possible for the nations of the world to address such problems as that of environmental deterioration in a serious way. Recent experience provides increasing evidence that it may soon be possible for the United Nations to be forced to fulfil the peace-making and peace-keeping purposes for which it was originally intended. It may then become possible to establish a world order based on institutionalized procedures for resolving international disputes by political and juridical rather than military means. There is an urgent need for a quick beginning of negotiations for a START II treaty, using the agreements on verification now adopted to achieve much greater reductions in these weapons and their means of delivery, initially perhaps to 5 per cent of their current levels, with the ultimate goal of complete abolition. The apprehension that this would leave the world susceptible to blackmail from clandestine nuclear weapons in irresponsible hands does not offer a reasonable counter to the great benefits which can flow from an agreement to attempt to reach a world free of nuclear weapons, in keeping with commitments made in the 1970 non-proliferation treaty. Nuclear weapons are both unnecessary and dangerous for all of us. The world will become safer when institutions are developed to settle international conflicts by non-military means in a world completely free of nuclear weapons. Those whose concern for peace and justice spurs them into political activism in an effort to bring about a world where safety and security will not depend upon armed forces and the threat of violence have plenty of work left to do. Their task undoubtedly will be long and arduous. Still, the goal is surely worth the struggle.

References

The factual material contained in this article with respect to such topics as the strength of armed forces, the provisions of disarmament treaties and agreements, and the character of additional measures which are needed, has been drawn from the following sources: The Defense Monitor, The Bulletin of the Atomic Scientists, the Pugwash News Letter, Science, Nature, Lancet, Scientific American, IEEE Spectrum, the Ploughshares Monitor, Disarmament Times, Disarmament (A United Nations publication), The New York Times, The Toronto Globe and Mail, The Vancouver Sun, Background Papers of the Canadian Institute for International Peace and Security, as well as briefing papers of the Union of Concerned Scientists, The Council for a Livable World, and Physicians for Social Responsibility.

CHAPTER 8

Children and War, Children and Peace

DR. JOANNA SANTA BARBARA

CHILDREN AND WAR

We, the children of the world, are the ones who suffer most when there are wars.

Gerald Hoyte, 10, Trinidad.[1]

I would like to stop people from fighting and having wars. I do not like the wars. People get killed. Some children get their mummys and daddys killed.

Yvette Austin, 8.[1]

This chapter begins with children as victims of war and ends with children as creators of a more peaceful, just, harmonious world. It begins with a story of one young person caught in war. It is important to face the pain of what war does to real people, especially young ones. From the sharing of this pain can grow a powerful motivation to stop its cause, war. Glib reference is often made, especially in defence of the theory of nuclear deterrence, to the last forty-five years of "peace" since the dropping of nuclear bombs on Hiroshima and Nagasaki. During this "peace" there were 127 wars causing 21.8 million war-related deaths.[2] The failure to notice these disturbances to the "peace" is presumably due to the fact that only two of these wars were in the developed world. With each passing decade, the proportion of civilian compared to military war deaths has increased, until in the 1980s, it has reached three-quarters of all the deaths. This proportion, of course, comprises mainly women and children.

Appalling as is this level of accumulated human suffering, it is small

Dr. Joanna Santa Barbara

compared to that caused by the absolute poverty of one in five people on the planet. In many cases this poverty exists alongside the wealth of a national elite, and is held in place by the oppressive might of the government's army. Very often the government *is* the army, and frequently the "stability" of this situation is supported by military aid and intervention by a superpower. When people, oppressed beyond endurance, arise in protest, the army strikes back and the country is at war. This dynamic underlies many of the wars currently killing children with bombs and bullets, while more children die of malnutrition and disease held in place by the war system. The debt trap is part of this phenomenon. According to this analysis, militarization is an integral part of a global order which ensures continued economic and political dominance for the developed countries and continued subordination for the underdeveloped. Militarization is the force that "enables the developed North to 'underdevelop' the South."[3]

Today in Colombia, Peru, Guatemala, El Salvador, Angola, Mozambique, Sudan, Ethiopia, Lebanon, Sri Lanka, East Timor and the Philippines, children are dying in large numbers by being bombed, shot, mined or hacked. Many more are missing limbs or eyes or suffer other injuries from the violence of war. Even greater numbers die because war disrupts immunization programs and other health services as well as food production.

Mozambique and Angola have the highest under-five mortality rates in the world.[4] Only Afghanistan (also war-disrupted) and Mali are at the same level—three in ten children die before they are five years old. A

Dr. Joanna Santa Barbara is a Child and Family Psychiatrist in private practice in Hamilton, Ontario. She is an Assistant Professor in the Department of Psychiatry at McMaster University. In addition, she consults to the Wentworth County Board of Education.

She is married, with three children, ages 10 to 21 years. She was born and trained in Australia, coming to Canada in 1976.

Dr. Santa Barbara became active in the peace movement about eight years ago, and is now President Elect of Canadian Physicians for the Prevention of Nuclear War. She has given speeches and workshops across Canada, in Australia, the U.S.A., and Central America. She travelled to Moscow in 1983, meeting with members of both official and unofficial peace movements.

Dr. Santa Barbara has taught Introductory Peace Studies, an undergraduate course at McMaster University, and is a Research Scholar associated with the Harvard Center for Psychological Studies in the Nuclear Age.

UNICEF study in 1986[5] estimated that almost 45 per cent of these deaths in Angola and Mozambique were from war and destabilization related causes.

Millions of children flee war-zones as refugees, most seeking haven in some of the poorest countries of the world such as Pakistan, Somalia, Sudan.

In addition to damage to a child's physical health, or even loss of life, there is less visible but important psychological and social harm inflicted by armed conflict and violence. Probably the most common form of damage results from children being separated, temporarily or permanently, from one or both parents because of the parents' death or "disappearance." In some cases, children may be witnesses or victims of direct hostilities or gruesome atrocities. Sometimes as a result of watching family members being killed while they themselves remain silent in hiding, children are ravaged by guilt feelings for long after. They may see the harrassment or torture of parents, the bombing of populated areas or the destruction of their home. Older children may themselves be deliberately killed to prevent their being used by opposition forces, tortured, taken away for sexual or other forms of exploitation or enlisted in combat units. Within family groups, or separated from their parents, they are often victims of mass evictions or other forms of displacement.

Economic hardships and the financial insecurity of parents reinforce the child's feelings of despair and insecurity...

War has an all-embracing impact on a child's development, on his [sic] attitudes, his experience of human relations, his moral norms and his outlook on life. Facing armed violence on a continuous basis creates deep-rooted feelings of helplessness and undermines the child's trust in others.[5]

These millions of children are made up of individuals, one child and one child and one child. Let us meet one of these children who did not die from bombs, bullets, starvation, disease or beating, although she almost did, and once wished she would. She is now twenty-six, an unusually beautiful, tall, graceful Somalian woman, a refugee in Canada, slowly rebuilding a shattered life. I first met Faisa over lunch in a restaurant.

"Do you have any brothers or sisters?" I asked brightly.

"They are all dead," she said. We both had difficulty finishing our meal. Later, over my kitchen table Faisa told me her story.

Until Faisa was six years old, she lived happily with her father, mother, three sisters and brother in a beautiful house on the Somalian side of the border with Ethiopia. Her father, a tall, handsome man, ran a business distributing camel's milk, gas, food and medication to rural households. They were well-off and the household had several servants. When Faisa was six, recently decolonized Somalia was taken over by a military dictatorship headed by Mohamed Siyad Barre. Serious persecution of certain tribal groups and all dissidents began, especially of supporters of the previous post-colonial government. Barre favoured members of his own tribe. He later sold a portion of beautiful coastline to the United States for use as a toxic chemical dump, according to Faisa. Resistance groups began to coalesce, plotting the overthrow of Barre. They sometimes were harboured across the border in Ethiopia. Faisa's father, sympathetic to their cause, delivered milk, food, medication and money to the rebels. He exchanged ideas with them and was drawn into their organization, soon becoming a local leader.

One night at 3 a.m., soldiers kicked in the door of Faisa's house, pushed her mother aside and hauled her father from his bed. The five children cried as he was dragged away, looking back at them, shaking his head. The mother, trembling all over in a kitchen smashed by the soldiers, tried to comfort the children. For the next eight years they had no news of the father. No visits were allowed. To speak of him would mean jail.

The family was constantly watched by government spies. The children could see soldiers patrolling outside. No one could visit or speak to them. An uncle, who tried initially to support the family financially, was jailed for two years. The mother, against all tradition, had to support the family by selling produce in the market.

The children left the surrounded house daily to go to school. There the children were unfriendly and the teachers harsh because the family was marked. "They used to slap us on the head and hands. My earring holes kept bleeding. I had no girl friends; nobody liked me. I just watched the other kids play. Other kids had parents who came to the school, but my mother was in the market. It was like having no parents." At the end of each year, everyone bought the class picture except Faisa, whose family could not afford it.

The family was very poor and the children did not have enough to eat. Sometimes there was only corn. They became thin and contracted skin diseases. Faisa wore the same dress for two years, frayed and torn. At thirteen she had a scalp problem. Her mother could not afford the medicine used to treat it, and Faisa's scalp was shaved instead, leading to further peer ostracism. Three times at school, her pen was stolen, a terrible event for Faisa. Her mother could not afford to buy another, and would weep and beat her daughter. Astonishingly, through all this Faisa was a very good student.

When Faisa was fourteen, one morning at 5 a.m. she heard shouts outside her house. She got up and joined her mother and siblings. Approaching the house was a man in a wheel-chair. He had map-like scars on his skin, no finger nails, swollen infected fingers, a burnt area on each temple. He was drooling, tremulous and incontinent. He did not recognize his wife, children or home. It was the shell of her formerly slender, tall, handsome, intelligent father, after eight years of torture. The children were afraid to go near him.

Faisa's mother sold the rest of her gold to pay a doctor to help her husband. The doctor said he could do nothing and Faisa's father never got better. Her mother cleaned and fed him before going to market and came home at midday to do it again. After school Faisa took her mother's place at the market stall until 7 p.m. Ten months later, soldiers shot her father through an open window. Faisa mourned his death. She understood that he had helped people fighting for their rights and felt proud of him. She vowed to take his place.

Meanwhile Barre's army had invaded Ethiopia. Three months after her father's death, Faisa's school was bombed by Ethiopians. She ran home. Her house stood apart from others, on the border. A Somalian war-plane had dropped a bomb on it. Faisa is sure it was deliberate, because her family was against Barre. A neighbour intercepted the child's flight, picked her up and covered her face with his robe. He took her to his house and told her that her mother and three younger siblings where dead. Faisa fainted. This happened on a Thursday, and every Thursday since has been a difficult day for Faisa.

She was taken to her older sister's house in another town. She was ill with fevers, vomiting, insomnia and nightmares for some time. Faisa was preoccupied by wanting to return to the site of her home, sure that there had been a mistake. Perhaps her family might still be alive. At least she could be shown the bodies. Her sister exerted herself to distract her, took her to doctors, prayed at mosques. After a year or two, Faisa returned to school.

At twenty, Faisa again felt spy surveillance closing in. She moved with her sister, brother-in-law, and their two small children to another town, joining the uncle who had initially risked himself to help her family. Faisa cared for the children of the two families. Her uncle and brother-in-law began again to get supplies to the resistance groups, and soon Faisa was spending most of her time in resistance activities. She organized secret meetings of students and neighbourhood children. Barre had poisoned the natural water supply of the area harbouring resistance fighters. Faisa organized the children to deliver clean water. She taught first-aid to the resistance fighters.

"I had so much to do. I was feeling proud and happy. Even though Thursdays were sad I kept working. I wanted to keep doing this for the rest of my life."

Faisa's activities were discovered in 1988. She was arrested at home and taken blindfolded to jail. The jailers wanted the names of all the children in her organization. Faisa decided she would die before telling them. They beat her with a device like a heavy baseball bat, breaking bones in her hand. They pulled two of her lower incisors out. In their efforts to extract information from her, they brought in a good friend of hers, pregnant, and the woman's husband. They raped the woman in front of Faisa and the husband and then killed the husband. Then they tried to rape Faisa. As she ran from them, a soldier tripped her. She fell dislocating and fracturing her jaw. As she lay bleeding, six soldiers raped her. They knew that by doing this they foreclosed the possibility of marriage for Faisa. She was taken, bleeding from ears, mouth and vagina, back to her cell. She expected to die. The other women surrounded her. Faisa looked at them wordlessly weeping and unable to speak. She received no medical attention, although her compound fractures became seriously infected.

Two weeks later the resistance group bombed the jail in an effort to free the captives. Faisa was carried out. On release she learned that her uncle, her sister and all the children of the two families had been killed by the army, who had torched their dwellings and shot the children. With no family left, Faisa was carried to former neighbours. They paid for medical attention. Unable to use her mouth, Faisa had an intravenous line inserted. Every night after dark, she was carried to a car and taken to a different house to sleep. The intravenous line stayed in for a year, until she could eat again. Also after a year she began to walk again and, after fourteen months, to speak.

At this point the leaders of the resistance movement said that Faisa must leave Somalia. She refused, begging to be allowed to continue to help her countrymen. They pointed out that those who gave her refuge were risking their lives and she sadly submitted. "Go, never look back," they said.

"I felt shame," Faisa said. "It hurts me when I think they are still sacrificing themselves and I am safe. I feel guilty."

Faisa escaped, in purdah, on a forged passport. After many frightening experiences en route, she arrived in Canada, knowing no one.

Faisa's story is that of one childhood, adolescence and young adulthood lived through insurgency, civil war and international war. Multiply it by millions and one knows with deep assurance that militarism and war must be abolished. Children long for this.

CHILDREN AND PEACE

Let me now discuss some of the practical steps which we as parents and teachers can take to help build a love for peace, and attitudes conducive to achieving world peace, among our children. Living in as rich and relatively non-violent a country as Canada, we surely have a moral responsibility to try to produce a generation of young adults who will seek to change the horrible world that Faisa grew up in.

PARENTING FOR PEACE

Working for peace, development and the environment is done not only "out there" in the public arena but also "in here" within our families, within ourselves.

Children want us to transmit values to them which, when broadly shared, will create a more peaceful world. What might these values be? At this point I'd like to encourage you, the reader, to stop and consider your own list of values for a better world, before reading on. You might even write them down.

This is my list.

Caring about others with *empathy* and *respect*. The others are at first very immediate—family members, the family pet, the spider on the wall, the flowers in the garden. Under the guidance of parents, the "circle of compassion" (to use Einstein's term) grows, to eventually embrace all the people of this planet, all the other creatures and plants who dwell here, and the rock, soil and air which sustain us. It leads inevitably to *non-violence* toward people and the environment.

Sharing begins small-scale and simple, with sharing toys and food with others, and develops under adult guidance into a sense of justice, recognizing the rights and needs of all on the planet.

Cherishing differences begins by guiding a child's early relationships with others of different skin colour or intellectual ability, for example, and develops toward celebrating the richness of and wishing to protect the diminishing cultural diversity and biodiversity of our planet.

Cooperating begins by working with others toward small goals in play or work, and develops toward an understanding of the need for international cooperation in the superordinate goals of peace, development and environmental protection.

Personal power and responsibility begins with experiencing respect for one's own opinion and limited right of self-determination as a young member of a family, together with the expectation of age-appropriate contribution to the needs of the family. From this develops a young person who believes s/he has the power to make a difference to the world and the responsibility to do so.

Commitment to truth regarding one's own word and outside information. This begins with a young child learning the importance of trust with the family and learning to be skeptical of the blandishments of television. It develops toward personal integrity and perspicacity in dealing with information about the world.

How do we rear chidren who exemplify these values? The following remarks draw extensively from the work of Dyke Brown and Daniel Solomon[6] who summarized research in children's "pro-social" behaviour. By "pro-social" they mean caring, sharing, helping, feeling resonsible.

All human beings have the potential to become caring and cooperative persons. There is an in-built neurological basis for this, just as there is for our self-caring or egocentric propensities. Development in this moral sphere begins from birth and can continue through adulthood into old age. I believe it is important for parents and others to see children as fundamentally "good," even when they seem very much otherwise at times. In fact, when parents convey this explicitly to their children in relation to specific behaviour, ("Thanks for putting your little brother's socks on; you're such a helpful child" or "I like the way you shared; you're a really generous person"), it is a more potent inducer of further pro-social behaviour than social reinforcement (the first part of the statement) alone.[7]

Secure attachment to a loving caretaker underlies development of caring, sharing and helping in pre-schoolers. This means the baby needs a parent who sensitively understands and promptly responds to his or her needs, and who provides an abundance of rich interaction and play. Support of the child's developing self-esteem is important. At a later point, self-esteem, optimism and confidence are found to correlate with pro-social behaviour.

Experiencing firm expectations from parents (or the family) for behaviour in these value areas is shown to develop social responsibility. This will begin with clear simple expectations that toys will be picked up and the cat's tail will not be pulled, and progress to the very complex expectations a family will convey to a teenager, covering attention to schoolwork, contribution to family work, expectations in areas of drugs, sex, etc.

Modelling behaviour in these areas is well understood to be particularly powerful in transmitting values to children. Parents who model empathy, who invite a Moslem friend to chant grace in Arabic before a meal, who

149

cooperate with their child as well as expecting the child's cooperation, will strongly convey these value messages. It seems to me that especially important modelling might take place when parents are visibly growing in value development, as many of us are in changing our lifestyles to live more harmoniously in the threatened biosphere. Some of these changes have an impact on chidren, who should be consulted as the family decides to eat less meat, or buy fewer things packaged in plastic.

Empathy-induction. Repeatedly guiding a child to imagine the feelings of another is considered an important component of developing pro-social behaviour. This begins when the mother cries "Ouch!" and grimaces when the baby pulls her hair or bites her breast. With toddlers one says, "How do you think Scotty feels when you've taken his car from him?" A child who has committed an antisocial act, for example theft or vandalism, should whenever possible hear of its effects directly from the victim.

As the circle of compassion expands in the older child, s/he may empathize with hungry children in Toronto or Guatemala, with dolphins drowning in drift-nets, with Indians deprived of ancestral lands.

Being given responsibility, expecially in caring for and helping others induces responsible and cooperative behaviour. This becomes especially apparent in cross-cultural studies where children in all other cultures studied (Asian, African, Latin American, Pacific Islands) are more nurturing and cooperative than North American children. The differences are attributed to expectations of children to care for younger siblings and contribute to the household economy.[8, 9]

Approval of pro-social behaviour by parents and disapproval of its absence are important, especially when, as mentioned before, the caring or cooperative or responsible behaviour is attributed to an enduring internal characteristic of the child.

Discipline. A good deal of research suggests that external rewards and punishments are not effective ways of inducing pro-social behaviour. Being spanked for hitting a sibling seems an especially confusing way of trying to convey a value. Coercive and authoritarian parental styles are less effective than the style where parents explain with empathy-induction the impact of a child's behaviour on others and provide reasons for desired behaviour.[10] It would seem consistent with these findings to replace punishment for misdemeanours in the family by the use of "natural and logical consequences" as described by Dreikurs[11] and elaborated by Dinkmeyer and McKay.[12]

In this method the parent dispenses with punishment and eventually, with practice, with shouting and anger. The child simply experiences the natural consequence of his or her undesirable behaviour. If he has come home too late, he cannot be trusted to go out the next day. The following day he'll be given another chance to prove himself trustworthy. If she refuses to clean her teeth, the next day she will have a sugar-free diet since she has now given her parents the responsibility of protecting her teeth. And so on. It demands a good deal of creativity and curbing the well-learned habit of responding with anger and punishment. In my opinion, it is very much worth the trouble as it so greatly reduces the hostility that follows punishment, and increases a sense of responsibility and self-determination.

Although there is copious research on the induction of pro-social behaviour, it mainly focuses on the child in the family or peer group. None that I know of deals with extending the "circle of compassion" more and more widely to all the people and creatures of the planet. I believe this is accomplished by the parent as the child's knowledge of the world expands. The parent explains to the child, models and elicits the child's help in ways of caring for others, from an elderly neighbour across the street, to the rainforest across the world.

The above remarks apply in general to guiding the development of all of the values mentioned. Some specific suggestions apply to each value in particular.

Caring. In developing this value the parent must deal with a cultural context that often conveys "Me first," "Look out for number one" and other such soul-deadening messages. In relation to caring for the environment, our culture conveys that technological progress will make life better, that the planet is ours to exploit, and, especially during the child's hours of absorbing television material, that we need to buy more and more things. Peers will reflect back the same messages. So the parent has a daunting task.

The principles, I think, are showing a deep respect for the child as a person, and from early on, expecting the child to respect and contribute to the needs of other family members, including one's own needs, and then slowly extending that caring outwards with knowledge, empathy-induction and opportunities to help. Participation in a Third World "development" program is one way to extend a child's circle of compassion. Opportunities for children to help with environmental protection are increasing.

Arousing children's capacity to care for nature can be one of the joys of life, involving their aesthetic sensiblities and their intellectual understanding. From hugging trees to canoe tripping, there are wonderful things to do with children in the back-yard, the park or the wilderness. "Sharing Nature with Children" by Joseph Bharat Cornell[13] expands the average parent's creativity. "Sunship Earth"[14] is a stunningly brilliant immersion experience in ecological principles. It is presented at certain summer camps in Canada and elsewhere in the world.

It was suggested earlier that an extension of the value of caring and respect for all people and all life is *non-violence*. This is a very troubling issue for many parents and leads us to the problems of violent television, war-toys, and play-ground fights. These issues will be dealt with briefly here.

Television violence. There is abundant evidence that exposure to television violence causes children to be more aggressive and less helpful in the immediately following time. There is a little evidence that it is related to long-term aggression. Large numbers of parents express unhappiness about the content of much children's television, but feel helpless to affect it. If you are among them, may I encourage you to join Canadians Concerned About Violence in Entertainment (C-CAVE). Write to the organization at 167 Glen Rd., Toronto, M4W 2W8, or telephone 416-961-0853. While you are helping the culture to change, discuss the issue and your own values within the family, guiding children to make decisions about whether they entertain themselves with violence. If they choose to do so, sit with them through a show (a considerable parental sacrifice!) and discuss with them the values conveyed. (The world is divided into "goodies" and "baddies." The "baddies" are often alien and dehumanized. Violence is the only successful strategy for dealing with the problem. Often it is very high-techology glamorous violence. It works. There is little suffering involved, and anyone who does suffer, deserves to.)

War Toys. Many parents are careful not to bring war toys into their homes but feel defeated by peer pressure (or gifts from relatives) and children's ingenuity in constructing guns from Lego, a twig, a piece of toast. The value messages conveyed by the parents' efforts are not lost. The make-shift war toys that appear can always be seen as opportunities for discussion of the values they represent. Preventive action can be taken by asking relatives and parents of friends coming to birthday parties not to buy war toys. As with violent television, there are community groups to support in their action against the invasion of militarism into children's play.

Playground fights and bullies. Do peaceful children have to be wimps? Emphatically, no! Children reared in these values are empowered children. (See particularily the section on Personal Power, below.) They know that as they are expected to be just in their dealings with others, they have a right to expect justice from others, and that they should not put up with injustice. They can be assertive in saying what they do not like, to their sibs, parents, playmates, teacher. Their parents are teaching them to solve problems and resolve conflicts cooperatively.

In my experience, children reared with these values and practices are socially attractive to others.

With the problem of being bullied, the following points may be helpful.

1. Validate that the child must not put up with being bullied, teased or put down.
2. Carefully check your child's contribution to the conflict.
3. Work first to support the child's own problem-solving:
   • assertive statements.
   • getting the children, if siblings or playmates, together for conflict resolution.
4. If this doesn't work, offer adult intervention:
   • contact the other child's parents.
   • problem-solve with the school principal.
5. Ask for school interventions. A number of creative programs in school playground conflict resolution are being used in Toronto, San Francisco, Ottawa and elsewhere.

Sharing. Beyond teaching children to share justly and generously with siblings and playmates, the aware family will be examining its "share" of the world's resources. Our "share" is provided partly by exploitation of the Third World poor and partly by exploitation and despoliation of the rest of the biosphere. Our "share" deprives other people and other creatures of their "share." With our children, we must pause again and again to rethink habitual patterns of our lifestyle, learning to consume less and differently.

Cherishing differences. It is fortunate if a child can attend a pre-school or day-care where there are others of different skin colour, ethnic origin, physical or intellectual ability. Parents can make use of the ethnic diversity of most Canadian communities to enrich their children's lives with music, dance, food and religious practices of other cultures. The periodic pow-wows held by many native communities offer an impressive experience of native Indian culture.

Parents need to be vigilant that when children are taught at school about other human groups, it is not as interesting but inferior curiosities, but with full respect for the humanness and cultural beauty of those groups. Watch carefully what your child is taught about the "discovery" of the Americas or of Australia. Curricula on these subjects are likely to be seriously Eurocentric.

Racism will be encountered by many children in one way or another in jokes or in put-downs. Whether one's child is victim, perpetrator or by-stander, a parent needs to act firmly, clarifying family values with the child, and dealing with the situation. If necessary, the school or institution where the issue arose should be called upon to act.

Cooperating. Cooperation means that shared goals are best reached by acting together with others. It comes up against a pervasive and cherished value in our society—competition. High valuing of competitive structures and competitiveness as a personality trait may pervade even the world of young children, in their sports and some class-room environments.

It comes as a great surprise to many to find that competitive learning environments ("You have to try to be the best and beat everyone else") are much inferior to cooperative learning environments ("You must work together to acquire this knowledge and skill") in both academic and social outcomes. Individual achievement-oriented learning environments, ("You must strive to do your personal best") are intermediate in outcome.[15] Furthermore, competitive personalities achieve at a lower level than non-competitive. These findings are beginning to be incorporated in the practices of some schools. Where they are not, parents may wish to discuss them with educators.

Cooperative large muscle games, including cooperative hockey, soccer and water polo have been extensively described by Ottawa researcher Terry Orlick[16] and are in use in many places. These games emphasize fun, fitness and participation and eliminate the typical casualties of competitive games, the dropping out of the clumsier, less skillful children who need the activity the most, and the hurt, hostility and humiliation that can be involved.

Cooperative table games have also been pioneered by Canadians. "Family Pastimes" of R.R. 4, Perth, Ontario, K7H 3C6 has a wonderful array of games for players from early childhood to adulthood. Some of their inventions such as "Harvest Time" are now produced by large companies and are available in toy stores.

An area where one might least expect the use of cooperative strategies is formal debating. But it has been done,[17] and the result is said to be superior in achieving a truthful understanding of the issue at hand.

Parents need to model cooperation to their children. Spending time with a child playing just the way s/he wants, becoming part of his or her fantasy creation, can be very rewarding to both participants. Children whose parents do this are more cooperative when asked to do a parent-determined task.[18]

Seeing the family as a cooperative enterprise may be important. Some families see themselves as parent-run organizations. Children may have no chores or few, and they are done "to help mother" as they are seen as basically her job. An alternative is to see the family as a cooperative group, with members of varying degrees of wisdom and ability to contribute. Chores are the child's necessary and important contribution to the whole family. Decisions are made by the whole family in regular meetings where everyone participates.[11, 12] The child learns about his or her rights and responsibilities in this small system, how to resolve conflict cooperatively, and how to help a family member with a problem. Many people see this experience not only as empowering for children, but also as splendid training for participation in a democracy.

At a global level, children need to slowly learn about the system of planetary cooperation embodied in the United Nations. Beginning with UNICEF at Halloween (it is a Canadian custom for children to collect money for UNICEF when they "trick or treat"), they may go on in some high schools to have a model United Nations event. Since supporting and strengthening the U.N. is one of mankind's best hopes, it is important for children to understand its present function and its potential for cooperative security, cooperative environmental management and cooperative development.

Personal power and responsibility. The comments above on the cooperative family where the child's feelings and opinions are treated respectfully are relevent to rearing an empowered child. Being offered even a limited range of choices fosters both cooperation and a feeling of personal power:

"What'll it be tonight—a bath or a shower?"

"Either you eat some spinach or get a lettuce leaf from the fridge."

As the child develops s/he is encouraged to act on the belief that s/he can make a difference to his or her classroom, school, town or the world. Naturally, s/he will be greatly helped in this if s/he has parents who believe and act on their own power to make a difference.

The heroes presented to a child may exemplify this, e.g. Jacques Cousteau, Martin Luther King, Mahatma Ghandi.

It is important not to raise an obedient child! The worst human cruelties have been defended by the claim of obedience to authority with surrender of personal moral autonomy. Consider Nazi war crimes, the My Lai massacre, the daily torture of men and women across the world—all of these were and are and will be done "only obeying orders."

At a more mundane level, our children will often excuse themselves from misdemeanours by saying that an older child told them to do it, or describing their need to conform, "Well, all the others were doing it." Sometimes parents accept this.

How do you rear a child who will not obey immoral orders or follow antisocial peers, who will make his or her moral decisions?

We do not know the answer to this, but my best guess is that it lies in the methods of rearing described above, where cooperation is maximized, coercion by authority is minimized, and physical violence to children is eliminated. Children are guided to understand the reasons for expectations and requests, to think through the consequences of their behaviour and to take personal responsibility for the consequence (which they experience when parents use "natural or logical consequence" rather than punishment). The child is helped to make his or her own moral decisions, rather than being told what to do. The parent raises the principles involved: "Would that be fair?"

"Is that entirely truthful?"

Sometimes the parent accepts "wrong" decisions and helps the child accept and deal with the consequences. I have been very tempted to become coercive when my child has refused a request to do a small errand. However, reasoning about the importance of family cooperation and the natural consequence of shortening or delaying my availability to play with him have led, I think, to a more morally responsible and cooperative child than demands for obedience to parental authority.

Commitment to truth. The expectation that people in the family can trust one another's word needs to be presented early and reinforced in family meetings when necessary.

A more difficult task is to help the child with the distortions of reality which are daily presented on television. I have referred above to television's representation of conflict and the success of violence. Truth in advertising is an issue which can be first raised quite early with small children beguiled by toy advertisements. Much later, media distortions of reality in news coverage of global issues needs to be addressed and children need to learn that leaders and spokespeople vary in their credibility. Noam Chomsky's writings[19] are very helpful in this area.

Knowledge. The children I spoke to referred to the need for knowledge to help make the world a better place. Beyond (or perhaps before) what they need to make a useful and satisfying vocational contribution and to enjoy cultural and leisure enrichment, what do they need to know? Here too, your list might differ from mine in interesting ways. Mine includes:
Knowledge:
- of the evolution of the earth in the universe.
- of the functioning of its ecological systems and the recent malfunction of these.
- of the human family.
- of global resources and economic disparities.
- of causes of war and conditions of peace.

- of human rights and the status of rights throughout the world.
- of international institutions and law.
- of science and technology in relation to values.

While some of this knowledge transmission occurs at home, much of it is advanced education appropriate to the school setting. Parents need to participate in helping schools prepare children to become effective global citizens. Many of the parenting processes described here can be appropriately transferred to the school setting. For example, classrooms can function democratically, with children taking responsibility for the maintenance of a good learning evnvironment.

Taking action for a more peaceful, just and greener world. Children say they want our support in their own beginning actions for a better world. Most parents who have read this chapter would be deeply thrilled to give it, seeing it as confirmation of their parenting for peace.

One last disturbing question remains to be addressed. The children now languishing in refugee camps, or fearing the worst for a disappeared parent, or gasping their last with diphtheria because immunization has been suspended by war—can they wait until we rear our children to create a better world? Of course not. Our political action in the world must proceed alongside our parenting which grows in depth and beauty with our own inner changes and growth. It is all of a piece, a seamless web. We are slowly harmonizing our lives with our wonderful planet. We are hand in hand with our children on a remarkable journey at a remarkable time.

References

1. Quotations by Children from Exley, Richard and Helen (1985) My World/Peace Passport Books, Chicago.
2. Sivard, Ruth Leger (1989) World Military and Social Expenditures, World Priorities, Box 25140, Washington, D.C., U.S.A. 120007.
3. Epp-Tiessen, Esther (1990) Missiles, Malnutrition: The Links Between Militarization and Underdevelopment. Project Ploughshares, Conrad Grebel College, Waterloo, Ontario, N2L 3G6.
4. UNICEF Report (1987) Children on the Front Line: The Impact of Apartheid, Destabilization and Warfare on Children in Southern and South Africa. UNICEF, 866 U.N. Plaza, New York, N.Y. 10017.
5. UNICEF Executive Board Report (1986) Children in Situations of Armed Conflict. UNICEF, 866 U.N. Plaza, New York, N.Y. 10017.
6. Brown, D. & Solomon, D. (1983) A Model For Prosocial Learning: An in Progress Field Study. In Bridgeman, D. (ed.) The Nature of Prosocial Development. Academic Press, New York.
7. Grusec J. E. & Dix T. (1986) The Socialization of Prosocial Behaviour: Theory and Reality. In Zahn-Waxler C., Cummins E. M. and Ianotti R. (eds.) Altruism and Aggression: Biological and Social Origins. Cambridge University Press.

8. Whiting, B. B. & Whiting J. W. M. (1975) Children of Six Cultures: A Psycho-cultural Analysis. Harvard University Press.

9. Graves, N. B. & Graves T. D. (1983) The Cultural Context of Prosocial Development: An Ecological Model. In Bridgeman D. (ed.) The Nature of Prosocial Development. Academic Press, New York.

10. Hoffman, M. L. (1970) Moral Development. In Mussen P. H. (ed.) Carmichael's Manual of Child Psychology Vol 2. Wiley, New York.

11. Dreikurs, R. (1987) Children, the Challenge. E. P. Dutton Publishers, New York.

12. Dinkmeyer D. & McKay G. D. (1989) The Parent's Handbook. American Guidance Service.

13. Cornell, Joseph Bharat (1979) Sharing Nature with Children: A Parents' and Teachers' Nature-Awareness Guidebook. Ananda Publications.

14. van Matre, Steven (1977) Sunship Earth. Library of Congress. American Camping Association. Martinsville, Indiana.

15. Kohn, A. (1986) No Contest: The Case Against Competition. Houghton Mifflin Co., Boston.

16. Orlick T. (1978) The Cooperative Sports and Games Book: Challenge without Competition. Pantheon Books, N.Y.

17. Peter, Ian. The Problem Solving Debate. CORE, P.O. Box 368, Lismore, New South Wales, Australia, 2480.

18. Parpal M. & Maccoby E. E. (1985) Maternal Responsiveness and Subsequent Child Compliance. Child Development 56: 1326-1334.

19. Herman E. S. & Chomsky, N. (1988) Manufacturing Consent: The Political Economy of Mass Media. Pantheon Books, New York.

CHAPTER 9
Low Intensity War and Mental Trauma in Nicaragua: A Study in a Rural Community

DR. DEREK SUMMERFIELD AND
LESLIE TOSER

The Nicaraguan people had barely 2 years of peace after the sacrifices entailed in toppling the oppressive and corrupt Somosa dictatorship after 43 years. From 1981 to 1990 the United States-sponsored Contra war inflicted enormous pain and destruction across a whole society, with 60,000 people (1.5 per cent of the total population) murdered, injured or abducted. The fatality rate was 10 times that sustained by U.S. society during the years 1965 to 1973 of the Vietnam War and thus the experience of bereavement escaped comparatively few Nicaraguans.[1] Fifteen thousand children were orphaned, 700 'disappeared', 450 were killed and 1,500 others were maimed or physically handicapped. Three hundred and fifty thousand people—at least one in six of the rural population—were uprooted from their homes and lands. In the worst war zones, some of the health gains fostered by the revolution were lost: infant mortality increased because of malnutrition and the diarrheal diseases which flourish in the conditions created by war; measles and tuberculosis, previously endemic but much reduced by mass vaccination programs, returned.

What was the basic nature of a war the U.S. Department of Defense called 'low intensity'? Defenceless peasant farmers (campesinos) and their families comprised most of the casualties, and the Contras were always less intent on combat with the Nicaraguan army or strikes at military targets. They ambushed and murdered randomly but also targeted health workers, engineers, literacy volunteers, community leaders, indeed anyone identified with programs to improve the lot of ordinary people. More than 100 health workers were assassinated or wounded, and the threat forced many of them to work in semi-fugitive ways, hiding their equipment and vaccines and removing the signs designating health posts. The

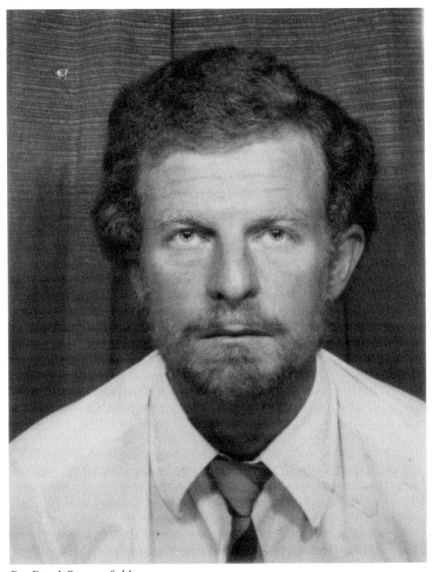

Dr. Derek Summerfield

Contras' sustained efforts to destroy the health service left 300,000 rural dwellers without access to health care of any kind.[2] The practice of torture of victims before killing them, and leaving their mutilated bodies near their homes to bear witness, was used too systematically throughout the war zones merely to represent random excesses by individual Contras. Acts of this kind were also committed deliberately in front of the families of the victims, including their children. Jacobo Timerman, witnessing similar scenes in Argentina (and a victim himself), has described the devastating blows that such acts deal to a culture which is based on familial love, devotion and the capacity for mutual sacrifice.[3]

It is clear that what was sought was the mass terrorization of civilians. This objective is in line with 'low intensity' warfare theory, defined by a Colonel in the U.S. Army Special Forces as "total war at the grass roots level."[4] Population, not territory, is the target, and psychological warfare is a central element. By means of terrorization wrought by a mercenary proxy army, the Contras, the aim was to paralyse rural life, to silence individuals and communities, to deny hope that personal struggle could ever bear fruit, and to insist that the revolution could not live up to its promises. This demoralization, as well as the damage to the infrastructure, to food-growing capacity and to the health services, was designed to augment the diplomatic and economic blockade in pressuring central government and hastening its political downfall. It is noteworthy that 'low intensity' warfare strategists used disease as a political metaphor: Nicaragua was repeatedly referred to as a 'virus or malignant tumour' threatening the health of the western hemisphere, and it was stated flatly that "there can be no negotiating with a cancer."[5]

Derek Summerfield qualified in medicine in London in 1977. He worked as a rural medical officer back in his native Zimbabwe in a war-ravaged area near the Mozambique border shortly before independence in 1980. Later he specialized in psychiatry at St. George's Hospital Medical School, London, where he was a senior registrar from 1986 to 1990. He is interested in the relationship between Western political and economic structures and poverty and violence in the Third World, the longer term health and social consequences of these issues, and in the rehabilitation of torture victims.

Leslie Toser is from Chicago. She has a Masters Degree in Business Administration and was an executive at the Chicago Stock Exchange. In 1988 she worked with the peace movement in El Salvador, in extended contact with progressive workers threatened with arbitrary execution or 'disappearance', and with traumatized communities. In 1989 she joined Witness for Peace in Nicaragua, a U.S.-based Christian pressure group documenting human rights abuses in the Contra war.

But statistics convey only the bare bones of the suffering over the past nine years. Relatively little has been recorded so far of the psychological trauma of the war, but it is likely to be substantial. A study in Ciudad Sandino near Managua showed that 25 per cent of those seeking mental health services had recently lost a family member in the war; staff in clinics in many parts of the country have made similar observations. In neighbouring El Salvador, at the height of the war in 1978 to 1981, psychiatric consultations rose from eighth to the third most common reason to seek medical attention.[6] Learning and behavior problems at home and at school have been noted in Nicaraguan children who have known little but war. There is concern about the social consequences of splintered families, and in particular about child abuse and neglect; several thousand children are estimated to be living rough on the streets of Managua, a new phenomenon. Ex-soldiers, particularly those who have been crippled, may be vulnerable to alcohol abuse.

What of the rural campesinos who have taken the brunt of the bloodshed and have had to contend with 'low intensity' warfare in their daily lives for eight years? The acute face of their suffering has been all too familiar, but the extent and nature of longer term effects has not been studied. This was the purpose of our survey. We chose a war zone community, a small farming co-operative, where most of the residents had suffered their worst traumas several years previously, and elsewhere. The community itself had never been attacked. It was thus a good place to document the emotional price that continued to be exacted from them by the war. One of us (LT) had become familiar with life in this community since early 1989 because of her work in documenting war-related human rights abuses in the region. The actual survey was conducted during several weeks' residence in August and in October 1989.

THE SETTING
La Urbina co-operative is situated across the Escondido river from La Esperanza, Zelaya, and is a 15 minute walk from the main Managua-Rama road. At the time of the study 215 campesinos, 86 of whom were over 18 years old, lived in 30 simple wood and iron houses. They had few possessions and were extremely poor. Their children were not overtly malnourished though parasitic infestations were endemic. Families were large: women had delivered up to 10 children, with 1 or 2 commonly dying in infancy. Some of the families were related to each other. Almost everyone was illiterate. They came from isolated farming communities in the Zelayan and Chontales mountains, sufficiently far-flung to have meant relatively little involvement in the revolution of the 1970s. The war had changed everything: many communities had been forced to exist for lengthy periods in a climate of terror, virtually besieged by mobile Contra

groups. Violence had been both focussed, like the killing of families with sons in the army or militia, and indiscriminate. Most of those at La Urbina had had close family members murdered, often in front of their eyes, and some had survived multiple attacks in different locations; everyone had lost homes, land and animals. After varying periods as refugees, some with as many as five moves, they had been given land by the government to start a new co-operative. Most families had been settled there for between two and four years. This was still one of the most active war zones in Nicaragua and the threat of attack on the co-operative had always been real. As recently as late 1988 everyone had been sheltering at night in trenches dug behind the houses. Between two and eight men did vigilance duty every night and the men were also required to be away in the army for four to five months each year, a substantial absence. This community was substantially pro-government in its political attitudes.

METHOD
We conducted interviews, each lasting one to two hours, with 43 residents (21 men, 22 women), a sample which comprised 50 per cent of those aged over 18. We asked each person to describe how the war had affected their lives and their emotional reactions to what had happened. Important issues from earlier periods of their lives sometimes arose and we asked about the way the war was colouring their expectations for the future. Their own words are given in this report in quotation marks. There was also a semi-structured component to the interviews; we used the 28 item General Health Questionnaire (GHQ), a screen for psychological disturbance in general populations.[7] The GHQ has been validated for use in many cultures and the Spanish version has been used in other parts of Latin America. The GHQ has four subscales: psychosomatic symptoms, anxiety and insomnia, social dysfunction and severe depression. Psychosomatization is the expression of emotional distress in the form of physical symptoms.

RESULTS
Overall GHQ scores revealed pervasive psychological disturbance. Sixty-two per cent of the men (average score 8.6), and 91 per cent of the women (average score 12.2), were above the score of 5 which usually represents significant psychological disturbance. Only 6 of the 43 (14 per cent) showed no evidence of disturbance.

1) Psychosomatic symptoms

Fifty-seven per cent of men and 86 per cent of women were plagued by patterns of psychosomatic symptoms which further contributed to their daily hardships. Most commonly reported were headaches, malaise, general bodily pains and dizziness. The most prevalent individual symptom, headache, troubled fully 95 per cent of women. Their descriptions were usually classical: a sensation of tightness around or inside the head, often present for most of every day.

The factors which shaped and propelled these symptoms emerged as people talked about what the war had done to their lives.

Josepha S., aged 60, said that she had been only occasionally sick until her husband, a literacy campaign organizer, was murdered at the beginning of the war. Since then she had been troubled by bodily pains, sudden exhaustion, feverishness, dizziness, and difficulty in walking, always at their worst when she felt most despairing or when her sons were away in the army. Her daughter had accidentally drowned four years earlier and at the funeral she had collapsed ("like a heart attack"), and was taken to the hospital. She said that "the sickness in my head" stopped her working properly.

Veronica G., 39, had had various bodily pains, headaches, or feelings of oppression in her head for three or four years. She said a cold sensation would start in her feet, move up to her head and make her tremble. She sometimes felt on the point of exploding and remarked on the need to keep conscious control of her "nerves." Recent years had been very traumatic for her family. Contras had burned their co-operative at Las Paras in 1984 and they had become refugees in the mountains, moving from place to place with sick children, always under threat. In 1986 her son Santiago, then 16, had been killed in the army. Veronica said she thought about him all the time, "a mother's grief never goes away."

Mercedes A., 33, described persistent fatigue, stomach pains, poor sleep, and feelings of desperation, all clearly dating back to when her husband was shot in the chest by Contras. Now these feelings were linked to her fears for the safety of her sons during military service.

Estefana B., 28, was in no doubt that her fevers, hot and cold flushes, back pains and headaches which made her feel she could go crazy, had all begun after her mother was abducted by Contras at Musuwaka. Before this she had felt healthy. These symptoms seemed more intrusive when she was feeling frightened.

Santos and Filomena M. were married and in their 50s. Santos described feverishness and said he went "almost deaf" with headaches. He felt sad and tremulous and had little energy for work, calling himself "half dead." Filomena had similar symptoms and blamed the war. Four years ago in the mountains, the Contras had forced the whole family to watch while they tied up a brother and a nephew of Filomena's and shot them dead. Nothing had felt the same since then.

Several others told how feeling anxious or thinking too hard about their predicament gave them headaches or dizziness.. They could also feel physically unwell when they heard rumours that the co-operative was under threat of imminent attack.

Estebana G., 56, who presented a strongly psychosomatic picture, said "I don't recognize my own body... it feels inflamed and heavy." Her headaches could be triggered by any news about the war. She had a particularly stressed and divided family; one of her sons had been a Contra and the rest were in the army.

Olga D., a young mother, had frequent faints which she called "epilepsy." Each faint was preceded by a strong desire to run. She had a sensation of pressure in her head which made it seem on fire, felt "tired all the time and empty," and could not enjoy anything. She spoke of a "sadness in my body," her way of conveying how the horror generated by the war penetrated the body as well as the mind.

This last phrase was also used by Felicita S., 18, who described how she would get waves of fear, would become acutely anxious and tearful, and would then faint. This had begun since the death of her husband Pablo at the hands of the Contras one year earlier ("they found him at his mother's house"). At almost the same time, their child had been born but died two weeks later.

When asked about her health, Midelba C., also 18, replied "I feel like my blood is frightened," connecting this and the onset of several psychosomatic symptoms to the abduction of her husband by the Contras at Tutuwaka three years before. Her sister had also suffered this fate and had been treated as the personal chattel of a Contra throughout her captivity. Both had eventually escaped.

2) Mental Symptoms

The majority of women were vulnerable to episodes of panic, trembling, and the feeling of being overwhelmed. These were triggered in various ways: when their sons were about to be mobilized, when the co-operative was on increased alert for an attack, when there was news of combat, or when the army came recruiting their 16-year-old sons. Sudden panics also happened spontaneously.

Nearly half the men admitted similar patterns. Leonardo L., 48, recounted how from a background of anxiety, intense feelings would rise up and overwhelm him "like a nightmare."

While resting, Ramon G., 42, would suddenly find his mind invaded by violent images that he was about to be killed, often by machete, and he would start screaming. He had been seriously wounded in an attack two years before. Olga D. had acute attacks of nervousness when she heard noises outside, particularly at night, and she would "think crazy things."

Even the wind could provoke a sudden fear that someone was about to kill her. This happened repeatedly, though she recognized it as irrational.

These were very common experiences at La Urbina. People seldom felt truly relaxed, and were startled or alerted much more easily than before the war. This became evident during interviews: despite apparent outward calm and composure, people were vigilant. Even in daytime, innocent noises like a pig snuffling outside could provoke a brief pause in the conversation, and slight turning of the head while the potential for danger was assessed. A sound of gunfire, however distant, provoked strong reactions. Each nightfall recreated some of the conditions by which the horror of past attacks was remembered, and raised the real possibility of another attack.

Several residents described experiences akin to depersonalisation/derealisation (unpleasant states of abnormal perception of one's own body or of external objects) that can arise during high autonomic nervous system arousal and emotional distress.

Christina S., 25, vividly recalled the time when almost daily she helped carry injured or dying victims of Contra attacks, often young like herself. One such had died in her arms and the shock had made her ill. She described a pressure surging up towards her head, her body feeling larger, as if it was not hers, and then "it turned into a big worry" and she became acutely panicky. These episodes recurred when someone mentioned a death or when her husband was mobilized, particularly since two Contra assaults on a co-operative at Cuadras Esquinas, near La Urbina. She felt different, "not exactly healthy," and that death haunted her. She ruminated about how she could run with all her three children in her arms.

Jose M., 20, son of Filomena and Santos (mentioned above) was shot during combat with 800 Contras in 1986, when eight of his comrades were killed. He wears a caliper on his paralysed leg. After injury he had episodes of intense anxiety, palpitations and a sensation that his body was suddenly much bigger. Three years later he is a little better psychologically, though sometimes he feels he wants to explode.

Depressed mood, perhaps better described as a pervasive sadness, was commonly evident during interviews and expressions of suffering became more overt as people told their stories. There was very little anger expressed. With one possible exception, no one had had suicidal ideas.

3) Sleep disturbances

No one reported peaceful sleep and nearly half of the sample had ongoing sleep disturbances. One or two men reported slightly better sleep in 1989, because the war had waned a little and they felt less oppressed. The tendency to startle easily, already discussed, was a significant factor, and

Mother of 12 children in La Urbina Co-op and Resettlement Camp, Zelaya, Nicaragua.

sleep was easily penetrated by small noises. People commonly woke up in a state of panic. There was more sleeplessness when there had been news of especially bloody combat or when a Contra group was believed to be close.

Alphonso M., 26, spoke also for other men when he said "if someone wakes you, you think it's combat."

Some reported waking up and wanting to run. In the middle of the night people could be possessed by irrational fears—for example, that their house was about to collapse—which often seemed to arise from a state of half wakefulness, half sleep. One mother spoke of a suffocating sensation when trying to sleep during periods when her son had been mobilized. Her fears for his safety were mingled with a sense of greater vulnerability in the co-operative in his absence.

Nightmares were very common. For Miguel L., 38, and other men, even in their dreams they could not escape from the war and they awoke in the mornings feeling disturbed. Miguel had dreams of magical escapes from situations of extreme danger, confronting superior Contra forces in the mountains (as he had done in real life); he dreamed that at the moment of crisis he was suddenly soaring above the battle and flying away.

Josefa F. repeatedly dreamt that she found her son dead. During the day she would recall the dream and panic afresh.

4) Work difficulties

The inability to work has grave implications in rural communities where its members depend upon manual labour for their living. Jose M., the young ex-soldier with the paralysed leg, was painfully aware of how little use he now was, and had devalued his life accordingly. The others interviewed did not have permanent physical injuries but could still feel impaired. Victorina R., 24, said he was dogged by a kind of tiredness he had never known before the war, which had brought him as much tragedy as anyone at La Urbina. The worst had been witnessing the fatal wounding of his daughter and the murder of his mother, "they called her a stupid old woman and blew her face off." His recollections about that night still distracted him, and at times his work in the fields was interrupted by a sensation of mounting pressure in his head, which caused him to pause until he had calmed down.

Many other people in the community were aware of a drain on their energies and powers of concentration. It seemed harder to get tasks started and to finish them efficiently. It seemed harder to plan and to be optimistic about achieving goals when the war threw up so many obstacles and seemed endless. Men said they felt atypically forgetful, slow and indecisive. The rigours of life in the mountains during successive spells of mobilization, each lasting several months, took a physical toll. And even when they were back in the community they had vigilance duties, sitting all night in a look-out post facing the river. "War wears you down, is hard on your body," Emilio A., 39, concluded. The wearing down was, of course, as much a consequence of a psychological as a physical assault. The result was they had less to give to the running of the co-operative.

There were a few men who were more globally incapacitated. Ramon, mentioned before, had defended two co-operatives under attack. At the second of these, La Victoria, in 1987, he had been shot in the back. He had endured another shock, notably the abduction of his son. Though he had recovered from his wounds without permanent damage, he had never felt the same. He continued to feel ill, weak and unable to work properly. The hospital had not diagnosed any disease to account for his disabilities, which were nevertheless real.

Cleofa F., 36, had never been wounded but presented a similar picture. Though he had not felt entirely well for six years, he was now worse and had no strength for work in the fields.

Eighteen-year-old woman holding her son, La Urbina Co-op and Resettlement Camp, Zelaya, Nicaragua.

Both these men, with what elsewhere might have been deemed a chronic fatigue syndrome, as well as their other psychosomatic symptomatology, seemed almost to feel as if they were 'burnt out' before their time. It was as if the physical decline of old age had been brought forward many years by the relentless accumulation of stresses wrought by the war.

5) Specific traumatic memories

For some, their mental and physical symptoms were centred on a particular traumatic memory. Such memories seemed 'live' because the horror embedded in them remained available to be activated; thus they had a haunting quality.

Edmundo Z., 49, was the deacon in the community. In Nicaragua such men are called Delegates of the Word. In 1984 he had been helping to found a new co-operative near Las Paras in Zelaya. Contras had attacked in July, and amongst others his nephew Tomas, whom Edmundo was raising, was killed. His son Evaristo, then 19, had been abducted and was never seen again. During our interview he produced a document which he and several other Delegates had written and circulated in August 1984. It was a protest at the terror and destruction being sown by Contra actions. Within three days of its circulation one of the signatories, Jose Rios, had been abducted, tortured and murdered. They found his body with multiple bayonet wounds and the tongue cut out. This grotesque piece of symbolism, a Delegate of the Word with no tongue, was doubtless not accidental; it was an act by which the dynamics of torture were extended beyond the body and mind of Jose Rios to assail others, like Edmundo, working for the same goals on behalf of their communities. And the continuing uncertainty over the fate of his son operated similarly.

Expectacion Z., 48, and his family, had survived Contra attacks on three different co-operatives between 1982 and 1987, in each of which people around them were killed. Expectacion himself also survived an ambush and still had rocket shrapnel in his body. He remembered those years as a period when he did not seriously expect the family to live much longer. One particular image came back to him frequently, encapsulating the horror of the times: the sight of his naked children running screaming under gunfire.

Juana R., 24, wife of Victorino, had lost at least five close family members to murder or abduction. In March 1987, their co-operative at Quisilali was attacked. Victorino's mother was shot at close range in cold blood, as noted above, and a grenade thrown at the rest of the family as they ran. Juana, pregnant at the time, was wounded by shrapnel, and four-year-old Lisbet was hit in her arms and in the abdomen. They travelled all night on foot and by canoe to reach help, and Lisbet was eventually sent to Juigalpa Hospital. She died three weeks later after a nightmarish battle for life. This period was still as vivid as ever in Juana's mind, and worst of all was her memory of Lisbet begging her for food or water and her being unable to respond because the doctors had forbidden any. Presumably Lisbet had a perforated intestine. Juana had bitterly reproached herself for not getting her daughter to Managua where she believed medical care might have saved the child. She could not think clearly or eat for a year afterwards and still felt far from normal. At times she could still hear Lisbet's clearly recognizable voice, calling out to her for water. Shortly after Juana had finished telling us her anguished story, she had an attack of psychosomatic chest pain.

6)   Other themes

The ever-present concerns about survival centred not just on the threat of murder and mutilation, but on poverty. The available land was relatively infertile, and food supplies were sometimes inadequate for 215 mouths. At times the co-operative was forced to seek hand-outs of rice or beans. "It's better not to be alive if children ask for food and you have none," a young mother, Norma Z., put it. There was little or no money to buy essential items.

The water at La Urbina, both from well and stream, was intermittently contaminated, but there were no alternatives. There had been less need of money in the mountains, and people remembered good land and pure water. Indeed, descriptions of life before the war often had an idealized quality, like a remembered happy dream, and the frequent mention of the fertility of the soil, where almost everything grew in profusion, seemed a metaphor for a wider richness. There had been poverty in the mountains, but for all the inherent hardships of campesino life, there had been no fear then, no major impairment of the sense of being in control of one's fortunes, God permitting. People were grateful to the government for the help that had enabled them, war refugees, to begin to build a new community. But while the war raged on, there was no escape from the feeling of dependence upon events far beyond personal control. These intangibles seemed part of the sense of enormous loss that people alluded to, directly or indirectly.

The war brought continuing strains to bear upon family relationships. The extended families of many La Urbina residents had been scattered, the fate of many members unknown, even after years. There were fears for elderly parents living without help in the mountains, but it was too dangerous to visit, particularly because the Contras were known to hate people who had organized themselves into co-operatives.

Several families were split by having one of their sons fighting against the government. Ramon's son, abducted in 1986, had been seen carrying arms for the Contras two years later. Ramon described himself as a staunch revolutionary, but said he was unable to be angry with his son and did not want to fight against him. He had tried to get a message to him, urging him to take amnesty. Compassion of this kind will be needed to effect reconciliation across the whole society in the post-war period.

With men away in the army for so much of the time, La Urbina could resemble a community of women and children. Anxiety about the safety of these absent men was a constant background element in day-to-day life, one which did not need to be verbalized. Stories filtered back about women loitering around army camps and had an upsetting effect on wives, sharpening fears of abandonment. Relations between some families were uncomfortable, but typically the community spirit at La Urbina seemed protective against the pressures of the war.

People were cautious but generally not hopeless about the future, saying, "if God wants, we might see the peace." They were desperate for a time when they would no longer be hunted "like deer," as Olga put it, for an end to the frustration of wielding a gun and not a spade, for the chance to give more to their children and for the re-uniting of splintered families. "The hope is in the family. If you abandon family you abandon life." Provided there was peace, the traditional uncertainties of life were manageable, and until peace came they could but keep up the stoic resilience of their parents and grandparents. "God put us here and we have to suffer. . . it's not up to us to decide," and "we believe God hasn't died yet, and we have the faith that He will care for us, perhaps not wonderfully but not badly."

Pride was also sustaining. Men expressed pride at their part in what they saw as a fight for freedom, characterized by Juana as the continuation of a struggle which had begun when her ancestors met the firearms of the Conquistadors with bows and arrows. For these people, defence of the revolution was not just a defence of the literacy, primary health, and agrarian reform programs begun since 1979 by the Sandinistas, but also seemed driven by a resurgence of pride in what it meant to be a Nicaraguan. Reymundo was one of the very poorest at La Urbina but was still able to be philosophical about his family's predicament. "Even though we only have tortillas and salt, others are poorer. People die of hunger in other countries but not in Nicaragua." And perhaps the war had matured some men faster, made them sharply aware of the real priorities and of their capacity to contribute at a time of crisis. With the recent electoral defeat of the Sandinista government, some may now feel that their sacrifices have been wasted.

We did not set out to survey the children of La Urbina. Child care was of course central to the life of the community, and it was largely the women who had to create the kind of stable and responsive emotional environment able to shield the children from the corrosive effects of the war. We could not but notice the emotional disturbance in three young brothers, so ravenous for affection from anyone, and wild and aggressive in their play. Their father, a Contra deserter, had been murdered by his ex-comrades, and their mother was the only resident embittered and despairing enough to say unequivocally that she constantly wished to be dead. Two children from another family were said to have talked little since they had witnessed Contra brutalities. It is likely that a systematic study would have detected some of the disturbances of emotional expression and behaviour found in children elsewhere in the war-torn areas of Nicaragua. Such disturbances may have long-term effects upon personality development.

DISCUSSION

We sought to show what might be called the 'silent face' of this kind of war, where rural peasants are the targets for systematic terrorization. The campesinos of Nicaragua, like those throughout the Third World, have not been accustomed to speaking of their feelings in the way we sought. The traditional toughness of life has not allowed them this 'luxury'; what was critical was to endure. Nonetheless those we interviewed responded, and for most this was the first time they had related the full story of the atrocities they had witnessed and survived. Their mental turmoil was testimony to the states of apprehension, fear and grief which terrorizers aim to create and sustain. To extrapolate from this sample to the rest of the rural population, in particular the 350,000 refugees, is to raise a spectre of psychological disturbance and distress on an enormous scale. 'Low intensity' warfare does not have low intensity effects.

There are pitfalls attached to the use of Western categories of mental disorder for organizing our comprehension of what those in non-Western cultures experience. Even concepts like 'stress' and 'coping' are culture and indeed class-bound. It is simplistic to assume that people respond to extreme events just by producing psychopathology. What, in any culture, is the 'normal' response to being tortured or witnessing the shooting of one's child? Moreover victimhood is seldom a purely passive state; even the most traumatized and destitute continue to have some active influence over what happens to them.

Psychological problems are not necessarily phenomena rooted in the individual and adjudged to be ''present'' or ''absent,'' but are socially mediated.[8] In the background are the culturally based sets of assumptions about what life inherently offers. These will reflect the particular history of a people: responses to current threat or tragedy are shaped by the impact of past events of this kind. As is true throughout Central America, most Nicaraguans see oppression as central to their history. All this will bear on the question of the 'meaning' that can be attached to events in the 1980s. And, in the more immediate situation, what is expressed will also reflect the kind of help perceived to be available, and even the way surveys of this kind pose their questions.

Despite such complexities, the similarities in adjustment problems and psychiatric symptoms between, for example, Southeast Asian refugees, World War Two refugees, and concentration camp survivors, does suggest that there are common denominators in human responses to war and terror.[9]

Posttraumatic Stress Disorder (PTSD) is an increasingly evoked formulation for the psychological responses over time, frequently years, following exposure to extreme and unusual traumatic events.[10] The major categories of PTSD are the re-experiencing of the traumas, numbing, and avoidance of stimuli and symptoms of increased arousal. There is some overlap with the features of major depression. We considered that 25 per cent of men and 50 per cent of women at La Urbina could merit a diagnosis of PTSD. Other studies have reported results of this order in war refugees and noted that women who had lost a child or spouse, or who had been raped, were particularly vulnerable.[11]

In relation to the higher symptom levels found in women compared to men, we wondered whether this partly related to their differing roles. With so many men away in the army, women were relatively alone with their children in vulnerable communities in the war zone, and could feel sitting targets, awaiting news that so often turned out to be bad. But for all the danger and discomforts, perhaps army duty allowed the younger men to feel engaged and able to influence events. Through military action they could 'externalize' some of their emotional stresses. Older men showed the same level of disturbance as women.

Full recovery from extreme trauma means a journey from the state of being a victim to the state of being a survivor. Those who have truly survived have come to understand and to accept their losses in the course of a process of mental healing, which eventually leaves them free to move on in their lives. But full resolution is impeded if the provoking trauma is not a finite event, or series of events, completed and receding into the past, as PTSD envisages. While the war continued around and through their lives, the campesinos were stuck in a traumatizing context which meant a kind of emotional suspension about their losses thus far. People at La Urbina were far from being 'pure' victims, but only with the ending of the war can they begin to be survivors in the full sense. It is hard for a woman to properly mourn the violent death of a child while under continuous threat of Contra attacks that could lead to the death of her others. And the families of the 'disappeared', people abducted by the Contras (and there have been thousands), could not but find it hard to mourn someone who may not be dead. The corrosive consequences of this predicament have become evident in Argentina, where, after more than a decade, many families are still in 'frozen' mourning. Perhaps we need an extended formulation of PTSD that encompasses the concept of continuous traumatization as well as the features of somatization.

LONG-TERM EFFECTS

The mental and somatic symptoms we have discussed may be just the crudest manifestations of terrorization. We have no reliable way of measuring damage to the most intimate functions of the mind—to people's innate capacity to love, laugh or achieve—and how lasting such damage could be. "One is never the same, one never goes back to being the same," was how a haunted old woman at La Urbina conveyed the sense of unrestorable loss the war had brought her.

In the medium term there will be multiple influences with the power to help or hinder personal and collective recovery from such a war as Nicaragua's. Healing at the societal level will be more tortuous because the Contras were also Nicaraguan, albeit under foreign command. Arguably, a post-war government interested in egalitarian approaches to reconstruction and able to allow the fullest possible acknowledgement of what everyone has suffered, can facilitate this process.

But wholesale terror across a whole society does seem capable of throwing a long shadow forward, even over an unborn generation. For instance, the children of Jewish survivors of Nazi persecution in the Second World War have been shown to be psychologically vulnerable when stressed[12] and, when soldiers, to get more PTSD.[13]

This conflict which we studied was but one of an estimated 150 in the Third World since 1945: many were the legacy of colonialism, or sprang from tensions created by gross social and economic inequities in which the dominant institutions of the Western world too frequently have an investment.[14] Terrorization has become common, and at least 85 per cent of the casualties of these wars have been civilians, mainly rural peasants. There are currently at least 13 million war refugees in the Third World. Most of the medical and anthropological literature has focused on the tiny majority who have been allowed to migrate to Western countries, and must face formidable acculturation problems there.

Relatively little has been written about the longer term mental and social effects of war, for the overwhelming majority who remain in or near the traumatized areas of their countries after such wars officially end. Tracing these effects may be complex, but is surely important. Firstly, there is a human rights dimension: a more complete counting of the actual human costs over time. Secondly, there are health/development issues, embracing such questions as the extent to which psychological numbing and devitalization, albeit operating under the surface, may comprise the efforts of terrorized communities to reorganize socially and economically, or to respond maximally to development projects.

References

1. Garfield, R., Frieden R., Vermund S. Health-related outcomes of war in Nicaragua. *Am J Publ Hlth* 1987; 77: 615–8.
2. Garfield R., Williams G. *Health and Revolution. The Nicaraguan Experience.* Oxford: Oxfam, 1989: 63–80.
3. Timerman J. In Stover E., Nightingale E. Eds. *The Breaking of Bodies and Minds. Torture, Psychiatric Abuse and the Health Professions.* New York: W. H. Freeman, 1985: 53.
4. Waghelstein J. Post-Vietman counterinsurgency doctrine. *Military Review* 1985; 1:42.
5. Kornbluh P. *Nicaragua, the Price of Intervention: Reagan's War Against the Sandinistas.* Washington DC: Institute for Policy Studies, 1987.
6. Garfield R., Rodriguez P. Health and health services in Central America. *JAMA* 1985; 254: 936–942.
7. Goldberg D. *Manual of the General Health Questionnaire.* London: NFER-Nelson, 1978.
8. Schwartz L., Levett A. Political repression and children in South Africa: The social construction of damaging effects. *Soc Sci Med* 1989; 28: 741–50.
9. Kroll J., Habenicht M., Mackenzie T., Yang M., Chan S., Vang T., Nguyen T., Ly M., Phommasouvanh B., Nguyen H., Vang Y., Souvannasoth L., Cabugao R. Depression and posttraumatic stress disorder in southeast Asian refugees. *Am J Psychiatry* 1989; 146: 1592–7.
10. American Psychiatric Association. *Diagnostic and Statistical Manual of Mental Disorders* (3rd edn. revised). Washington DC: APA, 1987.
11. Mollica R., Wyshak G., Lavelle J. The psychological impact of war trauma and torture on southeast Asian refugees. *Am J Psychiatry* 1987; 144: 1567–72.
12. Danieli Y. Families of survivors of the Nazi Holocaust: some long and some short term effects. In Milgram N. ed. *Psychological Stress and Adjustment in Time of War and Peace.* Washington DC, Hemisphere Publishing Corp., 1980.
13. Solomon Z., Kotler M., Mikulincer E. Combat-related posttraumatic stress disorder among second-generation Holocaust survivors: Preliminary findings. *Am J Psychiatry* 1988; 145: 865–8.
14. Zwi A., Ugalde A. Towards an epidemiology of political violence in the Third World. *Soc Sci Med* 1989; 28: 633–42.

CHAPTER 10
Peace, by Way of Truth and Justice

PETER DAVIES

This chapter is about a British soldier who spent many years of his life "keeping the peace" and "defending the free world." Two rather awesome jobs. The places where he was "keeping the peace" were coloured imperial red on the large oilcloth wall maps that used to hang in English classrooms. The biggest blob of red fifty and more years ago was, of course, Canada! The "free world" the British soldier was required to defend were nations which either supported or were controlled by the two or three white, western powers that had decided how the world was to be run.

This account is also about a Canadian civilian who, rather late in life, for he is a slow learner, came to believe that peace is neither the absence of war nor the presence of public order. Now, he's not so sure about that belief; he has met people whose most passionate desire is for war to end, order to be restored. Now, peace seems to him more like a goal towards which society flounders.

The British soldier and the Canadian civilian ·are one and—no, not quite the same; Canada can help even a British soldier change—just a little, mind you. And the world beyond "the true north strong and free" can force even a Canadian civilian to continue to search—however haltingly.

"The unexamined life is not worth living," Socrates declared at his trial. Most of his contemporaries, he maintained, pursued goals such as fame, wealth and pleasure without ever asking themselves if these objectives were worth a lifetime of striving. (America's Founding Fathers included "the pursuit of happiness" as one of their nation's goals. Two hundred years later their nation is sinking into a quagmire of pollution and

177

Peter Davies

some of its citizens are asking themselves if the pursuit of happiness through material acquisitiveness is worth the brutal assaults inflicted upon the physical environment and moral fibre of "America the beautiful.")

More than two thousand years after the death of Socrates most of us are like most of his contemporaries. Like them, we do not question our view of the world. Like them, we make no effort to discover the basis upon which our view is built. Like people of every age, most of us make little effort to search for truth. (Rabbi Rubin Slonim, a distinguished Canadian, has written—and I quote from memory—"To a conservative, truth is already in his possession and he guards it jealously. To a liberal, truth is just beyond his grasp yet always he strains to reach it.")

There are people, however, who *do* examine life. Moreover, some of them, a valiant few, do so from a most laudable perspective—that of the common good. (Among the few, I expect, will be found most contributors to this book and many of its readers.) To a tycoon of so-called free enterprise such people are probably dismissed as do-gooders up to no

Born in England in 1927, Peter Davies spent his first three years in a grim, damp fortress in Scotland—Stirling Castle—followed by three years on the shores of a tropic isle—Sri Lanka—where his father is buried. Eight years in the firm grip of a Victorian grandmother were an ideal preparation for life as a boy apprentice in the British Army where cold showers and runs over the Yorkshire moors before 7 a.m. breakfast were, literally, the order of the day. (He thinks joggers need help.)

Davies is a slow learner. He was forty-one when he escaped both military life and the dreary prospect of civilian life in the class-ridden society of Britain. (His timing was poor. After six years in the tropical heat of Malaya, he and his family headed straight into northern Alberta's worst winter in fifty years.) Within a year the intellectual challenges of the Legion hall and tupperware parties of Lac La Biche palled and the Brit Family Davies moved west—to "Sodom on the Coast" as some Albertans seemed to regard Vancouver.

Davies is also a late starter. He was forty-two before his working life came to life. Over the next sixteen or seventeen years he was a United Church of Canada worker in Vancouver's downtown eastside (known to some as "skid road"), a city social planner (a bird of prey that feeds off the oppressions or misfortunes of the poor) in Vancouver and Toronto, a radio journalist of sorts on Third World development issues (From a Different Perspective) broadcasting on community stations, a food co-op truck driver, a credit union worker (Bread and Roses), and a food importer (Bridgehead Trading). Now he is the unofficial, unpaid assistant to his wife who works for the Middle East Council of Churches in Cyprus as the international liaison staff person for educational travel.

179

good. To others they are uncommonly good and admirable people. And some of us see them as prophets, the pathfinders of society. When society reaches a crossroads on its long march through history they direct us to the right path. "Here it is," they call out, "See the signpost? 'To Truth and Justice'. Yes, we can read the notice telling us to watch out for potholes and falling rock. So what? If we want to reach Peace we must go by way of Truth and Justice, and that's a rough path." They beckon us forward. A few follow.

But what about the rest of us? What signpost do we read? What path do we follow? It seems that we prefer the one to Prosperity and Success. Which is hardly surprising; our parents, our teachers, and the whole value system of our society urge us in that direction. But why do we not see the notice on *our* signpost that tells us: Another Development of Deception and Illusion Inc.? In today's society, few indeed are those prepared to pay attention to the wisdom of ancient Greek philosophers—"Socrates? Wasn't that the winner of the Kentucky Derby years ago?" So off we set for Prosperity and Success until it becomes too dangerous with all those crazy guys with double ulcers and hypertension hurtling past us. Then we begin to look for another signpost; the one that says 'To Peace and Quiet'.

For many of my generation and origin—born in the 1920s in class-conscious England—and for many Canadians too, I imagine, Peace and Quiet is an appealing destination. It will be comfortable—we hope. Life there will be predictable—we expect. There will be no more "keeping up with the Joneses" that we tried to do on the path to Prosperity and Success. Instead, we will "keep ourselves to ourselves" (very British, that!) And if on our way we should be asked, "How's life then?", we shall reply with that profound gratitude for small mercies so characteristic of British working-class people in their sixties, "Oh, I'm making the best of it, you know." End of an examination of Life!

From time to time and as a change from "making the best of it," some of us will reply in a way that reveals both our age and our history: "How's life then?" "Oh, I'm soldiering on, you know."

That is what I did for twenty-six years; from when I enlisted as a fourteen-year-old apprentice in the British Army's Royal Corps of Signals, until I came to Canada as a forty-one-year-old veteran, I soldiered on.

* * *

The English language has many terms to describe military action between nations: to prepare for war, to go to war, to make war, are but three from a long list. But when governments take military action against their own citizens or, more usually the case for western governments, against people over whom they rule and whose territory they occupy, they prefer to describe the activity as "keeping the peace."

"Keeping the peace" was what British soldiers once did in "remote corners of the Empire"—a phrase beloved of the nationalist and racist sections of the British press. It was what governments told the British public their sons and husbands were doing across the seas in Palestine and Cyprus, in Malaya and Kenya, and a dozen other foreign lands that were, indeed, far from Britain. (These days, British soldiers are "keeping the peace" nearer home—on a disputed piece of real estate in Ireland.)

My first experience of "keeping the peace" was in Palestine. The year was 1947. I was nineteen. For more than fifty years Zionists had fought—ruthlessly at times—to establish a Jewish state in the land of Palestine. Now, in the post-war years, victory was imminent. To many of the Jews in Palestine, including youngsters of nineteen who had been hardened in the concentration camps of Europe, there was but one military obstacle between them and their goal—the occupation of "their" land by an alien military power. Killing British soldiers—including two with whom I shared a tent and whose booby-trapped bodies were found hanging in an orange grove—was their patriotic mission.

As a boy soldier I had read about the struggles of the British working class and decided that I must be a socialist—in spite of the disapproval of my widowed working class working mother. In Palestine my duties brought me in daily contact with Jews who were working in the Telephone and Telegraph Department. Not only were they the first "educated" people with whom I had had any close connection (two had Ph.D.s), they were also socialists. From them I learned much about the struggle of a people for self-determination. (Only later did I discover how distorted and one-sided my lessons had been.) However, I also learned, though not from my socialist technician comrades, that in the fight for the state of Israel I too had a role—as an enemy target. (Learning how to be an inconspicuous target for people whose objectives I supported at the time—even to the extent of passing military communications equipment to the Jews just before we pulled out—but whose methods of achieving them seemed likely to deny me a future, became an important part of my efforts at self-education. Today, would that part be called "Realpolitik 101?") That the Palestinian Arabs saw the Jews as occupiers and usurpers of "their" land simply added to the confusion of my education.

Slowly, I began to see that "keeping the peace" in an alien land has little to do with justice—for either Arab or Jew in the Palestine of 1945 to 1948—and a great deal to do with the political and economic interests of the occupying power. That the occupying power in Palestine was governed by a socialist party only deepened my confusion.

During my years of "keeping the peace," politicians were forever telling us ("the lads" in 1947–48, when Labour was in power; "the troops" eight years later when the Tories ruled) that we were "doing a splendid job." We told one another in basic Anglo-Saxon what we thought the politicians were doing and soldiered on.

In 1956 I was "keeping the peace" in Cyprus. The situation was rather similar to the one in Palestine: Greek Cypriots in an armed struggle against their British rulers. Their objective, however, was different. Greek Cypriots wanted Enosis, union with Greece, not an independent state of Cyprus. (Later, Turkish Cypriots would demand Taksim, separation of the two communities.) We soldiers were targets once again. I supported the people who were resisting being ruled by my country and once more I tried to be an inconspicuous target—this time for the manufacturers of state-of-the-kitchen-table-art landmines who took delight in carrying out field trials on British Army vehicles on mountain roads. (EOKA guerrillas had wild ideas about population control of the British in Cyprus thirty-five years ago. Today, I occasionally come across an old EOKA fighter. Retired from our former occupations, we'll sit in a coffee shop and swap yarns about the "old times." Enosis never did happen. Taksim is today's reality.)

As a change from "keeping the peace" far from home, British soldiers would be posted to the British Army of the Rhine where, with their Canadian comrades, they would chase across the northwest German plain every fall practising how to "defend the free world" against the Soviet hordes rolling westwards. With thousands of other NATO soldiers stationed in West Germany, year after year I took part in military exercises across a landscape that for a thousand years and more had soaked up the blood of young men fighting old men's wars. On cold nights we slept warm in German barns next to the horses and cows. We set up our headquarters in village inns. Our tanks tore up village streets and made them impassable before moving on to the farms and heathland. Gunners deployed their "Honest John" artillery and over our radio networks generals gave orders to fire, "notionally" of course, the nuclear missiles which were pointed towards East Germany. In East Germany meanwhile, year after year, soldiers of the Warsaw Pact countries were doing much the same—in reverse, so to speak; their nuclear artillery pointed at us.

It's hard to imagine a NATO general in the 1990s being anything but well-educated and technically literate. The same was true of British generals thirty years ago. Many of them had engineering and science degrees and could discuss matters technical on equal terms with scientists and engineers. Yet I cannot now recall ever hearing any senior officer, when chatting about the activities of the day over a beer in our village pub headquarters, ever question the devastation this nuclear mayhem would bring to a densely populated and industrialized region of Europe. Was it because, Hiroshima and Nagasaki notwithstanding, no general had ever *experienced* the havoc and carnage that battlefield nuclear weapons would create? As Socrates once asked, "Can we learn what we do not know?"

Soldiers tend to avoid analyzing the geopolitical causes and effects of their activities. Most of them, Canadian, I imagine, as well as British, leave to politicians, newspaper columnists and, when the dust has settled, historians, the job of finding out why their country went to war or why their country is "keeping the peace" far beyond their national borders. Such analysis, most soldiers would say, only leads them into swamps of confusion. What soldiers want above all, especially in the fog of war, are firm ground and simplicity.

*　*　*

When I came to Canada in 1968, I had been a civilian for all of three weeks. I came with no thought of analyzing the causes and effects of the events in which I had played an insignificant part in my quarter century of military service. I came with no intention of "facing the challenge of new thinking." I came to Canada to get away from a Britain littered with broken-down signposts most of which seemed to point back whence we had come—to some fantasy land called Hope and Glory. (Even socialist governments seemed unable to uproot them. In 1982, Mrs. Thatcher set them upright, gave them a fresh coat of paint, and dispatched an armada to fight a war on islands in the South Atlantic ocean that, until the bands began to play, a benighted public had barely heard of.)

Although I came with no thought of facing the challenge of new thinking, nevertheless, following a spell in the northern Alberta village of Lac La Biche learning to be Canadians, my family and I arrived in Vancouver on Canada Day 1969 and within weeks the challenge faced me. That it had to do with the Vietnam War was hardly a surprise. (In common with others in my line of work, I had a tradesman's interest in the war. With the benefit of years of experience in jungle warfare, the British Army generally, and the Brigade of Gurkhas—in which I was then serving in Malaysia—in particular, were convinced that the U.S. Army was doing a poor job! From a soldier's perspective it was the Vietcong that gained our professional respect.)

My political re-education about the war started at the Peace Arch on the Canada-U.S. border in the company of The United Church of Canada. And to this old Brit and new Canadian, that *was* a surprise. Here were people (members of an institution to which I now owe an unrepayable debt of gratitude) challenging me not just to do some new thinking (which in my own muddled way I had been working at for years) but to take new actions. And before long they had me stumbling along the path to Truth and Justice when I had been trying to find the one to Peace and Quiet. So much for an old soldier's map-reading skills.

* * *

During the past twelve years I have travelled in Africa, Asia, Latin America and the Caribbean. Now that I live in Cyprus, I travel in the Middle East as well. Because my journeys are not vacations, many of the people I meet live in towns and villages far from the centres of tourism. We meet as friends, often as colleagues engaged in some venture or other. I see them in their workplaces, I know their families and I stay in their homes. Few of them deal with the issues of justice and peace in the way most of my friends and associates in Canada do.

Friends in Canada seem to be forever on the point of rushing off late to or returning angry or depressed or both from a meeting, a workshop or a seminar. Their living rooms look as if they have just been raided by the RCMP. Leaflets and notices, books and assorted correspondence—all in such profusion as to delight Chief Executive Officers of pulp and paper companies and copying machine makers—are scattered in planned confusion. Peace, to my friends in Canada, is a precious child whose life is under threat by mindless power structures over which the architects and builders have lost control. Peace is what, in our way, we try to keep and defend.

Friends in non-western countries do not deal with the issues of justice and peace in the way friends in Canada do for some rather obvious reasons: they don't have the time (daily life is a daily struggle for many of the people whom I know in Africa and Asia); they don't have transportation and other communication facilities; they don't have the money. And they don't have the freedom and security that most of us do. But what they have is what most of us are spared: personal experiences of injustice and war. Theirs is not a matter of debating resolutions about how to achieve the ideal of justice; it is a matter of how to battle the reality of injustice. Theirs is not a war of words waged to protect the fragile flower of peace; it is violence in the combat zones.

A different approach to a common issue does not mean that the people I know beyond the western world are only trying to survive as individuals. Their courageous history of fighting for justice is enshrined in the initials of their movements—ANC, PLO, SWAPO, ZANU, FSLN.* And their different approach certainly does not mean voices are not raised in public protest about the issues. On more than one occasion I have heard church

---

* Editor's note: ANC = African National Congress; PLO = Palestine Liberation Organization; SWAPO = Southwest Africa People's Organization; ZANU = Zimbabwe African National Union; FSLN = Frente Sandinista de Liberacion Nacional.

and community leaders speak out passionately, fearlessly and at great personal risk as they demand justice and call for peace. (I have a memory of one open-air meeting in Guyana when sugar workers had gathered to commemorate the shooting in British colonial days of old comrades—the Enmore Martyrs. A Jesuit priest whom I accompanied to the meeting made a demand for justice for his oppressed and exploited fellow citizens of present-day Guyana directly to the senior officers of the large force of armed riot police surrounding the gathering.)

In Guyana, Fiji, Sri Lanka, Nicaragua, Palestine, Cyprus . . . the roll-call goes on. . . . Justice and Peace have been for many people I know the hidden faces of two coins whose visible faces are marked Injustice and War.

"There can be no peace without justice." Philosophers discuss the exhortation, moralists argue it, radical action groups shout it, politicians declaim it. The words are preached from pulpits and used as foundation stones in keynote speeches. We are in danger of losing their impact upon our consciousness. We quote them to one another at meetings and we hurl them at each other over beer and pizza in local pubs after the meetings. They help to strengthen our resolve to continue the struggle and at times they bring us back to the essentials of the struggle when one of us becomes "intoxicated with the exuberance of his own verbosity." They are, indeed, powerful words. But are we sure the significance the words have for many of us in western liberal democracies is shared by people elsewhere?

After some years of living among people of different races, cultures, religions, economic and political systems, and historical experiences, I have come to realize that humanity does not form a homogeneous society with identical ethical and moral values. This is not a realization that is easy to accept. It contradicts much of what I have been taught about unity: "Workers of the world unite!"; ". . . keep the unity of the Spirit in the bond of peace;" ". . . the global village." Yet, as rural people know, strife in a village can be vicious. And, as immigrants know, old animosities can be transferred with even greater intensity to new lands. We are still far from a global ethical and moral unity.

From Lebanon and Sri Lanka, Afghanistan and Haiti, from Central America and many another war-ravaged country around the world, scores of thousands have found refuge in Canada and have given thanks for being here. To them, Canada is a land of peace where people live in peace. Canada is where they expect to find, if not for themselves, at least for their children, the signpost that points to Prosperity and Success. Yet Canada is also a country where people from the war zones, together with immigrants from the Caribbean and Africa and the native people of this land, are denied justice almost daily. They are denied it because of their colour, their religious beliefs, their customs and traditions, even the way they speak our national languages. Do these Canadians think that "There can be no peace without justice?"

In the Middle East today, justice is a body violently dismembered. With unconcealed contempt it has been torn apart with cruelty and rapacity. It lies bleeding among the barren rocks, the forested hills and the awesome deserts of the eastern Mediterranean. Cyprus is divided. Lebanon is divided. Palestine is divided. The wounds of these divided countries are visible in refugee camps and abandoned towns and villages. They can be seen in the blackened shells of burned-down schools, in bombed-out hospitals, and along mined and barbed-wired frontiers patrolled by occupying armies and the soldiers of UN "peacekeeping" forces.

Cyprus, a member of the Council of Europe, is now Europe's only divided nation. Upon first meeting a Greek Cypriot here in the island, I very often ask where she or he comes from simply to find out whether or not the person is a refugee. During and after the invasion of Cyprus by the Turkish army in July 1974, over 200,000 Greek Cypriots, 40 per cent of the Greek Cypriot population, either fled or were forced to leave their homes in the Turkish-occupied area. Now they are refugees in their own land. More than one third of The Republic of Cyprus is ruled by a puppet regime—the so-called "Turkish Republic of Northern Cyprus"—that has all the legitimacy and international recognition of a South African homeland. Turkey, a NATO ally of Canada's, has 30,000 soldiers in the illegally occupied area and has settled many thousands of peasants from the Turkish mainland on Greek Cypriot-owned land. Now, the soldiers and Anatolian peasants outnumber the Turkish Cypriots. The so-called "government" prohibits movement across the cease-fire line, the "Green Line," that separates the Greek and Turkish Cypriot communities. For twenty-six years (there had been inter-communal strife for ten years before the 1974 Turkish invasion), soldiers of the United Nations' Force, including a large Canadian contingent, have patrolled the line. The fathers of some of the Canadians now serving here were themselves on "Green Line" duty twenty years ago.

In the free part of Cyprus, people enjoy unprecedented prosperity, much of it a result of tourism. More than one million tourists come to Cyprus every year—almost triple the population of the country. (Each year some west Europeans and many Turks go to the occupied area where practically every hotel and restaurant belongs to a forcibly exiled Greek Cypriot.) There are no hostilities here in Cyprus; there is peace of a kind. But it is a nation deprived of justice.

Lebanon has been a country at war with itself and with invaders for seventeen years. At present there is a lull in the battles among the complex and confusing groupings that make up society in that small nation. Among people in Cyprus with whom I am in close contact are many Lebanese Christians who support Michel Aoun, the leader of one of the two warring Christian factions in and around Beirut. These friends have not given up on their country. Their work requires them to be here temporarily. They travel back and forth as often as circumstances allow. They have families in Lebanon and responsibilities there. Yet when I ask, "Why do you support Aoun? Why should the Lebanese support any of the leaders of the various factions? They all seem to be tearing your country apart," they say, "Because Aoun is honest and fights for justice."

It is not possible for me to know if what they believe about Aoun is worthy of the man or not, but the sincerity of their words goes some way in explaining why fighting in the country has continued for so long. Perhaps they are among the valiant few Lebanese who, having examined their national life from the perspective of the common good, are now expressing in their actions what in Canada we put into our resolutions: "There can be no peace without justice."

More than fifty years ago Palestinian homes were being flattened as reprisals for alleged acts of terrorism against the British mandatory authority. The "law" the British used to justify their actions is today used by Israel which now occupies Palestine. "Demolition of family homes is a barbaric punishment," a professor at the Hebrew University said to Amos Elon of the *New Yorker*. And he went on, "Administrative detention without trial is just as bad. You are taken out of your bed in the middle of the night. They throw a hood over your head and lead you away. Then they throw you into an overcrowded cell for practically indefinite periods without being charged, without trial, without even being told what you are accused of." On visits to Palestine in the past two years, I have met with young men and boys who have experienced these very injustices. Some of them knew I had been a soldier in their country forty years before. They may even have known that the "laws" under which they were put into detention camps in the Negev desert far from their homes were the same "laws" that the British had enacted. I was grateful to them for not reminding me.

Hospitals in Canada, I suppose, produce regular summaries of admissions to their emergency rooms. Hospitals in the Gaza Strip do the same and the information contained in their summaries is, up to a point, much the same as that found in the Canadian ones. But at that critical point similarity ends. One hospital had recorded this information in its summaries of admissions for one month:

Gunshot wounds: live/plastic, 179; rubber, 78.
Beatings: 278.
Gas inhalations: 63.

Casualties under 15 years of age: 143 (5 brought in dead).

The Israeli Border Police and the Israeli Defence Force soldiers whose actions caused the casualties had no doubt been told that they were "keeping the peace."

I was given a copy of that summary one Saturday afternoon when I visited the hospital. Shortly before I left, a boy was brought to the emergency room by his friends. His hands were badly bruised from a beating. Outside, in the hospital garden, I spoke with a youth in a wheel chair. He is a paraplegic as a result of his wounds. To me he is a war casualty. Our brief meeting brought to mind visits I had made forty-three years ago to some of my mates in a British military hospital not many miles from Gaza. They too were war causalities. There is a difference, however, even though to a paraplegic Palestinian and to legless and blind British veterans it is cold comfort. My mates had been "keeping the peace." The young Palestinian in the Gaza Strip hospital had been fighting for justice.

Throughout history, injustice has been the fundamental affliction of humanity. I have now come to believe that in the fight against this foe, Peace is neither the goal nor the reward for victory. Only Justice can be that. In the Middle East today, injustice corrodes the foundations of national life and permeates the structures of society. Peace is but a mirage, an illusion, a distant object turned upside down that shimmers through "the dust of death" churned up by tanks moving into battle positions. The arms manufacturing states of the world that equip the armies of Middle East rulers, attempt to use the *hope* of Peace as a tool to control events in the region. When the tool fails them (which is when their client states fail to do their bidding), the presidents and prime ministers give the order: "Let loose the dogs of war!"

Justice will continue to be defined imperfectly with barely concealed self-interests and self-delusions. Like truth, it will always be just beyond our grasp. Yet we *must* strain to reach it. In the name of peace, of Shalom, of Salaam Aleikum, justice must not be sacrificed.

CHAPTER 11

Letter to Tessa, Born Canadian, September 1990

MS. MEREDITH WADMAN

Dear Tessa,

I have known your mother since she and I were five years old, a stretch of time that becomes important when you reach the age of thirty, as we are both doing within months of your arrival. Thirty is a frightening condition; one is supposed to be wise enough to know better and young enough to be whole. But as I look at you, Tessa, with your black hair thick and damp across your head and your wondering blue eyes, so much like your mother's, I know that wisdom is not a product of time, but of courage and pain, and that wholeness is, humanly speaking, and whatever they may tell you, unachievable. This is what, I am sure, David meant by his guilty and remorseful outburst so long ago—*in sin did my mother conceive me*—and this is what you must accept, not as your sentence but as your blessing.

Nonetheless, you, now one month old, will spend much of your life fighting to regain the state of beatitude that you now enjoy and that time and pain and experience will attempt to take from you. These are formidable forces, but they can only defeat you with your consent. If you will embrace them, and learn what they have to teach you, you will make of yourself a miraculous creation. This, I believe, is what it means to be born again. It is also the only journey that can save you from sleepwalking or despair.

But I am supposed to be writing to you on the subject of peace—dismal topic to be considering at this particular juncture. You will no doubt read in your history books, fifteen years hence, if we are all still here, of the autumn that the world—your world, which is why the following is unfor-

Meredith Wadman was born and raised in Vancouver, attended Stanford University in the United States, and began medical school at the University of British Columbia. She completed her medical studies as a Rhodes Scholar at Oxford University in England. She also studied in France, and later travelled widely in Africa and Asia. As a medical student, she worked in rural and urban health centres in Ghana, South Africa and Sarawak. She now makes her home in Vancouver, where she has been active in the church-based peace movement.

givable—sat poised on the brink of yet another appalling and useless round of madness and destruction. The books will explain that the war was about Arab nationalism, and about oil, which is to say, Western fear. But they will not tell you what it did to people, will not relate, for instance, the eyewitness reports out of Iraq this week: the father who watched his wife and small daughter raped before his captors blew his head off; the men made to lie face down in asphalt in the ruthless heat of the Arabian noonday. Nor will they paint the agony of the countless women, western and Arab, whose tears will inevitably, and forever, soak the fields of destruction. And you should know, incidentally, that women in wartime pay a price far worse than death.

Your books will not record those details because it is imperative for the warmakers that you not see, ever, the unbelievably brutal human facts of war; that you and your generation, like those before you, learn to think in terms of heroes and flags and oil, and not of life. Life is anathema to the warmakers, whose business is death; because of this you, Tessa, the groaning thighs and messy agony of love from which you issued, are the greatest, and finally, the only threat that exists to them. They know this, in their guts, and, knowing it, are afraid of you. They will therefore go to many and subtle lengths to prevent the world from considering your existence.

But you exist, nonetheless, and that is already a great victory for the forces of life. For there have been many moments, in the thirty years that your mother and I have been around, when your future—any future—looked very dark indeed. It may not be less so now—the track record of your race does not give one very great cause for hope in this regard—and yet your every breath is a pledge and a struggle against that unthinkable day for which your elders, if it arrives, will not be forgiven.

It is a strange concept to bend one's mind around: the end of all life, forever. As hard to conceive of as it would have been for you, one month ago, to imagine the other side of the dark, cursing and inevitable tunnel that beckoned you. But whereas your journey opened onto life in all its ragged glory, the promise of that other ending—whether bang or whimper—is always and forever the cold and black and infinitely impersonal void.

You might think that your elders, faced with such a terrifying possibility, would have long ago developed ways to stop their race from destroying itself. But it is a fact of human life that courage, love and rationality rarely prevail over greed, fear and the lust for power, with the result that, at the time of your appearance, three-quarters of humanity is hungry at least some of the time and weapons exist that can destroy the planet and everything on it several times over. (They are presently signing treaties that will eliminate some of these; they neglect to mention that those remaining are being developed into devices so sophisticated and deadly that the ones on the scrap heap will scarcely be missed.)

Nonetheless, there has been much made of the end of the Cold War—a development which, for the three-quarters mentioned above, is at best of passing interest. (It is difficult, after all, to be interested in much of anything when you are dizzy with hunger and your children are sick and dying.) And, although the crumbling of the Soviet empire is already engendering great change in the white-skinned lands, it is clear, and the three-quarters know this, that this change has little if anything to do with them. (An exception may be made in the area of foreign aid, which quantity the three-quarters now see retreating to a decidedly distant shore. Whether such aid actually does harm or good is another question altogether, about which the people of the countries involved would best be consulted.) At any rate, their babies are as hungry as they were while the Wall still stood; their shacks are as dilapidated; their sons and daughters as bitter and defeated. And this is why, although the one-quarter does not believe it, or cannot see it, the millennium is not now upon us because a few grey-haired men are shaking hands.

We are already seeing evidence of this in the Gulf, where a dictator currently holds the power he does because Arab nations are festering with the wounds of three hundred years of humiliation. Incidentally, what the western media will paint for you as Arab fanaticism is the inevitable byproduct of Arab humiliation. Humiliated people will rally to any flag, bow before any god and embrace any martyrdom if by doing so they can wrest back some measure of their self-esteem. (They intuit, rightly, that without this their days, spiritually speaking at least, are extremely numbered.)

In this sense, the eager followers of Saddam Hussein are not the least bit different from your elders, whose rationality and magnanimity are, on the whole, exactly as long as their circumstances are kind. Push them a little—integrate a neighbourhood, blockade a commuter bridge—and you will soon see that they are capable of throwing stones with the best of them.

I suspect it was a nasty shock to many of your countrymen to discover, during the days of this long, chaotic and difficult summer, the seeds of hatred sprouting so close about the hearth. The scenes we saw at Oka we had not been accustomed to call Canadian—not, at any rate, in the Canada we inhabit. (And you will hear it said, Tessa, often: The Holocaust could not happen here!—a notion so amply refuted by Canadian history that it is astonishing that anyone at all is able to maintain it. For if nothing else, the history of your country demonstrates that genocide requires neither gas chambers nor ovens—centuries of poverty, degradation and abuse at the hands of a conquering majority will do.) The fact is—and which is a mortal blow to the seemingly indestructible myth of western moral superiority—not only is this the Canada we inhabit, it is the Canada that inhabits us. This recognition—so threatening and so foreign to us who have been schooled in the goodness of our intentions—strikes at the heart of the desperate and fatuous thinking which is endemic, I am afraid, not only in your country, but in the entire western world, and which is grounded in a delusion that runs something like this: "We are a fine, upstanding people. We may be guilty of a few trifling sins, but we have never, really, done anything wrong." Like any delusion, this one serves to protect its adherents from a reality which, in the dark recesses of their minds, they suspect would be too difficult to bear. The reality is themselves, in front of the mirror, stripped of the mask of delusion—a prospect at once so painful in its truth and so frightening in its implications that most people will go to nearly any length to avoid it. (And for the purpose of avoidance, work or profit, sex or television and always, especially, insatiable acquisition, serve equally as well as the driest of martinis.) Furthermore, it is not exaggerating to say that the all but unmitigated chaos that your forebears have propagated in the lives of the three-quarters these many centuries is a necessary consequence of their refusal to face this reality. What I can't abide in myself I will soon find reason to locate in another; God only knows how many tortures have been refined, how many peoples been cut down, as the ineluctable result of the working of this particular spiritual law.

The real tragedy of all of this, Tessa—and I think it is, still, possible to conceive of tragedy beyond the continuing, unbelievable and certainly unquantifiable misery of hundreds of millions of human beings—is that unless and until your elders face reality, which is to say themselves, they will be neither alive nor free, although they will attempt to persuade you and themselves otherwise with an enterprise and an ostentation that is perhaps only possible in a society as wealthy and desperate as yours. For living, as opposed to sleepwalking, requires, above all, the honest and consistent confrontation of oneself—all of oneself—and freedom, in spite of what the advertisers will tell you, all day long, every day, for as long as you live, does not proceed from the power to purchase (a bomb, a body, a city, the world), but from looking at and loving what you find in the mirror. And by "love" here I do not mean the soulless and deadening narcissism in which you will also be well-instructed by the advertisers, nor the dangerous and sentimental romanticism that is the province of Hollywood and (not accidentally) women's magazines. I mean, rather, that impossible and essential tenderness which acknowledges and forbears with the unspeakable and the intolerable in you, and that carries this burdensome weight the length of the journey.

The journey is long, Tessa, but we have not stopped walking yet. Only fear—which is the real enemy—can inhibit your progress, and drive you to despair. But you are strong—you have your mother in you—and you have the thousands who have gone before, who often looked despair in the eye, and laughed; who watch and wait for you to carry on.

God bless you, now and always,
Your friend, Meredith

CHAPTER 12

Peacemaking: A New and Powerful Role for Cities

COUNCILLOR LIBBY DAVIES

Each April in Vancouver, tens of thousands of citizens take to the streets, usually under threat of rain clouds, to participate in an extraordinary event: a walk for peace. Under the auspices of End the Arms Race—a broad coalition of more than 230 peace, church, labour, community and professional groups—the diversity of people, colours, religions, classes and political beliefs are woven together in an outpouring of humanity striving to secure a world of peace and disarmament.

It would seem only natural that the City of Vancouver would endorse and indeed co-sponsor such a prestigious and important event. And in reality the city of Vancouver does co-sponsor and even help defray some of the financial costs of the walk. But this has not always been the case.

In decades gone by, and even into the early 1980s, municipal governments were not even faintly expected to give credence to, let alone fully support, events such as peace walks that were international in scope. For the conventional thinking—not only in Vancouver but in most Canadian municipalities—was that City Councils concerned themselves solely with the day-to-day affairs of running a city. Streets, planning, sewers, and parks have everything to do with city government. But peace and the threat of nuclear war? This was something better left to national government and international forums!

Thankfully, that kind of narrow perspective has changed. Our cities have grown, not just physically, but in the way we view ourselves in relation to the world.

In Vancouver, as in other Canadian cities, the early 1980s produced a significant change for the peace movement. Disillusioned and fed up with far-removed, unsympathetic provincial and federal governments, peace

Councillor Libby Davies

activists turned to local governments as a possible expression for the pent-up energy and consciousness of growing numbers of Canadians who felt compelled, in the face of nuclear madness, to turn the world around.

Faced, on the one hand, with a debilitating sense of powerlessness to prevent a nuclear holocaust, and yet on the other hand faced with no choice but to struggle for individual, community and planetary survival, the peace movement broke all bounds and forced civic attention to the skies above and the missiles that could soon annihilate us. It was sheer terror that propelled many of us to finally act: terror for our children, terror about the politicians who so easily accepted and justified nuclear militarism as civilized policy-making.

It was in the cities that the momentum for change and an end to the arms race found its due process. Day by day, year by year, the peace movement found its strength in the urban environment. After all, it is cities that are targets for missiles: cities made up of workers, women, children and families, whether in Canada, the Soviet Union or the United States. As the fear and outrage grew, it produced a powerful movement of people dedicated to removing the threat of nuclear war.

There are so many slogans in the peace movement that aptly describe our feelings, but one of my favourites has always been: "If the people lead, eventually the leaders will follow." It describes well the change of events that led to the involvement of municipal governments in an arena until then uncharted. But lest I leave the impression that civic governments are an unwilling partner for peace, let me hasten to place the situation in its political and historical context.

Libby Davies has been a member of Vancouver City Council since 1982, and serves as a liaison to the Council's Special Committee on Peace. Born in England, she has lived in British Columbia since 1969, and has a long record of public activism for women's rights, better housing, an end to poverty, peace and international solidarity. She represents the Committee of Progressive Electors (COPE) in Vancouver City Council, and played a major part in Council's decision in 1983 to declare the City of Vancouver a nuclear weapons-free zone and in the ongoing work of the City to be active for peace. Her political activism stems from her family background of commitment to social change. (Her father, Peter Davies, currently a resident of Cyprus, is also a contributor to this book.) Libby and her husband, Councillor Bruce Eriksen, also a COPE member of Vancouver City Council, have both played an important part in the progressive movement in Vancouver. Councillor Davies recently won re-election to the Vancouver City Council for a three-year period and topped the polls. She also has just been given an important Peace Award by the Y.M.C.A.

There are elected representatives who deplore civic involvement in peace issues. They dismiss such involvement as spurious and political grandstanding. There are others who, worse still, blindly swallow the nuclear mind-set and would likely be grateful to be home base for a nuclear arsenal. Fortunately, a growing number of politicians fervently believe that the level of government closest to the people—civic government—has a significant role to play in matters that go beyond our municipal boundaries.

Starting in 1982 many municipalities across Canada conducted public referenda on general nuclear disarmament. In most cases the referendum process was initiated by local peace groups collecting signatures, lobbying city councils, etc. The ease with which many of these referenda passed was a signal from the general public that there was widespread alarm and massive concern about the nuclear arms race. These referenda sent a strong message to Ottawa—via a municipal vote—that disarmament was an immediate necessity for human and planetary survival.

In many instances local governments were sympathetic to the issue, but there were also political, and later legal challenges concerning the jurisdiction of municipalities to act on peace initiatives. Nevertheless, the stage was set and local and national peace organizations seized the opportunity to work in concert with local government for peace and disarmament.

CITY GOVERNMENT SUPPORT FOR PEACE IN VANCOUVER

In Vancouver in 1982, the burgeoning peace movement, combined with a slim majority of sympathetic left-leaning City Council members, produced the necessary ingredients to elevate peace activism in the city to new heights. Things progressed rapidly. A supportive City Council declared Vancouver (on April 19, 1983) to be a Nuclear Weapons Free Zone. In 1984 City Council co-sponsored the already-established annual Walk for Peace. A special Council Committee on Peace was established in 1985, made up of citizens and City Council representatives. The Committee, the first of its kind in Canada, was mandated to liaise and network with other Canadian municipalities, and to advise Vancouver City Council on peace matters.

In 1986, a highlight of Vancouver's Centennial Celebration was a peace festival and Symposium culminating in the adoption of the *Vancouver Proposals for Peace*. (See Appendix A.) (The proceedings of the Vancouver Centennial Peace and Disarmament Symposium have been published in book form, *End the Arms Race: Fund Human Needs*, Eds. T. L. Perry and J. G. Foulks, Gordon Soules Book Publishers Ltd., West Vancouver, B.C., 1986.)

City Council approved the distribution of two informative and educa-

April 1990 Walk for Peace coming over the Burrard Street bridge in Vancouver. Photo courtesy Pacific Tribune.

Walk for Peace closing rally, Vancouver, April 1990. Photo courtesy Pacific Tribune.

tional leaflets in 1984 and 1986 to every household in the city, on the dangers of nuclear war and what could be done to prevent it. A second referendum was held in 1984, where 57 per cent of the respondents supported the cancellation of cruise missile testing in Canada.

Vancouver City Council acted in numerous ways to foster greater cooperation with a rapidly developing peace movement, so that by the mid-1980's attendance at the annual Walk for Peace climbed over the 100,000 mark, and Vancouver became known as the Peace Capital of North America. Vancouver became a conduit for communication and assistance for other local governments across Canada. Public support for City Council's peace initiatives was very evident, and indeed, many residents saw the city's leadership as a ray of hope in what sometimes appeared to be a losing battle to prevent the nuclear time-clock from reaching midnight.

Municipal involvement in the peace movement has grown in leaps and bounds across the breadth of the country. In 1986 there were an estimated 80 nuclear weapons free zones (NWFZs) in Canada. That figure has now risen to over 200, including the major cities of Canada, the Provinces of Manitoba and Ontario, and the Northwest Territories and the Yukon. (See Appendix B.) Such phenomenal growth, and the many other peace initiatives of local governments are indications that the people of Canada understand very well the popular slogan "Think globally—act locally."

A poll conducted by Greenpeace in May 1990 clearly demonstrates public support. Close to 70 per cent of respondents in B.C. supported B.C. being declared a Nuclear Weapons Free Zone. Sixty per cent of B.C. lower mainland respondents favoured a ban on warships carrying nuclear weapons from entering Vancouver's harbour.

MUNICIPAL GOVERNMENTAL SUPPORT FOR PEACE IN EASTERN CANADA

The City Council of Montreal has taken the Canadian lead in securing an amendment to the City's Charter that allows it to implement an advanced strategy for securing a nuclear weapons free future. Under active consideration are policies that would require a company doing business with the City of Montreal, to declare that it does not produce or store nuclear weapons. The Montreal City Council could also refuse to do business with companies manufacturing, processing or conducting research on nuclear weapons, and that Council is also considering pension fund investment policies based on non-nuclear involvement.

The Cities of Toronto and Ottawa have also passed key resolutions giving effect to concerns of local residents. In June 1990 Ottawa City Council passed a motion urging the federal government to actively support efforts for a comprehensive nuclear weapons test ban treaty. Similar to an earlier motion passed by Vancouver City Council in September,

1989, the resolution stressed the significance of a test ban treaty being the single most important step to be undertaken to prevent nuclear war. Subsequently, similar resolutions calling on the Federal Government to support a comprehensive nuclear test ban have been passed by the city councils of Victoria, Calgary, Winnipeg, London, Toronto, Hamilton and Montreal. And in July, 1990 the City of Toronto passed a resolution expressing its opposition and concern about nuclear capable warships in its harbour. In view of the large number of Canadian cities opposing nuclear weapons testing, it is difficult to see how Ottawa can continue defying Canadian public opinion.

NUCLEAR WEAPONS FREE ZONES NETWORK

Nationally, efforts are underway to establish a network of Canadian NWFZs. Over the past five years a number of local councillors have kept in contact, and doggedly pursued the idea of trying to form a national municipal peace network. Taking advantage of the annual convention of the Federation of Canadian Municipalities (FCM), interested local councillors have managed to meet once a year to discuss the concept and its implementation. In 1989, at the FCM convention held in Vancouver, a number of us agreed to proceed with establishing the NWFZ network. Councillor Jack Layton from Toronto, Councillor Michael Fainstat from Montreal, and I have become the core group to advance the concept. It has not been an easy task, due to lack of finances and difficulties of meeting to sort out logistical problems. However, knowing that there now are over 200 NWFZs in Canada, with interest growing all the time to form a network, we are determined to do as much as we can to make the network a reality. An interim national clearing house of municipal NWFZs has already been established under the volunteer efforts of the Nuclear Weapons Free B.C. Committee. This clearing house has already begun to fill a strategic need to collect data on new NWFZs in Canada, and to coordinate the exchange of information between municipalities. Though the task is difficult and financial resources scarce, the development of a national network signals a new and more sophisticated level of activity that propels municipalities to work together for common goals for the betterment of our cities. A similar concept has already taken root in the United States, as well as in Europe and Japan.

Internationally, there are also significant developments linking cities in a common struggle for peace. In 1989 I was fortunate to be able to attend the 4th International Conference of Nuclear Free Zone Local Authorities, held in Eugene, Oregon. Over 200 delegates from 70 cities representing 16 countries, attended. There are now over 4000 NWFZs in the world! What is particularly interesting is the fact that NWFZs have become much more than symbolic declarations. Many municipalities have developed policies on selective purchasing and peace conversion. For example, in some U.S. cities, selective or ethical purchasing policies require the municipality to purchase goods and services from companies not involved in armaments work. This concept is still relatively new in Canada, although some local governments (Vancouver included) have already established the principle of "ethical purchasing," by agreeing to boycott Shell Oil for its investment and business holdings in South Africa.

The whole notion of ethical purchasing has significant implications. Collectively, local governments expend billions of dollars on goods and services. Criteria of low bid and quality of product are well established, but what about ethics? I believe strongly that a municipality does have choices to make about with whom to do business. The cheapest price and of course the quality of product are very important, but so are the corporate practices of the company.

Vancouver's Special Council Committee on Peace has already received a report on ethical purchasing. However, translating this concept into an institutionalized civic decision-making process is not easy. There will, no doubt, be resistance on grounds that civic government is overstepping its bounds and interfering with private enterprise.

NEW WAYS OF THINKING IN MUNICIPAL GOVERNMENT
Striving for peace in our cities and between the cities of the world has produced a profound change in the way we define ourselves. Municipal peace-making and struggling to end the arms race have opened new avenues for cities to assert themselves and their place in the world. And rightly so. As we face our urban problems of inadequate housing, health care, education, shrinking federal assistance, over-burdened transportation and infrastructure systems, and growing poverty, even in affluent North America, we witness growing military expenditures that are literally robbing needed resources, public expenditure, and expertise from our human problems.

As more and more of us live in cities and the quality of life becomes harder to sustain, we are challenged to address questions and problems that previously were not considered part of the civic agenda. Citizens are desperately concerned about air and water quality and creeping pollution. We have to make choices about our future growth, including transportation, health care, housing, lack of agricultural land, and so on. Thus comes a growing consciousness that the cities of the world are not isolated entities but, on the contrary, are interdependent with the state and health of our global political, economic and environmental systems. There is also a growing realization that senior governments are just not dealing with their responsibilities in a way that corresponds to local needs.

There is every reason and great urgency for our cities to become *more* active in peace-making, the environment, and the social health of the community. Unquestionably, progressive urban thinkers are realizing that it will be cities that have the flexibility, ingenuity and boldness to take on many of the enormous challenges facing us in the decades ahead. I think that cities are on the threshold of a new and powerful role in the world. As it becomes more evident that national governments have failed miserably to deal with serious national and international problems, it will be our cities that people turn to for help, involvement, and leadership. It is in our urban environment that we can begin to make concrete changes for a safer, healthier world. I don't want to minimize the very important and necessary responsibilities that national governments have. But as problems seem to grow and the federal response correspondingly becomes more illusory, municipalities have the opportunity, and challenge, to deal with the real problems and issues we face. This movement of cities is not, of course, confined to Canada, but is reflected in increasing dialogue, activism, and co-operation of cities around the world.

It must be emphasized that municipal involvement in peace and disarmament is not based on a transitory whim, nor a passing fad. It is a profound issue that has pioneered the way for local governments to involve themselves and provide leadership on issues that concern us as human beings in our living environment.

There is no question in my mind that the public has a growing expectation that local government should deal with issues in a holistic and integrated way. So, where does the municipal boundary lie? Most likely in the sky above us and the deep earth below and everywhere in between! Constitutionally speaking, senior governments have imposed severe jurisdictional limits on local government. But as the pressure and indeed support from citizens grows, so will the initiative of local government have to advance to meet the challenges of not only pursuing a peaceful and just world, but facing a diversity of human issues in our urban environment.

However, this expanding role of municipalities is dependent to a large degree on the political philosophy, program, and commitment of a local council to embrace a broader agenda. I was motivated to run for a civic office, largely because of my activism in my local neighborhood, and my frustration with our City Council's lack of concern and action on very pressing and serious issues in the community. Ensuring the well-being and quality of life in our local communities is still a prime motivation for me and my political associates. But over the years I have experienced an evolution of consciousness that has established stronger and stronger bonds between the issues that arise from the "backyard," to those of a more global nature. These issues *are* connected. The livability of our streets, homes, and cities is part of an international order concerning the wealth and resources of the world and how they are used and by whom.

Obviously, not all locally elected representatives share this kind of broad vision. While one would be hard-pressed to find politicians who will say publicly they are not in favour of peace, it becomes quite another matter when assessing a Council's commitment to go beyond pious platitudes in favour of substantial policy development that firmly establishes a municipal stake in broader questions.

One of the challenges of the peace movement in Canada in the 1990s will be to sustain and expand the pioneering peace work done by municipalities across the country. The peace movement must ensure that we are not left with a few token peace resolutions here and there as a legacy of our fear about nuclear war in the early 1980s. If we want to elect local politicians who are part of a global movement that recognizes the connections between peace, a healthy environment, poverty, use of resources, human rights, and our cities, and are firmly committed to municipal programs that reflect these connections, then the peace movement must politicize itself to bring this about.

There are many ordinary voters who, with genuine concerns about the future of the planet, don't know the power they have and could use at the municipal level. Ironically the level of government that is closest to its voters has, generally, the lowest voter turn-out during elections. The peace movement, along with the other people's movements, can be instrumental in empowering ordinary people to realize the strength they have to make civic government and our cities advocates for positive change that can literally change the world.

NUCLEAR ARMED WARSHIPS UNWELCOME IN VANCOUVER'S HARBOUR

This chapter would not be complete if I did not give special mention to one extraordinary struggle still in progress: nuclear armed warships on our seas. For the past decade Vancouver has been in the forefront of a campaign to rid our seas of nuclear arsenals. The campaign poses some interesting twists because it directly involves federal jurisdiction over Canadian ports. Greenpeace, Save Our Seas, and other groups have worked vigorously to educate the public on the danger these floating nuclear arsenals pose. Vancouver's 1983 NWFZ declaration did not include the port or waters of Vancouver, which are under Federal jurisdiction.

As visits to the Port of Vancouver of American naval vessels carrying nuclear weapons have increased, so has the indignation of Vancouverites. Numerous delegations to Vancouver City Council eventually pressured a

Zodiaks manned by Greenpeace activists protest visit of U.S. Aircraft Carrier Independence, carrying a large number of nuclear weapons, to Vancouver harbour in August 1989. Councillor Libby Davies was one of a group of long-distance swimmers who protested by swimming completely around the anchored warship. Photo courtesy Pacific Tribune.

majority of Council to support a recommendation in 1989 from the Peace Committee to urge the federal government to declare the Port a NWFZ. This initiative was not without controversy. (An earlier resolution in 1988 had failed before City Council, but the peace community—undaunted and determined to convince City Council of the public's feelings—brought the matter back.)

The issue resurfaced in a different way in April 1990, when the City Council Peace Committee resolved to urge City Council not to provide funding to any organization which invites nuclear-armed vessels to the Port of Vancouver. This motion was defeated by City Council. The Sea Festival Society, partially funded by the City of Vancouver under its cultural grants, has consistently invited nuclear capable warships to participate in the Sea Festival, oblivious to the strong opposition of Vancouverites and City Council. That a majority of City Council would not follow through on its earlier 1989 resolution urging a non-nuclear port, but was willing to fund an organization inviting visits from nuclear capable warships, points to the need for the peace movement to be ever vigilant in monitoring the actions of politicians who say one thing and do another. Nevertheless, despite some setbacks, and thus far no positive action from the Federal Government, the campaign to de-nuclearize our seas is gaining ground and, I have no doubt, will eventually win. The efforts of the peace movement have been tremendous. The sight of peace flotillas bravely confronting huge warships and the military and nuclear might they represent, has become an inspiring symbol of the power that ordinary people can attain to change society.

In August 1989, when the aircraft carrier USS Independence dropped anchor in Vancouver with approximately 100 nuclear weapons on board, I joined a group of swimmers to swim around the warship in protest. It was only a small action, which I knew wouldn't of itself stop these floating fortresses of death from being in Vancouver. But it gave me a sense of the vast human chain of events and actions that I was part of, that will inevitably be more powerful than nuclear warships.

Concluding remarks

What we do today *does* make a difference tomorrow. When I entered elected office ten years ago, there was a terrible fear about nuclear annihilation. It was the power of people, determined to face this fear head on, that produced such a powerful movement for peace to turn the world around. The world *is* a better place, as dialogue and understanding between the Soviet Union and the United States emerges to check the pace of nuclear escalation.

But as we know only too well, we cannot afford to rest on gains made. The military industrial complex is still intact and very resilient. There are still huge profits being made in the armaments business. The ability to create "new" enemies means the military infrastructure still has enormous power to influence world events and drive the economy. We still witness the horror of human suffering in war-torn areas of the world. We still face governments who too easily reach for military solutions to address human problems.

We have to make sure that active participation in the peace movement does not flag, due to optimism and confidence by the public that somehow we "won," and that the fear of nuclear war or nuclear accidents is gone. It hasn't. The institutions and economics for war still remain.

Our challenge in the 1990s may be different, but no less difficult than what faced us in the 1980s. In Canada our defence policy is still dragging itself through a 1950s mentality, as we face low level flight testing, cruise missile testing, and obedience to NATO.

We must now begin the task of converting our society from war readiness to sustaining peace. Jobs and industries that supported a militaristic society must be traded in for activities that use our resources in a way that protects our environment and enhances the health and quality of life for people. Such a transformation, it needs to be said, cannot confine itself to industrialized countries, but must include a recognition and redress of inequities between poor and rich countries. Such vast and complex problems nearly always seem just too much to deal with. It is overwhelming—for we do face so many obstacles to a peaceful and just society. But it's not impossible to deal with. The cities of the world have the ability (and every reason) to be part of the human struggle for social and economic change, and finally an end to the arms race. Our cities are a place to begin setting the agenda for peace and justice. Local governments that are bold, progressive, accessible and democratic, can and must reach to fulfil the aspirations of ordinary people for a better, safer world.

Appendix A. *The Vancouver Proposals for Peace*
These Vancouver Proposals were drawn up by the invited speakers at the 1986 Vancouver Peace and Disarmament symposium under the leadership of two Nobel Prize laureates who attended the Symposium, Sean MacBride of Ireland, winner of the 1974 Nobel Peace Prize, and Professor Dorothy Hodgkin of England, winner of the 1964 Nobel Prize for Chemistry. The Proposals were adopted by acclamation by participants at the Symposium on April 26, 1986, and are reprinted here from *End the Arms Race: Fund Human Needs*, Eds., T. L. Perry and J. G. Foulks, Gordon Soules Book Publishers Ltd., West Vancouver, 1986.

THE VANCOUVER PROPOSALS FOR PEACE

"End the Arms Race—Fund Human Needs"—this is the message of Vancouver's Walk for Peace in the year of its 100th anniversary.

It is natural that this city, which has declared itself to be a nuclear-weapons-free zone and which has, on many occasions, urged the cause of peace, should have chosen this occasion to sponser the Vancouver Centennial Peace and Disarmament Symposium.

The people of Vancouver and their elected representatives are only too conscious of the threat posed by the arms race to the survival of humanity and of the tremendous waste of resources which it causes. This waste of resources has serious consequences everywhere, and we cannot ignore the fact that in many parts of the developed world there is unemployment, hardship and poverty which, although less severe, is otherwise not unlike that in the Third World.

In the nuclear age, war is no longer a way of resolving conflicts between nations. In 1961, the United States and the USSR came to the conclusion that war could be eliminated only by general and complete disarmament and agreed on eight principles upon which all further negotiations should be based, and this was agreed by the United Nations General Assembly. Eight years ago, the United Nations General Assembly declared unanimously we must end the arms race and proceed to disarmament or face annihilation. Yet, despite this and other resolutions of the United Nations, we face the fact that no progress has been made towards nuclear or any other form of disarmament, despite the fact that most, if not all, of the thousands of nuclear explosive devices that have been piled up are militarily useless.

On the contrary, we are moving into a new phase of escalation and counter-escalation of the nuclear arms race and, if this process is not stopped and reversed, the inevitable outcome will be a further reduction in the security of the nuclear-weapons powers themselves and indeed of the whole world. We are rapidly approaching the point at which there will be equality of security only in the sense that there will be no security for anyone.

The catastrophe we face is not inevitable. There are immediate opportunities to check this suicidal process and gain time to reverse it:

1. A Comprehensive Test Ban Treaty, stopping all further testing of nuclear weapons. We urge the United States to respond to the Soviet initiative by immediately ceasing nuclear testing and urge the Soviet Union to extend its moratorium. We call upon other nuclear states to stop all nuclear weapons tests.

2. A ban on all weapons in space.

3. A freeze on development, testing or deployment of new nuclear weapons and their delivery systems.

4. Immediate and substantial reductions in the existing nuclear arsenals.

5. The establishment of nuclear weapons-free zones in Central Europe, the Nordic and Balkan regions, and the Indian and North Atlantic Oceans, and compliance by the nuclear-weapons states with the newly established South Pacific Nuclear-Free Zone Treaty.

6. Renunciation by all states, and in particular by the nuclear-weapons states, of the use or threat of force and intervention in the affairs of other states, and a commitment to negotiate an agreement to that effect.

7. Recognition that the arms race is having serious negative effects, both on the nations involved and on the whole world, and that it is now urgently necessary to reduce substantially all military budgets and transfer the resources thus saved to the promotion of human well-being.

These are steps that can and must be taken now. None of them need wait for long negotiations and formal treaties. The process must be started and independent intitiatives are therefore needed. The Report of the Secretary General of the United Nations on unilateral or independent nuclear disarmament measures, adopted in December 1984 by 126 votes to 1 by the United Nations General Assembly requires far more serious consideration and action.

We feel that the proposals made by General Secretary Gorbachev on 15th January, 1986 could lead to significant progress. We urge, therefore, that the existing disarmament forums consider these proposals and develop a mutually acceptable approach to the achievement of nuclear disarmament which can then be jointly agreed and implemented.

The measures we have proposed are essential first steps back from the edge of oblivion and toward a peaceful world. It is within the power of the people of each and every country to exercise their right to determine and preserve their own future, to intervene and compel a change of course. We particularly commend to the smaller nations the positive role they can play in bringing about this change.

Parallel with these changes, new creative initiatives are needed to address the problems of hunger, disease, education, environment and other global problems, and indeed to the establishment of a just international economic order.

From this peaceful city we appeal to our sisters and brothers everywhere:

Let us act together now to end the arms race and to fund human needs.

Appendix B. *List of Nuclear Free Zones (NFZs) in Canada*
(List is as of June, 1990. Additions can be obtained from, or reported to, Nuclear Weapons Free British Columbia Committee, Councillor Libby Davies, Vancouver City Hall, 453 W. 12th Avenue, Vancouver, BC, V5Y 1V4.)

Provinces and Territories which have officially declared themselves NWFZs are:

Manitoba	Northwest Territories
Ontario	Yukon

Municipalities which have declared themselves NWFZs:

Alberta:

Calgary	Edson
Cochrane	Elk Point
Didsbury	Lethbridge
Edmonton	Red Deer

British Columbia:

Alert Bay
Burnaby
Campbell River District
Castelgar
Central Coast District
Coquitlam
Courtneay
Cranbrook
Creston
Delta
Denman Island
District of Kitimat
Fernie
Fort St. James
Grand Forks
Hornby Island
Houston
Hundred Mile House
Kamloops
Kaslo
Kelowna
Kimberly
Ladysmith
Lake Cowichan
Lasqueti Island
Maple Ridge
Nanaimo
Naramata
Nelson
New Westminster
Nimpkish Valley
North Cowichan District
North Vancouver (City)

North Vancouver (District)
Nee—Chah—Nulth
    Tribal Council
Parksville
Penticton
Port Alberni
Port Coquitlam
Port Moody
Powell River
Prince River
Prince George
Queen Charlotte Islands
Richmond
Saanich
Saltspring Island
Sidney
Smithers
Sointula
Squamish
Squamish-Lillooet District
Summerland
Sunshine Coast District
Surrey
Terrace District
Tofino
Trail
Vancouver
Vernon
Victoria
West Vancouver
Whistler
White Rock
Williams Lake

Manitoba:

Winnipeg

New Brunswick:

Bathhurst	Nackawic
Beresford	Petit Rocher
Mathers Island	Pointe Verte

Newfoundland:

Corner Brook	St. John's
St. Anthony	Wabush—Labrador

Nova Scotia:

Bridgewater	Mahone Bay
Chester	Trenton
Lunenburg	Wolfville
Lunenburg Municipality	

Northwest Territories:

Yellowknife

Ontario:

Ancaster	Latchford
Barry's Bay	Loughborough Township
Bastard and South Burgess	McGarry Township
Bath	Morley Township
Bedford Township	Muskoka District
Borough of York	Newmarket
Black River Matheson	Niagara Falls
Brethour Township	Niagara On the Lake
Brockville	North Algona Township
Chamberlain Township	Orangeville
Charlton	Owen Sound
Dover Township	Parry Sound
Dymond Township	Port Stanley
Emo	Red Lake Township
Fort Frances	Sarnia
Geraldton	Sherwood/Jones/Burns
Goderich	Simcoe
Grattan Township	South Algona Township
Gravenhurst	South Crosby Township
Hagarty/Richards	St. Thomas
Hamilton	Sudbury

Harris Township
Hensall
Hudson
Ignace
Kapuskasing
Killaloe Lake
Kitchener
La Vallee

Thunder Bay
Timmins
Toronto
Vespera Township
Welland
Wellesley Township
Wilmot Township
Windsor

Quebec:

Ancienne Lorette
Ascot
Austin
Ayer's Cliff
Beaconsfield
Boucherville
Bristol
Bryson
Canton d'Eaton
Canton de Stanstead
Drummondville
Hull
Joliette
Jonquiere
La Haute-Cote Nord
La Pleine
Lachenaie
Lachute
Lennoxville

Les Basques MRC
Les Iles de la Madeleine
Leslie, Clapham et Huddersfield
Magog
Mascouche
Mont St. Gregoire
Montreal
North Hatley
Ogden
Plessisville
Rock Island
Rouyn-Noranda MRC
Sherbrooke
St. Alexandre
St. Valentin
St. Felicien
Ste. Catherine de Hatley
Waterville

Saskatchewan:

Melfort
Regina

Saskatoon

Yukon:

Faro

CHAPTER 13
Nuclear Power: A Difficult Question

PROFESSOR ALAN F. PHILLIPS, M.D.

"Electricity too cheap to meter" was the prediction in the days of "Atoms for Peace," when nuclear reactors had been proved to work, and a few dozen nuclear bombs were said to be sufficient for "deterrence." Thirty years later, nuclear-generated electricity has been found to be as expensive as that generated by fossil fuel, there are 50,000 nuclear bombs in the world that threaten complete extinction of civilization, and a few reactor disasters have harmed the health of thousands and frightened millions.

The people of the world must now decide whether to allow their governments to go on building nuclear reactors. The question is not a simple one. Many who are concerned for peace and the environment believe that nuclear generators should be phased out. Others, including some scientists active in the peace movement, maintain that the advantages outweigh the dangers. Others again remain undecided and might be in favour of nuclear power, but only if the possibility of using products from the reactors for manufacture of bombs could be ruled out.

In this chapter we shall look at the main issues involved, trying to start from an unbiased position. In my own field of radiation therapy, nuclear reactors gave us the great benefit of radioactive cobalt: many people with cancer have been cured by its radiation. In different fields of medicine, and in biological research, artificial radioactive isotopes are also important. However, there are now other sources of radiation for treating cancer and for making radio-isotopes. Reactor-produced isotopes are cheaper but, at a price, medicine could manage without them.

The science and engineering of nuclear reactors are complex, and most of those who are expert in the technology depend on it for their liveli-

Professor Alan F. Phillips, M.D.

hood, so it is difficult to get an unbiased account of the facts. The experts minimize the risks, while many who are not expert have understandable fear of radiation and express exaggerated concerns. The extraordinary history of secrecy, the concealment of risks and accidents, the attempts to manipulate public opinion by government agencies in every country that uses nuclear power, all add to the suspicion that there may have been an underlying military purpose. When the deceits are discovered, people rightly refuse to accept new official reassurances, either in a threatened emergency or regarding the ongoing use of nuclear generators. In this complicated situation, it is difficult to form a soundly based opinion as to whether we ought to generate more electricity by nuclear fission, or phase out nuclear reactors entirely.

CONNECTION WITH MANUFACTURE OF NUCLEAR BOMBS
The artificially produced element plutonium, and the naturally occurring element uranium, are the two elements used for nuclear fission both in nuclear power reactors and in nuclear bombs, whether of the "fission" or the "fusion" type.

Plutonium is made in a nuclear reactor. It is formed by the action of neutrons on the uranium fuel of the reactor. Most plutonium for bombs is

Alan Phillips was an honours student in Physics in the famous Rutherford Laboratory at the University of Cambridge, England, when World War II began. His class was probably among the first thousand people to learn of the theoretical possibility of the nuclear bomb. He and his fellow students quickly calculated that the explosive energy available could be a million times that of a high explosive bomb. This compares with the jump from 50 kilograms of molten lead (dropped from the battlements) to 50 kilograms of high explosive, which is only a jump of a thousand times in terms of energy.

Some of Alan's friends were drafted to work at Chalk River, Ontario, on the atomic bomb project. He was drafted to radar research. After the war he switched to medicine, graduating M.B.,Ch.B. at the University of Edinburgh, and then M.D. with a gold medal for his research thesis on medical applications of radiodioactive isotopes. He specialized in radiotherapy, and spent his working life in the clinical practice of radiotherapy in England, U.S.A., and Canada.

At the start of the Reagan era, Dr. Phillips became acutely concerned about the risk of nuclear war and its terrible consequences. Since retirement in 1984 he has spent all his energies working for peace. He is a Board member of Canadian Physicians for the Prevention of Nuclear War (CPPNW), and PeaceFund Canada, and a member of Veterans Against Nuclear Arms (VANA) and Project Ploughshares.

made in special military reactors designed for that purpose. In the U.S.A. and the United Kingdom, there are laws against using plutonium from civilian reactors for nuclear bombs. In Canada, there are regulations to prevent the export of radioactive materials for use in their manufacture, but once material is out of the country it is impossible to exert effective control. It is widely believed that governments do not feel themselves bound by such rules if they can ignore them without public outcry. It is now admitted that British plutonium made in civilian reactors was used for American bombs in the early days of nuclear power, though it was repeatedly denied in Parliament.

Uranium is a natural element, obtained from a mineral ore. In nature, it is a mixture of the isotopes U-238 (99.3 per cent) and U-235 (0.7 per cent). Some types of nuclear reactors, and all uranium fission bombs, require "enriched uranium," which has had the proportion of U-235 artificially increased. A much larger degree of enrichment is needed for bomb manufacture (93 per cent) than for nuclear reactors (3 to 6 per cent).[1] Enrichment is done at present by an elaborate process in large plants that cannot easily be concealed from satellite monitoring. A more compact, but still elaborate and expensive laser method of separation, has recently been developed, and is in use in the U.S.A.[2]

(a) "Vertical Proliferation"

The question here is whether continuing or increasing the use of nuclear power adds to the ability of the superpowers, and other "nuclear weapons states," to manufacture even more nuclear bombs than they have already. It is said that there is now a surplus of plutonium in the countries concerned.[3] If that is true, they have no need for it from civilian sources. One must bear in mind, however, that the Pentagon, and no doubt the military establishments of other countries, have departments devoted to "disinformation" (or lies), so information about military stocks is always uncertain.

There is a very direct connection between nuclear power and nuclear bombs in the incidental production of *tritium* by CANDU reactors. ("CANDU" is an Atomic Energy of Canada, Ltd., trade name for its major electricity-generating reactor, which uses deuterium oxide, heavy water, as coolant and moderator.) Tritium is a radioactive isotope of hydrogen (H-3), that is formed as an unwanted by-product in all reactors that use "heavy water." U.S. commercial reactors do not use heavy water.[4 (p.95)] Tritium is an essential component of modern nuclear bombs. It is needed to make the boosters for new bombs and to replenish the old ones every few years. This represents the current use of 95 per cent of the world supply of tritium.

The present situation in North America is that the U.S. military tritium-producing reactors are shut down for safety reasons. The Pentagon complains that its bomb production program will be limited by shortage of tritium. The price has been arbitrarily raised to $29 million per kilogram by the U.S. Department of Energy.

Ontario Hydro has good safety and operational reasons to remove the tritium from its stocks of heavy water. Its Tritium Separation Facility at Darlington, Ontario, has just started operation, and will produce tritium at the rate of 4 kilograms per year. This is enough to fulfil almost half of the U.S. military "requirement," but "Hydro" is bound by federal and provincial government regulations, and by the public assurances they have given, not to sell it for bomb manufacture. There are peaceful uses, world-wide, for at most 50 grams a year.

Governments of nuclear powers may attempt to acquire tritium regardless of law, regulations and stated government policies. There must be a strong temptation for theft by any criminal organization that can find a way to sell it to a government that wants it, and tritium has in fact been lost in transit. If the U.S. government really thinks the Pentagon needs tritium from Canadian reactors, it is hard to believe that they do not have the means to acquire it, one way or another. This Canadian tritium, together with certain economies and re-use of residues from old bombs, could allow the U.S. Department of Energy to go on building several new nuclear bombs a day, and delay asking Congress to authorize the expense of building new tritium-making reactors for many years.

(b) "Horizontal Proliferation"

Following the example of the present "nuclear powers," the government of a country still without nuclear bombs may think its security or prestige would be enhanced by acquiring them. Does the operation of nuclear power plants in such a country (or elsewhere) make it easier for its government to acquire bombs? And do nuclear power plants make it easier for the countries with undisclosed stocks of nuclear bombs to go on making more?

The big concern here is the formation of plutonium during normal reactor operation, but the possession of used fuel rods containing plutonium is a long way from having plutonium in a form usable for a bomb. The used fuel has to be "reprocessed," that is, plutonium has to be separated chemically from the many other highly radioactive substances present. The chemistry is straightforward, but an elaborate plant and special expertise are needed to do it safely, because of the radioactivity.

Next, reactors designed for power production do not normally make plutonium of the quality required for bombs. The plutonium isotope that fissions reliably is Pu-239, and "weapons-grade plutonium" must contain no more than 6 per cent of Pu-240 and heavier isotopes. Power reactors are designed to use their fuel elements for much longer than military reactors, allowing the proportion of Pu-240 to increase far beyond the "weapons-grade" level. Purifying reactor-grade plutonium to weapons-grade is essentially the same process as enrichment of natural uranium; in fact if a country had the facilities to do it, they could make uranium (U-235) bombs without a nuclear reactor at all. Most writers opposed to nuclear power evade this issue by ignoring the difference between weapons-grade and reactor-grade plutonium.[e.g.5] It has been stated that reactor-grade plutonium can be used to make bombs that will explode with lower and more variable force.[6 (p.201)] but an army would surely prefer reliable U-235 bombs. In CANDU reactors, it is feasible to remove the fuel rods early and obtain weapons-grade plutonium by chemical reprocessing. Ten or twenty times as many fuel rods a year would have to be re-processed as in normal use, which would not escape the notice of International Atomic Energy Agency (IAEA) inspectors.

However, the government of a country intending eventually to make nuclear explosives might well choose first to develop a nuclear power program so that its scientists, engineers and technicians would gain experience in nuclear technology, with help from a country already using nuclear power. The Indian nuclear explosion on 18 May 1974 was of plutonium reprocessed from fuel of the CIRUS research reactor obtained from Atomic Energy of Canada, Limited (AECL). Official spokespeople insisted that the explosion was "for peaceful purposes," but, like statements by other governments on nuclear matters, this was generally assumed to be untrue.

WHAT IF NUCLEAR WAR CAN BE RULED OUT?

All other risks of a catastrophic end to our civilization, and an unprecedented ecological disaster, pale beside the idea of a major nuclear war. With over 50,000 nuclear bombs in the world, many thousands of them mounted on rockets, aimed and ready to go, the risk of war being started, even accidentally, is always present. We are lucky to have survived so far. *If nuclear power adds to the risk, we have to do without it and the sooner it is phased out the better, whatever that may do to our standard of living.*

There are hopeful signs that the governments of some countries are beginning to act on the realization that the threat of war is no longer a rational instrument of statecraft. It is worth considering whether nuclear fission might, if war is renounced, become a boon to humanity, at least until better sources of power are developed. Provided the "breeder" technology is used, there is enough uranium to supply the world's energy needs for at least 1,000 years.[7]

Alan F. Phillips

Aerial photo of the Bruce Nuclear Power Station, 1980.
Courtesy of Ontario Hydro Archives.

All large-scale production of usable power carries risks to the environment and to the health and safety of its workers. For example, the dangers to health and life in mining coal, and the environmental and health damage caused by burning millions of tonnes of coal, are substantial. Modern demands for power are so vast that even the scale of construction for "benign" sources of energy, like solar radiation, water or wind power, would be so enormous that environmental damage and accidents to workers would be far greater than in the *construction* of equivalent nuclear generators. Nuclear generators are a very compact source of electrical power.

WHAT ARE THE RISKS?

Nuclear reactors are a source of "ionizing radiation," the form of radiation of which X-rays are the best-known example. Apart from possibly adding to the risk of nuclear war, and from dangers to workers that are common to most large industrial undertakings, the special risks are all related to radiation.* Many activities in our civilized life give us tiny doses of radiation, and there is and has always been a "natural background" of ionizing radiation everywhere on earth. This natural radiation forms the greater part of the total radiation received by most individuals. The amount of it varies from place to place, in some places being as low as half the average and in others as much as a few times the average. These variations make no obvious effect on health, though some careful statistical work suggests a slight effect. Actually, in both North America and the United Kingdom, the areas with the highest natural radiation are on the average the healthiest,[8] (p.56) probably because they happen to be mainly rural.

Workers in occupations that involve extra exposure to radiation have their actual exposure checked regularly. Currently accepted limits are defined at about 25 times average natural background. Few workers in nuclear plants receive anywhere near the legal limit. Artificial radiation reaching members of the public not subject to this monitoring, is limited to a calculated dose of one tenth as much. Medical X-rays are not included in the totals. Guidance for national legal limits is given by the International Commission on Radiation Protection (ICRP), which is a body of scientists and physicians whom we trust to make the best recommendations they can in light of current knowledge. The ICRP has recently issued a draft report indicating that the general guidelines will probably be lowered, in light of continuing research, to one half or one third of present levels.

Let us consider the radiation hazards from nuclear power plants under the following headings:

(1) normal operation
(2) management of highly radioactive waste
(3) accidents
(4) earthquakes
(5) sabotage
(6) decommissioning at the end of useful life.

(1) Normal Operation: Here we are concerned both with exposure of workers, which is measured, and of the regional population, which is calculated on various assumptions. The mining of uranium, unlike the min-

---

* "Radiation" in this chapter means "ionizing radiation," except in the context "solar radiation."

ing of coal, requires great precautions to keep radiation to the miners within accepted limits. Also, mining uranium sufficient to produce the same amount of energy as a million tonnes of coal, results in "tailings" containing a significant amount of radium (about 20 grams).[8 (p.171)] Radium continually forms a radioactive gas, radon, which, if it reaches the atmosphere, poses a possible danger to people living nearby. The tailings can be buried, which makes them harmless, because the radon decays in a few days to solid products. Often they have not been buried, and the mining companies have been rightly criticized for that. Coal also contains a tiny amount of radium (as do most rocks), and combustion of a million tonnes of coal leaves about 1 gram of radium in the ash, of which a small portion is discharged into the atmosphere, and is absorbed into foodstuffs over a fairly large area. It is probably enough to add significantly to the total radiation received by people living downwind of coal-fired generating stations,[8 (p.222)] particularly if they grow their own vegetables.

As regards risks to people living near a nuclear power plant, a small amount of radioactivity is discharged into the atmosphere and into natural bodies of water in the course of normal operation. According to measurements and calculations available, the resulting radiation dose to the public outside the perimeter fence is far below that due to "natural background."[4 (p.115)] There is concern because several studies have shown an increased frequency of leukemia, a rather rare disease, in the vicinity of some nuclear facilities in the United Kingdom, where usually workers at the plant have formed a large addition to the regional population. The leukemia has *not* been correlated with increased radioactivity in ground or atmosphere, either measured or calculated. Increased leukemia has also been found in some new towns unconnected with nuclear activities.[9] A recent report seems to indicate that an increase in childhood leukemia may be due to radiation exposure of the child's father, if he worked in a nuclear plant prior to conception of the child and received radiation doses near the legal limit.[10] Unless this theory is disproved, stricter standards of permissible dose to prospective fathers will be necessary in all occupations where there is exposure to radiation. The new ICRP recommendations mentioned above may be adequate.

(2) Management of highly radioactive waste: The used fuel from nuclear reactors is highly radioactive. Opponents of nuclear power calculate how many millions of people could die if the radioactivity were divided up and each person given exactly one lethal dose. The number is frighteningly large, but similar calculations can be done on the toxic products of other industrial processes. For example, in generating the same amount of electricity using coal, the sulphur dioxide actually liberated into the atmosphere amounts to 1000 times as many lethal doses as there are in the

radioactivity encapsulated in the reactor fuel for disposal after routine storage for 10 years.[11]

Atomic Energy of Canada, Ltd., and the appropriate bodies in other countries, have done extensive research on waste management. The most favoured plan is, after a few years' natural decay, to render it insoluble, encase it, and bury it very deep (e.g. 1 kilometre) in stable rock formations. The AECL research is reviewed annually by a Technical Advisory Committee selected from nominees of major scientific and engineering societies.[4 (p.125),12] Opponents of nuclear power may not know of this very careful research and apparently independent review, which impresses me as being thorough and unbiased. They point to the lifetime of the radioactive material (up to millions of years), the uncertainty of geologists' predictions, and other factors they believe to be ignored by the experts. This is an area where the experts sound more convincing.

Another possible management method is re-processing, i.e. chemical separation of the stored fuel rods, which would yield useful amounts of several precious non-radioactive metals and fissionable elements, usable again as reactor fuel. The final residue could be rendered safe by radiation with neutrons in a special reactor for the purpose to form mainly non-radioactive elements.[11]

Very little of the many tonnes of high-level waste produced by nuclear reactors over the past 40 years has actually been permanently disposed of. It is being stored at reactor sites, where it does represent a gradually increasing hazard.

A factor that is always omitted in expert calculations, is that cheaper and quicker alternatives to the correct procedures may at times be adopted for individual loads of waste or as a regular regime. We know that criminal practices such as clandestine dumping at sea, or unethical deals with the governments of Third World countries, have been used for toxic chemical wastes, and have been strongly suspected in the case of radioactive wastes. There has also been evidence of criminal negligence, especially in military nuclear facilities, for example allowing known leaks of radioactive material awaiting final disposal to go unreported and uncorrected.[13]

(3) Accidents: Occasional accidents are inevitable, and may be more frequent than is predicted by those who calculate risks. No calculation of the risk of an unpredicted or unpredictable type of event can be valid. Expert calculations tend to omit allowance for defects in specifications or construction, that somehow get past checks and routine inspections, and are often found in all types of buildings long after they have been put in use.

Accidents in the nuclear power industry over the last 40 years have involved far fewer immediate deaths than in any other method of power

Alan F. Phillips

production, relative to the amount of power generated. However, they have inconvenienced and frightened millions of people who had no connection with the industry, leaving them with anxiety for the rest of their lives about long-term effects, notably an increased risk of cancer. To compare with that, a terrible number of coal-miners have died in pit disasters, many of them entombed alive underground. Oil rig workers have died in ghastly circumstances by fire or drowning. Dams have burst and obliterated whole villages in the valley below.

Some nuclear disasters, notably those at Kyshtym and Chernobyl in the Soviet Union, have left thousands of square kilometres of land uninhabitable. The feared disaster of a complete "melt-down" has not yet occurred, and newer designs of reactor are said to make this more unlikely or even impossible. Containment vessels are designed to prevent release of radioactivity in the event of a chemical or steam explosion in the core.[7] A major nuclear explosion (like a nuclear bomb) is impossible in most reactors, because the fissionable material (uranium or plutonium) is mixed with large amounts of non-fissionable substances. Some scientists believe it may be a remote possibility in the fast neutron (breeder) type of reactor.[6] (pp. 127ff)

(4) Earthquakes: Popular protests alleging risk of nuclear catastrophe from an earthquake have several times prevented the building of proposed new nuclear generators at particular sites in the U.S.A. and caused temporary or permanent closure of others. Some aspects of the risk have clearly been exaggerated in people's minds. It appears that the mere shaking of the ground in even a major earthquake would not damage a reactor sufficiently to release radioactivity; only a large vertical shear occurring in bedrock right under the foundations could do this. This would be an extremely rare event, unless the reactor were built over or very close to an active fault (i.e., one where movement had occurred within say 30,000 years). Even then, major movement would be rare, and if it did occur, a well-built reactor container would probably survive intact. Nonetheless, the licensing procedures in the U.S.A. do not convey confidence, and there is no reason to suppose they are better in other countries. The hearings tend to be adversarial rather than objective fact-finding or risk-assessing, and it seems to be quite difficult to be certain whether a particular site does or does not overlie a fault in an area (such as coastal California) that is prone to earthquakes.[14]

(5) Sabotage: The danger of terrorists blowing up a nuclear generator and spreading radioactivity over the neighbourhood may have been exaggerated. So far such a bombing has not happened, except in the Israeli bombing of an Iraqi nuclear plant under construction. (If that action

caused radioactive contamination, it must have been kept secret.) I am told there has been one threat with a hijacked airplane that the U.S. authorities took seriously.[2] Reactor buildings and the containment vessels are very robustly constructed. Terrorists wishing to cause a dramatic disaster could more easily do so by setting fire to a large petroleum or natural gas store, or by blowing up a chlorine store, though the results would be immediate and visible, unlike the actual or feared long-term contamination from a destroyed nuclear reactor.

If a terrorist organization wanted to disseminate radioactive contamination, or to threaten to do so, stealing plutonium from a nuclear bomb plant, and using a simple explosive charge, would be easier than blowing up a nuclear generating station. If they wanted a nuclear bomb, it might be easier and safer to steal one intact, than to steal the essential components and try to make one. The danger exists, but military stocks of plutonium and bombs may be a greater hazard than civilian nuclear generators. It is only after reprocessing that the danger of misappropriation of plutonium arises.

(6)Decommissioning at the end of useful life: When, at the end of its useful life, or for any reason, a reactor is to be shut down permanently, the first step would be to remove the used fuel and deal with it as at routine refuelling. The reactor vessel and its remaining contents (already well shielded), would still be very radioactive, mainly with relatively short-lived isotopes. A period of natural decay, perhaps 50 to 100 years, would reduce this radioactivity by a large factor. The rest of the installation would contain much material of low radioactivity.[6] (p.93),[8] (p.214)

During the decay period the site might be in use running remaining and new reactors, in which case casual access would be prevented. Otherwise the reactor building would have to be physically sealed and guarded to prevent access and unauthorized removal of radioactive components. This is easy to state, but in practice it is impossible to guarantee reliability of guards over a long period. Contractors' employees, in one instance in the United States, have been convicted of sale of contaminated tools scheduled for burial as "low-level waste".[15]

In theory, at least, final dismantling of the plant and management of the large bulk of low-level waste would be tedious but not dangerous. The cost is allowed for by adding 0.1 cent per kilowatt-hour to the price of the electricity, which in 25 years would yield some $200 million (plus interest) for a large reactor.

ENVIRONMENTAL BENEFITS OF NUCLEAR POWER

We are told there is serious danger of irreversible damage to the environment by non-radioactive pollutants that are emitted in large amounts by industrialized society. These include carbon dioxide (a "greenhouse" gas), oxides of sulphur and nitrogen (causes of "acid rain"), and many other harmful chemicals. Some 10 per cent to 15 per cent of pollutants are currently being formed in the generation of electricity by burning coal or oil, and could be eliminated if all coal-fired and oil-fired generators were replaced by nuclear power or other power sources that are free from chemical pollution. Then, if automotive power and heat for buildings could be switched to electrical sources, pollution from them would also be eliminated. Emission of chemical pollutants is virtually zero from a nuclear power plant, and from electric power at the point of use.

Large-scale replacement of fossil fuel by non-contaminating energy sources (wind, tides, solar), is at best several decades away. No doubt economy in use of electricity will help, but it appears that more, not less, electricity will be required world-wide. As a practical matter, proponents of nuclear power reasonably argue that starting to build more nuclear generating stations now would reduce the "greenhouse effect" ten years hence more certainly than other proposed changes.

POWER FOR THIRD WORLD
One of the pressing needs for development in the Third World is an ample supply of electricity. Because of emission of CO_2, large-scale generation by burning any of the available fuels would add to the greenhouse effect. Water power (rivers), wind power, tidal power, geothermal power, and solar radiation are possible sources for some locations, but, except for the first, they are unproved for large-scale electric generation. Nuclear power may or may not be the best way for those countries to go. For some, many small generators may be better than a large nuclear one. A matter of concern is that, in the event of a Chernobyl-like catastrophe, evacuation of the area and damage control would be far more difficult and less effective in the non-industrial countries than in developed countries, because of lack of roads and transportation and of heavy and airborne equipment. Construction and start-up cost is high, and Third World debt is already crippling. Direct aid, not further loans, is required. Any success in development pre-supposes a drastic cut-back in world military expenditure, and release of those funds for useful purposes.

Nuclear fission power is a proved technology, despite its drawbacks, and may be the only way to supply very large amounts of power to the developing world within fifty years.

COST
The original hope of "electricity too cheap to meter" has by no means been realized. The cost of nuclear power is far above the early projections for many reasons, not least the attempts to ensure safety and reliability.

Repairs are also inordinately expensive and take much extra time because all parts in the reactor and many parts outside it are radioactive, and cannot be handled by ordinary maintenance techniques.

Ontario Hydro estimates the cost of electricity (cents per kilowatt-hour) from their several sources to be:[16] (p.49)

nuclear	3.2
coal and oil	3.7
hydro-electric	0.9

The close relationship between Ontario Hydro and the Ontario government, and with AECL, which itself is a subsidized Crown Corporation, makes it impossible to rely on these figures as realistic. The cost of "down time" is subsidized by the Ontario government and AECL.[16] (p.34) The cost of safe management of high-level waste can hardly be properly estimated, since the methods to be used have not yet been decided. And it should be remembered that the initial cost of research and development of nuclear reactors was borne by tax-payers of this country and others, much of it included in military budgets.

The cost of a possible major disaster, to the community and to the world, is obviously not included in Hydro's calculation. All other big enterprises have to buy insurance, but governments of countries with nuclear reactors have changed laws to exempt the corporations running reactors, and their suppliers, from civil liability for negligence, and from carrying full liability insurance. No insurance company would accept the risk. In Canada the corporations are exempt from liability insurance above $75 million for a reactor disaster, and part of this is supplied by the government.[4] (p.42ff) No government compensation for injury, life or property, is guaranteed.

In discussing the cost of electric power from different sources, it has to be realized that the cheapest in dollars and cents is not necessarily acceptable. We may all have to pay more because we must use sources of power that minimize environmental damage.

POWER FOR A PEACEFUL WORLD

Suppose our descendants lived in a world where security was assured by non-military means, and nuclear bomb technology was effectively and completely outlawed. It may be long before such a world order is achieved, but it has to come if our civilization is to survive. War between countries possessing nuclear bombs is no longer compatible with the survival of the belligerent countries, and alternative security is possible. The American civil war was only 130 years ago, but the states of the U.S.A. do not need to stockpile "deterrent" arsenals. It is inconceivable that one of them would use a nuclear bomb on another.

Suppose, during the next century, a similar degree of stability could be achieved between the states of the world, what then would be the best source of power? Could it be nuclear power as available now or as might be available in the foreseeable future?

I have not studied the degree of ecological damage caused by the construction and use of generators depending on alternative sources of power such as water (fresh-water dams and tidal barrages), wind, geothermal energy, and direct use of solar energy. Objections to most schemes have been expressed by those who are concerned with the environment. Only water power has been exploited on a really large scale at present; the others await development. Also awaiting development is nuclear fusion. Present-day nuclear reactors obtain their energy by "fission," that is by splitting large atoms (uranium or plutonium) into two or more parts. In theory it is possible to obtain even more energy by forcing the smallest atoms to combine into larger ones, which is called "fusion." Research has been going on in this field for many years. Tritium and deuterium (two isotopes of hydrogen) are the likeliest atoms to be used. Nuclear fusion would be a great deal "cleaner" than nuclear fission from the point of view of radioactive waste, and there would be no danger of an uncontrolled reaction like Chernobyl. It will be a long time before this process will be ready for use on a significant scale.

Many years later still, a much more difficult fusion reaction might be achieved, using a non-radioactive isotope of helium (He-3) from which power could be obtained leaving almost no radioactivity.[17] He-3 happens to be the end-product of radioactive decay of tritium.

Until nuclear fusion or other environmentally acceptable sources of power become available, a peaceful world might have to accept the risks of radiation from nuclear fission reactors, rather than the harm to people and to the environment caused by other sources of power on the scale needed. While people in the industrially-developed countries obviously have to accept a much more economical life-style, the idea of avoiding trouble mainly by using less electricity is not a good one.

Electricity is environmentally "clean" at the point of use. It is much more practical to control the emissions from a central generating station than those from a hundred thousand small buildings and a hundred thousand vehicles.

For supplementary heating of homes and all buildings, beyond what can be done with built-in solar collectors, electricity offers significant advantages if it can be generated in an environmentally acceptable way. Heating by burning fossil fuels (oil, coal or natural gas) generates carbon dioxide, and the older furnaces lose a lot of heat up the chimney. Heating with simple electric heaters puts 100 per cent of the heat energy into the building, and does not pollute, while heat pumps use electric power even more efficiently.

Automotive transportation in the industrial countries produces a large proportion of the atmospheric pollution. No good solution seems to be in sight. Electric cars at present have only short range because of the weight and bulk of batteries. Hydrogen is sometimes advocated as an ideal fuel for transportation. It can be made cleanly by electrolysis of water, and has the unique advantage that it produces no carbon dioxide on combustion. Burned with oxygen it produces only water vapour, but in practice when burned in air some oxides of nitrogen are formed, as in combustion of any fuel in air. Whether it is stored under pressure in cylinders, or as liquid in a vacuum bottle, or as metal hydride, the weight and bulk of containers at present make hydrogen unsuitable for personal automobiles, though feasible for trains and possibly for commercial vehicles.[18,19] More research is needed before electricity can be widely used, either directly or through the intermediary hydrogen. We must also expect much more limited freedom of transportation and personal mobility.

A MODEST CHALLENGE FOR THE 90s

At present there is an acrimonious debate in Canada between many public interest groups on the one hand, who are opposed to all nuclear power, and on the other hand AECL who want to make and sell CANDU reactors, supported by provincial utility corporations, notably Ontario Hydro, and by federal and provincial governments.

The public interest groups admit no possible benefit from nuclear power. They enlist public support largely by emphasizing the dangers of radiation, which have been underestimated by regulatory bodies. The dangers have been greatly exaggerated by some, but they rightly point to the possibility of catastrophic accidents, and to the connection with nuclear bombs.

The proponents of nuclear power say there is need for more generating capacity both in North America and abroad. They point to environmental benefits in reducing use of fossil fuel, and lack of other convenient sources of energy. AECL and its allies have spent large sums of our money on advertising campaigns, and they have used or condoned underhand methods to discredit the public interest groups.

Confrontation between these groups is not the way to find the best course of action for the benefit of the country and the world. I appeal to both parties to seriously try to resolve the conflict, realizing that our world is not perfect, and no solution will appear to be ideal.

As a start, I have a suggestion for each:

For the opponents of nuclear power, my suggestion is to find scientists and health professionals whom they can trust, working in the fields of energy, nuclear physics and radiation safety, and learn from them more about the actual dangers and possible benefits. At present they seem to regard everything "nuclear" as unacceptably dangerous, and by feeding exaggerated fears they risk depriving us of beneficial uses of nuclear and radiation technology. Also, they lose credibility with the experts and with government agencies by this attitude. There are many honest scientists working in those fields, who also hold health, safety, and the future of our planet very dear. In Canada there is a fine organization, "Science for Peace," where such scientists can be found.

For the other side, the task is far more difficult. The motives and the reassurances of governments and their agencies, of corporations working in nuclear engineering, and of all their employees and consultants are mistrusted. To reach a position where constructive resolution of the conflict can begin, they will have to establish their credibility, but not by advertising campaigns or other attempts to manipulate public opinion. If there are concealed motives behind the push for more nuclear power, then as long as they remain concealed honest discussion is impossible. Motives that are openly admitted are no bar to dialogue. The chief concern should be the future prosperity of the country and the world, with full respect for the environment, health and safety; but acceptable issues for negotiation include job security, career prospects, corporate profits, and the like.

If there is in fact a military purpose, then that itself is a point of conflict which has to be resolved.

The nuclear power protagonists have to begin a policy of consistent honesty and reach a point where they can be trusted. This may take more than a decade, and the best time to start is now.

I would like to be able to suggest some interim compromise, such as a moratorium on construction. But that does not deal with the "proliferation" question or the waste management problems. Tritium and highly radioactive waste are still being produced as long as the existing reactors are operating. I personally think the waste can be managed, but while nations still want to build nuclear bombs there must be no compromise in Canada that allows CANDU reactors to help them.

ACKNOWLEDGMENTS
I am grateful for the help of several colleagues and friends, especially Drs. Rosalie Bertell, David Goodings, Jim King, Jim Phillips, Elinor Powell, Ms. Barbara Starr, and my wife Joy Phillips, who made suggestions I have used. They do not necessarily agree with all that I have written.

References
1. A. DeVolpi, "Fissile Materials and Nuclear Weapons Proliferation," in *Annual Review of Nuclear and Particle Science* (1986)
2. R. Bertell, personal communication 1990

3. D.H. Albright, T. Zamore, D. Lewis, "Turn Off Rocky Flats," in Bulletin of Atomic Scientists, *46.6* (June 1990) 12–19

4. "Nuclear Energy: Unmasking the Mystery," Tenth Report of the Standing Committee on Energy, Mines and Resources, to the House of Commons, Ottawa, August 1988

5. R.H. Williams, H.A. Feiveson, "How to Expand Nuclear Power Without Proliferation," in Bulletin of the Atomic Scientists, *46.3* (April 1990) 40–45

6. Walter Patterson, "Nuclear Power" ISBN 0-1402-2499-8 Penguin 2nd.ed.1983

7. W. Hafele, "Energy from Nuclear Power," Scientific American *263.3* (September 1990) 137

8. J.H. Fremlin, "Power Production: what are the risks?" ISBN 0-85274-479-X Adam Hilger 1985

9. L. Kinlen, "Evidence of an Infective Cause of Childhood Leukemia: Comparison of a New Town with Nuclear Re-processing Sites in Britain," Lancet, II.1988, 1323–1326

10. M.J. Gardner, M.P. Snee, A.J. Hall, C.A. Powell, S. Downes, J.D. Terrel, "Results of case-control study of leukemia and lymphoma among young people near Sellafield nuclear plant in West Cumbria," British Medical Journal 1990; *300*: 423–429

11. J.V. Johanovich, " How to Live with Nuclear Power," Physics in Canada, March 1989, 68–79

12. Technical Advisory Committee on the Nuclear Fuel Management Problem, 8th Annual Report, 1987.

13. P. Loeb in "Nuclear Culture," 1986, New Society Publishers, pp. 209ff. ISBN 0-86571-087-2

14. R.L. Meehan in "The Atom and the Fault: Experts, Earthquakes, and Nuclear Power" M.I.T. Press, 1984. ISBN 0-262-13199-4.

15. S. Saleska, "Low-Level Radioactive Waste: Gamma Rays in the Garbage," in Bulletin of the Atomic Scientists, *46.3* (April 1990) 18–25

16. Ontario Hydro Annual Report, 1988

17. A. Harms, personal communication 1989

18. J.S. Wallace, C.A. Ward, "Hydrogen as Fuel," International Journal of Hydrogen Energy, *8* 255–268, 1983

19. J.S. Wallace, personal communication 1990

CHAPTER 14
A Revolution in Thinking: The Role of Science in the 21st Century

PROFESSORS GEORGE B. SPIEGELMAN AND
LUIS SOBRINO

When we look at the critical state of the world today, we see the results of chaotic technological growth. This growth was not designed or willed, but arose from the symbiosis of science and technology, impelled on the one hand by public demand for better living conditions, on the other by the desire for profit in private enterprises. This technological transformation has produced both good and bad results. What makes the present situation critical is that the bad results have accumulated in the course of less than two centuries, to produce unbearable inequalities among the peoples of the world and to threaten the ability of the planet to sustain life as we know it.

The World Commission in Environment and Development in its 1987 report[1] described in detail the threat to humankind posed by the inequalities between peoples in the world and the possibility of dangerous radical changes in their physical environment, and went on to suggest areas of scientific research that might lead to their amelioration. Examples of these research areas are:

Agriculture and biotechnology.
Fisheries, forestry and other renewable resources.
Health and epidemiology.
Alternative, unharmful energy sources.
Environment assessment and renewal.

As the World Commission report pointed out, current technology in the above areas has been developed to serve the needs of the industrial nations. If we are to solve the problems of underdeveloped nations, and at the same time protect the environment, we will require new technological

Professor George B. Spiegelman

tools. Developing these tools will in turn require reorienting research and reallocating resources away from weapons development and economic development based on resource exploitation.

A Role for Canada?

To examine Canada's possible role in developing this new set of technologies, let us first look at current research directions in Canada. Research directions are relatively easily traced by examining the distribution of research funds. In general, scientific research funds are allocated by two types of agencies: governments and private institutions (industries and foundations). Grants and contracts from private sources usually closely fit the mission of the industry or foundation, as defined by its board of directors and clarified by a scientific advisory group. Government research policy is set through the budget process, which allocates money to governmental departments having research mandates. The budget decisions include input from a variety of sources, including panels of experts and the political advisors of elected representatives.

Of seven leading industrialized countries (U.S.A., U.K., West Germany, France, Japan, Netherlands and Canada), Canada devotes the smallest percentage of its gross national product to all forms of research. This value is approximately 1.4 per cent in Canada, whereas it ranges from 1.8 per cent in the Netherlands to 2.1 per cent in France, 2.4 per cent in the U.K., 2.5 per cent in Japan, 2.6 per cent West Germany and 2.7 per cent in the U.S. A surprisingly large fraction of Canadian government research (13 per cent) is devoted to promoting competitiveness of Canadian industry. Basic research is supported to a very low level in Canada, receiving only about 20 per cent of the federal research expenditures.[2]

Table 1 shows the total dollar amounts spent in research funding by Canadian government departments (in constant dollars).[2] The total increase from 1984 to 1989 was 30 per cent, or about 5 per cent per year, which accounts for inflation. Some departments did better than others. The Department of National Defence (DND) increased its funding during the pe-

George B. Spiegelman received his Ph.D. from the University of Wisconsin (Madison) in molecular biology. He joined the Department of Microbiology of the University of British Columbia in 1978. He is currently an Associate Professor and Acting Head of the Department. He has published numerous papers in the field of molecular genetics. A long time activist in environmental preservation, he joined the disarmament movement in Canada in 1982, as the first President of the B.C. Chapter of Science for Peace. He has served as the National Vice President of Science for Peace, and is currently the President of the B.C. Chapter.

Professor Luis Sobrino

riod by 70 per cent, while Medical Research Council funds increased by 24.1 per cent. It is encouraging that during the period the Canadian International Development Agency (CIDA) increased its funding by 65 per cent, to constitute 1.8 per cent of the total Science and Technology budget in 1989. Although this amount seems very low, given the dimensions of global problems, it compares favourably with the percentage spent by other developed countries (data not shown in Table 1).

It should be emphasized that the Canadian Government allocates less than 10 per cent of research dollars to DND (although some additional money for military research is allocated through other departments). This is in stark contrast to countries like the U.S., the U.K. and France, which devote a much larger proportion of research dollars to military research.

What can be concluded from these numbers about Canadian research policy? First and foremost, in terms of percent gross national product, Canada does not invest in science and technology to the level that other developed countries do. Since Canadian society is highly industrialized and needs advanced technology, it would appear that our government relies to a large extent on importing ideas and equipment to satisfy that need. Second, leaving aside those countries, like the U.S., the U.K. and France, that historically have relied on the force of arms to achieve a preeminent status in the world, the distribution of Canadian research dollars between military and non-military areas is comparable to that of other industrialized countries. Third, the majority of funds spent on science and technology in Canada is aimed at economic development within the country.

Luis Sobrino was born in Spain. In 1947 he entered the Escuela Naval Militar, the Spanish naval officers' academy, where he graduated as Sub-Lieutenant in 1951. He served aboard naval ships until 1957, when he went to the Massachusetts Institute of Technology to do graduate studies in Nuclear Engineering. He obtained an M.Sc. in 1958 and subsequently enrolled in the Sc.D. program. After obtaining his doctorate in 1960, he immigrated into Canada and became a member of the Department of Physics at the University of British Columbia, where he is now a professor. In the course of his career at U.B.C. he has done work in Plasma Physics, Statistical Mechanics and Quantum Mechanics. Since 1982 he has been a member of Science for Peace, and has served as President and Vice-President of its British Columbia Chapter. Since 1985, he has been a member of Canadian Pugwash. He has co-authored papers on the Cruise Missile and the Strategic Defence Initiative, and has given numerous talks on these and other topics related to peace and disarmament.

Table 1 Federal Expenditures on Science and Technology (Millions of dollars)

Year	83–84	84–85	85–86	86–87	87–88	88–89	%/Yr
Total	3484	3875	3929	4179	4168	4409	5.1
Agriculture	354	391	405	409	393	415	3.2
Atomic Energy Canada	138	150	140	171	143	107	-5.0
CIDA	48	50	52	66	72	79	10.5
Energy, Mines & Resources	89	338	388	397	399	397	6.6
Environment	316	342	348	378	398	405	5.1
Fisheries & Oceans	212	254	246	224	207	229	1.6
Internal Development	64	76	82	91	96	103	10.0
Medical Research Council	141	157	162	168	175	185	5.6
National Defence	162	195	214	225	240	272	10.9
Health & Welfare	110	118	115	123	142	150	6.4
National Research Council	412	485	424	468	484	480	3.1
NSERC	282	313	311	321	339	356	4.8
Regional Industrial Expansion	164	173	203	189	168	281	11.4
SSHR	61	63	64	71	71	73	3.7
Statistics Canada	230	249	283	361	276	282	4.2
Transport	39	44	37	31	33	35	-2.1
Other	376	382	397	422	457	483	5.1

George B. Spiegelman and Luis Sobrino

Science, Technology and the Past

As we pointed out at the opening of this article, our current world situation is, in considerable part, a reflection of the combined successes and failures of science and technology. Inasmuch as the outputs of these two endeavours have not been entirely beneficial, it is reasonable to ask whether they can be counted on to eliminate the problems they have created.

In thinking about this question, it is useful to explore the distinction between "science" and "technology," words that are too often linked together in the expression "science and technology."

In essence, science is a particular way of understanding the natural world. Science is carried out by observing natural phenomena and, from these observations, formulating scientific "facts" or "laws" that describe the observed phenomena. Simple steps of reasoning are then applied to the facts or laws to arrive at predictions of new events. If further observations determine that the predicted events actually occur, then the hypothetical facts or laws are confirmed. Scientific facts are "true" only as long as they continue to survive experimentation. Through this process of "basic research," science accumulates a body of "scientific knowledge" about the world.

In contrast, technology is simply the art of making tools. Technology is the domain of "applied research." Today's technology is partially, but by no means entirely, based on science (this is probably the reason why science and technology are often confused). In many cases, we use our scientific knowledge of the natural world in the design of tools. In other instances, the method of trial and error is used. Even when the design of a tool is based on scientific knowledge, it is often the case that the design is refined by trial and error.

Problems can arise in developing new technological tools for two reasons. First, new technologies are typically deployed before their negative impacts are assessed. Historically, this has been the case because many new developments are pushed by both industrial and military-industrial interests. These interests exert enormous pressure, pressure that transcends political borders.

The second problem relates to the fact that our technologies and economic systems are tightly linked. Technology creates new economic opportunities (and problems), and the economy presents demands for certain technologies. Less widely realized is that the economy inhibits the development of some technologies. There is a current example in the field of waste management. In developing technologies to solve the garbage crisis by implementing the Three R's: "Reduce," "Reuse" and "Recycle," the market economy concentrates on "Recycle" because it least threatens continued consumption. However, it is clear that the first R, "Reduce," would lead to a more fundamental solution to the problem. The combination of our economy and our technology has created a society which is inherently nonsustainable. The question is whether changing our technology without changing our economy can create any other kind of society.

Science, Technology and the Future

We will not be secure until the chaotic development that has characterized the past century is organized and directed towards the goal of providing a good quality of life equitably to all peoples—"without compromising the ability of future generations to meet their own needs." Realizing this goal will require more than redeployment of technology from the "haves" to the "have-nots." It will require a fundamental shift in our world view. We need a change in our attitudes towards "growth"—economic growth as well as population growth: a revolution in human thinking and behaviour.

Revolutions on the scale we are suggesting have occurred in the past— the emergence of the nation state and the emergence of modern democracy are but two examples. Such revolutions are cultural, not technological. They belong to the world of ideas, not tools. Thus these revolutions are more profoundly influenced by developments in science than by developments in technology. As we do not have the space for a full discussion of this point, suffice it to direct attention to the discoveries of Galileo and Darwin, which brought about radical changes in the understanding of the place of human beings in the universe. These changes, in turn, led to revolutionary changes in the social and political mores.

The technology we have developed over the past 150 years has been based on the "reductionist" paradigm which framed the methods through which scientists explored the natural world. Reductionism has encouraged society to deal with social and environmental problems in isolation. Over the past 30 years, and in particular over the past 10 years, the inter-relationships between components of the natural world have begun to appear much more important. The importance of this interconnectedness, increasingly demonstrated by scientific research, has begun to penetrate a wide spectrum of human activities. As we come to grips with scientific evidence that the ecosystem of the planet is threatened, we are witnessing and experiencing the beginning of revolutionary change.

In light of the impending change, what types of scientific issues will need to be explored to allow, in turn, the development of sustainable technologies yielding security and well-being for the great majority of people on this planet? Many of the questions to be answered before we can achieve sustainable development (a term that certainly does not describe our profligate society), can only be answered by looking into social issues—the social ecosystem which humans have created. We know precious little about how our society acts, and next to nothing about what controls the economy. It may be found that many of the concepts which appear to be key to the neo-capitalistic economy prevalent in the West will have to be revised if we are to develop a stable relationship with our resources. For example, the laws of incorporation, whereby responsibility can be dispersed, and the laws of land ownership, have profound implications on how we view ourselves relative to our environment.

If we in Canada are to make a significant contribution to the solution of the problems outlined by the World Commission,[1] there will have to be significant policy changes. While it will be important for our science to redirect its efforts away from destructive technologies and to develop tools to reduce the inequities in the world, this is not enough. The pursuit of technological solutions alone will lead to the proliferation of inappropriate technologies, unless it is guided by insights derived from basic scientific research. Continued and more attentive public support for these endeavours is essential.

Finally, in order to accomplish a revolution of ideas, discerning and informed public involvement is critical. Education is the key to the ability of citizens to understand the issues we are facing, and to influence policy. The need for improved public education is not confined to the nations of the underdeveloped world. Citizens, particularly in North America, need to lobby harder and harder for increased education not only in science, but in history, social science and communications areas as well. Without this involvement and understanding, it will not be possible to navigate through the dangers that lie ahead.

References

1. *Our Common Future*, World Commission on Environment and Development. Oxford University Press, Oxford, New York. 1987.
2. Federal Scientific Activities. Statistics Canada, Catalogue 88-204, 1989.

Professor Michael Pentz

CHAPTER 15
Global Warning:
The Present Threat to a Sustainable World

PROFESSOR MICHAEL PENTZ

Contents of Chapter

Professor Emeritus Michael Pentz now lives in Provence, where he retired in 1986 after 17 years as Dean of the Faculty of Science at The Open University (UK). Prior to joining the Open University at its inception in 1969, Mike Pentz (as he has always been known to colleagues and friends) worked for 11 years in the Accelerator Research Division at CERN (the European Organisation for Nuclear Research) in Geneva. Before that, he was for eight years at the Imperial College of Science and

241

INTRODUCTION

This chapter is about three related global problems: population growth, energy conversion, and the environment. In the past two years, international attention has become focused upon a threat which incorporates these and other problems—the threat of **global warming.**

The final statement adopted at the World Conference on the Changing Atmosphere, held in Toronto in June 1988, defined the nature of this threat in the clearest possible terms:

> Humanity is conducting an unintended, globally pervasive experiment whose ultimate consequences could be second only to a global nuclear war. The Earth's atmosphere is being changed at an unprecedented rate by pollutants resulting from human activities, inefficient and wasteful fossil-fuel use, and the effects of rapid population growth in many regions. These changes represent a major threat to international security and are already having harmful consequences over many parts of the globe... Far-reaching impacts will be caused by global warming and sealevel rise, which are becoming increasingly

Technology, where he was a Lecturer in physics and did research on controlled fusion. Mike was born and educated in South Africa, but left that country in 1947 and adopted British nationality in 1948. When asked whether he ever thought of going back there he has always replied: yes, when Nelson Mandela is Prime Minister!

Apart from his work as a scientist and educator, Mike has been active in the peace movement since 1947. He helped found Science for Peace (UK) in the early 1950s (and edited its Bulletins for several years), and in the very different situation of 1980, organised the foundation of SANA (Scientists Against Nuclear Arms) of which he was the national chairperson until his retirement to France. In the 1980s he was also active in CND (the Campaign for Nuclear Disarmament). For the three years before his retirement he was an elected national Vice-Chair of CND—of which he is still an appointed Vice-President.

Apart from scientific papers (mostly on particle accelerator research), Mike Pentz has written extensively on problems of the nuclear arms race and disarmament, on the nuclear winter and related topics (including a number of contributions to Symposia in Vancouver). His interest in the topic of this chapter dates from 1976 to 1979 when he was the principal author of the final unit in the Open University's Science Foundation Course (of which he was also the course team chair and general editor), Science and the Planet Earth—problems of survival, *dealing with the related questions of population growth, energy needs and climate change.*

242

evident as the result of continued growth in atmospheric concentrations of carbon dioxide and other greenhouse gases.
Other major impacts are occurring from ozone layer depletion,
resulting in increased damage from ultraviolet radiation. The
best predictions available indicate potentially severe economic
and social dislocation for present and future generations; this
will worsen international tensions and increase the risks of
conflict among and within nations. It is imperative to act now. [1]

These problems are not going to be solved in a world embroiled in wars
and preparations for war, because their solution requires massive investments and international collaboration. What's more, the longer they
remain unsolved the more will they become a source of international conflict. So there is a two-way link between world peace (which does not
mean just the absence of war in the world) and the preservation of a planetary environment in which it will be possible for humans to go on living
and evolving.

The present crisis in the Persian Gulf (which could become a war before these words are printed) is essentially due to the dependence of the
United States and other industrialized countries upon imported petroleum. Yet this "dependence" could be completely eliminated by economically profitable fuel economy measures, which would at the same
time greatly reduce atmospheric pollution by gas-guzzling automobiles.

The 1986 Vancouver Centennial Peace and Disarmament Symposium
had as its title: *End the Arms Race: Fund Human Needs.* I will argue in
this chapter that the most important of all the many human needs at this
time is to stabilize the world's population at a sustainable level, to deal
with the problems of *real,* as distinct from *apparent,* energy poverty, and
at the same time to protect the environment from catastrophic damage. It
is obvious enough that these global problems can only be solved if a large
proportion of the resources, both money and people, now being wasted
on armaments and armed forces is applied to their solution. But is that all
that is needed? I very much doubt it. It seems most unlikely that any of
the measures needed to solve these problems will be taken in time, if at
all, so long as what is done—and especially what is invested in—depends
first and foremost, and perhaps only, on whether it will be profitable in
the short term. World peace and disarmament are undoubtedly a *necessary* condition for planetary survival, but I fear that they are not a *sufficient* condition. It seems that we shall also need to change quite radically
a set of entrenched economic and political structures and relationships,
and this is likely to be a difficult and lengthy business.

This book's avowed purpose is to provide Canadians, especially young
people, with the new ideas they need to shape the world they will live in.

If that purpose is to be achieved, there is an educational job to be done that extends far beyond what can be achieved in a book, let alone in a single chapter. My purpose in writing this chapter, then, is to show how urgent this educational task is, and to spell out the warning that, if we do not tackle this task world-wide, with the utmost vigour and skill, the chances of creating a sustainable world for our children and grand-children to live in are poor indeed.

1. TOWARDS SUSTAINABLE DEVELOPMENT?

The World Commission on Environment and Development characterized *sustainable development* as paths of social, economic and political progress that "meet the needs of the present without compromising the ability of future generations to meet their own needs."[2] Sustainability implies that economic growth and development must be maintained within the limits set by ecology, by the context created by humans and their activities, and by the physical, chemical and biological properties of the biosphere.

> ... Many present efforts to guard and maintain human progress, to meet human needs, and to realize human ambitions are simply unsustainable—in both the rich and poor nations. They draw too heavily, too quickly, on already overdrawn environmental resource accounts to be affordable far into the future without bankrupting those accounts. They may show profits on the balance sheet of our generation, but our children will inherit the losses. We borrow environmental capital from future generations with no intention or prospect of repaying. They may damn us for our spendthrift ways, but they can never collect on our debt to them. We act as we do because we can get away with it: future generations do not vote; they have no political or financial power; they cannot challenge our decisions. But the results of the present profligacy are rapidly closing the options for future generations...[2]

Sustainability implies also a concept of economics very different from the "standard," neo-classical economics that dominates the world's marketplaces today (and the activities of institutions like the World Bank and the International Monetary Fund). In her chapter on *Managing the Global House: Redefining Economics in a Greenhouse World,* in the recently published book *GLOBAL WARMING—The Greenpeace Report,* Susan George reminds us that the term "economics" stems from the Greek *oikos,* house, and a derivative of *nemein,* to manage, and that "we now know that our house is the world."[3] Standard economics is concerned only with the production, consumption and distribution of wealth as quantified in monetary terms, and is not concerned with comprehensive management. The economy is seen as a perpetual growth machine, with no points of contact with the environment, unless these can be quantified. Thus the so-called "development" financing agencies have consistently funded ecologically devastating projects in the Third World, including those that have destroyed forests, in the name of "economic development," based on a conception of unlimited growth and a rooted belief in the notion that "more is always better than less." They do so on the criteria of standard accounting practice, which takes note only of those factors that can be expressed in monetary terms, and in which "economic efficiency" is judged according to short-term profitability. To them, "the long-term costs of forest destruction, including climatic change,... and the disruption or death of indigenous forest-dwelling communities is not quantifiable and is therefore not quantified."[3]

As we enter the last decade of the twentieth century, decisions are due to be taken, starting this month (November 1990) at the Second World Climate Conference, and continuing in 1991 (and probably beyond) with the expected international negotiations on a "Greenhouse Convention," which will critically affect the destiny of humankind.

Will we seize this unique opportunity to move nations and people in the direction of sustainability? "Such a move would be a modification of society comparable in scale with only two other changes: the agricultural revolution of the late Neolithic and the industrial revolution of the past two centuries. Those revolutions were gradual, spontaneous and largely unconscious. This one will have to be a fully conscious operation, guided by the best foresight that science can provide—foresight pushed to its limit. If we actually do it, the undertaking will be absolutely unique in humanity's stay on the earth."[4]

Yet, unless there is immediate and effective political intervention from "below"—from outside the "policymakers'" council chambers—it looks very much as if the opportunity may be lost, perhaps irretrievably.

The World Climate Conference (WCC) is due to consider the reports of the three Working Groups of the Intergovernmental Panel on Climate Change (IPCC). The IPCC was set up in 1988 (soon after the Toronto Conference) by the World Meteorological Organisation and the United Nations Environment Programme. At its first meeting in November 1988, IPCC set up three Working Groups, on *science* (IPCC WG1), on *impacts* (IPCC WG2) and on *policy responses* (IPCC WG3). It is the integrated results of these three working groups, combined as an overall IPCC Report, that will now go to the WCC. The scientists' report was published in May, and the policymakers' report in June.

The scientists' report was unequivocal: "We are certain that emissions resulting from human activities are substantially increasing the concentrations of the greenhouse gases. . . These increases will enhance the greenhouse effect, resulting on average in an additional warming of the Earth's surface."[5] They predicted that if greenhouse-gas emissions continue at their present rates, the global average temperature would rise by as much as a degree (Celsius) within thirty years, and would go on rising beyond that time at an accelerating rate. The record of past climates shows that changes of this rapidity have never happened before—global temperatures have probably fluctuated by little more than 1°C in the 10,000 years since the last glaciation. Within less than half a century we shall be experiencing average temperatures never before felt while humans have walked on the planet. Furthermore, the IPCC scientists warned that their assessment is likely to be an underestimate, because a number of effects left out of their computerised climate-simulations are likely to cause "positive feedback," that is, increased rates of accumulation of greenhouse gases (such as methane) caused by the global warming itself. If we continue with "business-as usual," global temperatures could rise by as much as 3 to 5°C above the level of the nineteenth century; such climate conditions have not existed for more than 125,000 years (3°) or even 3 million years (5°).

The impacts group (IPCC WG2), predicted extremely serious effects of such temperature rises upon ecosystems of all kinds, on agriculture, on urban populations, on coastal communities and on human health—even in the absence of possible positive feedback effects. Throughout the report of this group it was emphasised that the many remaining uncertainties entail massive risks to humankind.

It was immediately obvious that the policymakers (IPCC WG3) were unwilling or unable to take the findings of the two scientific groups seriously. They completely glossed over the findings of both. They avoid mentioning "global warming" and refer instead to "climate change" or even "potential climate change," and to "potential impacts" of such climate changes. They do not even discuss the merits or demerits of policies that could buy insurance against the global-warming effects described by the first two IPCC groups. Instead, they put the emphasis on the need for increased research to reduce the uncertainties. They do not recommend—or even discuss—any cuts in greenhouse-gas emissions or even advocate a freeze on emissions. They consistently emphasise the perceived costs of policy action, but ignore the costs of inaction. They do recommend the negotiation in due course of a Climate Convention, but only one which "lays down general principles and obligations for addressing climate change."

The IPCC policymakers' report was firmly rooted in a frame of reference which refuses to countenance appreciable change from present conditions.[6]

It is against this inauspicious background, then, that the next stage of international negotiations will soon be starting in Geneva. Far from providing clear policy guidelines upon which serious negotiations could be based, the IPCC policymakers will give those participants in the World Climate Conference who would like to avoid any effective action, ample pretexts for so doing. It will be surprising (though it cannot be altogether ruled out), if the Conference gets as far as agreeing upon the outlines of a "Framework Convention" to be ratified in 1992. Such a Convention could include formal recognition of the problem of global warming and of the need for some form of international response. It could outline the widely accepted scientific understandings and establish a centralised assessment process for continually updating the parties' understanding of the science and potential impacts of global warming. It could include a set of initial global targets and timetables for the limitation of greenhouse gas emissions, but it would *probably not* attempt to prescribe specific targets for individual countries or regions. It could establish an overall goal of stabilizing global emissions at the levels reached during the year the convention entered into force, to become effective by a specified time (such as 10 years) thereafter. It might even include certain sub-targets, such as:

requiring the OECD countries to stabilize their CO_2 emissions at the level existing when the convention comes into force, and requiring each party to the convention to improve the ratio to its GNP of its CO_2 emissions from fossil fuels by some percentage (such as 2 per cent) per year over a 10-year period after the convention enters into force;

obliging each party to ensure no net loss of forests on an annual basis by the end of the 10-year period;

requiring each country or regional grouping to prepare a national or regional strategy for dealing with greenhouse warming and to update that strategy at regular intervals (say every two years) thereafter.

It could establish some procedure for revising the targets, timetables, and other obligations in the convention through *subsequent protocols,* based on the result of the assessment process and the first round of national strategies. The most important of these protocols could be one that allocated to individual countries or regions their shares of the overall ceiling on global greenhouse gas emissions.[7]

These limited objectives for a greenhouse convention are based upon the judgement that, "there is little to be gained by putting forward policies which are clearly unacceptable to any of the major countries or groups of countries—developed or developing—that will need to agree and implement such measures."[8]

However, what is "acceptable" or "unacceptable" to the government of any particular country is not immutable. It is "acceptable" to the Swedish government today that all nuclear power stations in Sweden should be closed down by the year 2010, because a referendum obligates it to do so. But the referendum itself would not have been held, and its outcome would not have been what it was, but for the political pressures developed by environmentalists. If more significant, and above all more rapid progress is to be made towards reducing (at least) the future impacts of global warming, there will have to be a great increase in public political pressure in all countries.

This implies an entirely new approach to the problem of public information and education. Effective modern methods and media need to be deployed to inform people at all levels, from policy-makers through intellectuals, professional and business people to the masses of working people and consumers. It is all these people who, in principle in all countries and in practice in most, can influence political decisions. Their responses, as citizens and as consumers, to legislative and/or market incentives or pressures, will determine what is or is not going to be done about global warming. For these responses to be effective, these people must be informed. There is a huge educational job to be done, and it must be done with the methods of the present century, not the last one. I shall return to this point at the end of the chapter.

If political campaigning is going to be essential for the achievement of a sustainable world—and I am sure that is so—there needs to be a set of "campaigning goals" on which to focus the efforts of the campaigners. And who *are* these campaigners? Most people would probably reply "environmentalists," or something similar. I think one of our primary aims must be to abolish the implied distinction between "environmentalists" and "everyone else." What is at stake now is more than the preservation of wildlife or of biodiversity in tropical forests—important as these aims are—but the preservation of human civilisation and of a biosphere that will still be habitable a century or two hence. This is no longer just the concern of "environmentalists," but of everyone.

Before we return to the question "what can be done?", we should briefly take a closer look at the question of global warming itself and its underlying causes.

Michael Pentz

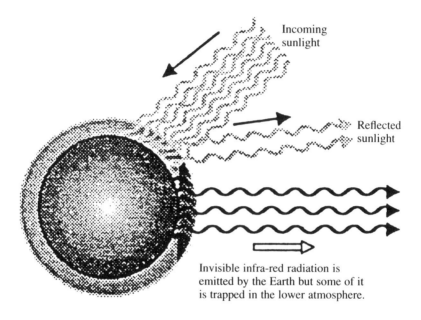

Fig. 1: How the greenhouse effect works. Energy from incoming solar radiation reaches the Earth. Some is reflected. Most readily penetrates the atmosphere and warms the Earth's surface. Invisible infra-red radiation is emitted by the Earth and cools it down. But some of this infra-red is trapped by greenhouse gases in the atmosphere, which acts as a blanket, keeping the heat in. (Source: UK Department of the Environment, Global Climate Change, *May 1990).*

2. THE GREENHOUSE EFFECT AND GLOBAL WARMING

Figure 1 and its caption explain (in a simplified way) how the greenhouse effect works.

When the climate system is in equilibrium, as it was before the Industrial Revolution, the energy in the incoming solar radiation is exactly balanced by the energy of the radiation reflected back into space plus the (infra-red) radiation radiated away from the Earth and passing through the atmosphere. The effect of injecting gases that absorb this infra-red radiation ("greenhouse gases"), is to reduce the amount of infra-red energy radiated away, thereby upsetting the balance. The surface temperature of the Earth then increases to the point where the additional infra-red radiation emitted by the warmer surface and escaping through the atmosphere into space is enough to restore the equilibrium. The process is not instantaneous. If we were to suddenly stop injecting greenhouse gases into the atmosphere, it would take decades (or perhaps even centuries) before the equilibrium temperature corresponding to *earlier* injections is reached. That is why a certain amount of global warming is now inevitable. Our future actions can now influence only the rate and degree of *further* global warming.

Current estimates of the contributions of the principal greenhouse gases to global warming in the 1980s are summarized in Table 1.

Current predictions of global warming due to continued injection of these greenhouse gases at present rates, are illustrated in Figure 2.

The "realized" warming predicted by IPCC WG1, is about 1°C above present levels by 2025, and 3°C before the end of the next century. The "committed" warming due to the greenhouse gases emitted between 1880 and 1969 would involve an additional rise of between 0.5°C and 1.5°C at some time in the future. It is clear that the *rate* at which the global temperature is rising at the turn of the 20th century is many times greater than the rate at the turn of the 19th century.

To understand the implications of these predictions, it is useful to compare them with the record of the recent geological past. Figure 3 shows the variation of the global average surface temperatures since the last glacial period (10,000 to 20,000 years ago). It is obvious that the temperature changes predicted for the 21st century are not only much greater than any that have occurred in this period, but also very much more rapid.

In a "business-as-usual" world in which greenhouse gas emissions continue at today's rates, we can expect the temperature to rise more rapidly than at any time in human history. This is likely even if there were to be none of the natural positive feedback effects which the world's scientists believe to be "likely" if greenhouse gas concentrations continue to build up in the atmosphere. Furthermore, these predictions do not extend beyond the next 50, or at most 100 years; if temperatures can rise

Table 1   The main greenhouse gases and their contributions to global warming

Gases	Current annual rate of increase per cent	Contribution to global warming per cent
Carbon dioxide (CO_2) from fossil fuels (77%) from deforestation (23%)	0.5	55
Chlorofluoro carbons (CFCs) and related gases (HFCs and HCFCs)*	4.0	24
Methane (CH_4)	0.9	15
Nitrous oxide (N_2O)	0.8	6

* *Production of CFCs began only a few years before the Second World War. Now that these gases are known to deplete stratospheric ozone, the chemical industry is preparing replacements—hydrochlorofluorocarbons (HCFs) and hydrofluorocarbons (HFCs). Though they do not deplete ozone so badly (and are yet to be produced in commercial quantities), they are potent greenhouse gases.*

Tropospheric ozone is another significant greenhouse gas. It is omitted from the table because of difficulties of quantification. It forms in the troposphere as a result of chemical reactions between uncombusted hydrocarbons and nitrogen oxides, produced by fossil fuel combustion (particularly by automobiles), in the presence of sunlight.
Source: From GLOBAL WARMING (Ref. 3), based on IPCC WG1 Report, Policymakers' summary.

by 3°C in a single century, can we simply rule out the possibility that they might rise by 10 to 15°C in the next few centuries? These are the temperatures which geologists estimate existed during the age of the dinosaurs some 100 million years ago, which seems to have been the warmest the Earth's atmosphere has ever been in the 600 million years' history of animal life.[9]

It is sometimes said that if we just "carry on as usual," we shall be playing Russian roulette with the future climate and hence the future of human civilisation as we know it. It could be that the stakes are even higher.

What, then, can be achieved by *not* just carrying on as usual, by reducing the emissions of greenhouse gases?

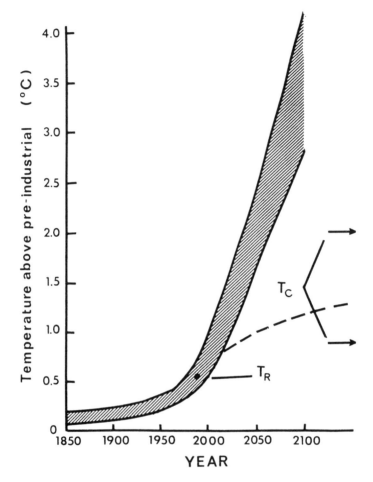

Fig. 2: A semi-quantitative picture of global warming (based on IPCC WG1 estimates).

T_R = *the "realized temperature" in 1990. It is between 0.3°C and 0.6°C above the pre-industrial level.*

T_C = *the "committed temperature." It is the equilibrium temperature that would eventually be reached as a result of the greenhouse effect up to now.*

IPCC WG1 predicts temperatures of about 1°C above the present level by the year 2025 and about 3°C above the present level before 2100.

The shaded area between the two curves indicates (approximately) the range of uncertainty. There is an even greater uncertainty about the present "committed temperature" and about when it would be reached.

Michael Pentz

Fig. 3: Generalized global average temperatures during and immediately before the history of human civilization. (a) The past 20,000 years. (b) The past 1,000 years. The averages depict a range of analyses from sediment- and ice-cores. Note how temperatures last rose quickly around 12,000 years ago as the world emerged from the last ice age. Global average temperatures rose some 5°C over several millennia at that time. The average temperature rise predicted beyond 1990 by the IPCC scientists is many times faster. In (a) the temperature-rise would be lost in the thickness of the line which forms the right-hand margin of the figure. In (b) the grey peak is the "best guess" of the IPCC scientists. The black peak is the upper range of the estimates from the IPCC models. As the IPCC scientists observe, however, the likelihood of positive feedbacks—many of them unaccounted for in climate models—means that the real temperature rise in the next century is "likely" to be even higher than that predicted. (After International Geosphere Biosphere Program Report no. 6, Global Changes of the Past, July 1988, and UK Department of the Environment, Global Climate Change, May 1990, modified to include the IPCC scientists' results).

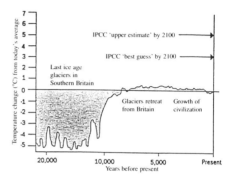

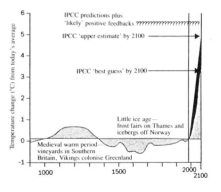

253

It is important to bear in mind that the atmospheric concentrations of carbon dioxide, nitrous oxide and CFCs will only adjust slowly to changes in emissions, because these gases have relatively long atmospheric lifetimes. This means that "the longer emissions continue to increase (at present-day rates), the greater would reductions have to be to stabilize (concentrations) at a given level. If there are critical concentration levels that should not be exceeded, then the earlier emission reductions are made, the more effective they are."[10]

The implication of the term "critical concentration" should be noted: it is likely that when a certain concentration has been reached, the consequent unavoidable warming would reach a "critical" point at which natural amplification, or positive feedback, effects "take over":

> The possibility exists that the warming will proceed to the point where biotic releases from the warming will exceed in magnitude those controlled directly by human activity. If so, the warming will be beyond control by any steps now considered reasonable. We do not know how far we are from that point because we do not know sufficient detail about the circulation of carbon among the pools of the carbon cycle. We are not going to be able to resolve those questions definitively soon. Meanwhile, the concentration of heat-trapping gases in the atmosphere rises.
> —*Dr. George M. Woodwell, President and Director of the Woods Hole Research Center, Massachusetts.*[11]

The aim must clearly be at least to stabilize the atmospheric concentration of greenhouse gases at the present level. The IPCC scientists, and other scientists who did a recent study for the US Environmental Protection Agency, have calculated the cuts in the rates of emission that would be required to achieve this. See Table 2:

Table 2   Cuts in emissions needed for stabilization of greenhouse gases at present atmospheric levels

Greenhouse gas	IPCC estimated at %	EPA estimated at %
CO_2	>60	50–80
CH_4	15–20	10–20
N_2O	70–80	80–85
CFC-11	70–75	75–100
CFC-12	75–85	75–100
HCFC-22	40–50	n/a

Source: *GLOBAL WARMING* (Ref. 3)

254

The immediate causes of the greenhouse effect are the rapid increases since the Industrial Revolution in the rates of emission of carbon dioxide, methane and nitrous oxides, and, much more recently, of CFCs, all of them due to human activities. What, then, are these activities, and how can they be changed?

3.   THE UNDERLYING PROCESSES

The processes and activities underlying the emission of greenhouse gases are summarized in Table 3:

Table 3 Sources of greenhouse gases from human activities

Gas	Source	Principal human activities
Carbon dioxide (CO_2)	Fossil fuel combustion	Electricity generation Motor vehicles Other industrial activity
Chlorofluorocarbons (CFCs) and related gases (HFCs & HCFCs)	Chemical industry	Refrigeration Foam blowing solvents
Methane (CH_4)	Agriculture	Rice cultivation Domestic animals Agricultural burning
	Biomass burning	Deforestation and domestic heat
	Fossil fuel production and combustion*	Leakage and venting of natural gas Motor vehicles*
Nitrous oxide	Agriculture Fossil fuel combustion Biomass burning	Fertilizers As for carbon dioxide As for methane

* *The effect is indirect, via the competition between motor-vehicle emissions and methane for the hydroxyl radical OH.*

Source: GLOBAL WARMING (Ref. 3)

Reductions in the emissions of these gases on the scale necessary to stabilise their atmospheric concentration (Table 2) will evidently have major implications for a range of activities that are fundamental to the life-style and even the existence of the world's growing population. Since carbon dioxide has contributed 55 per cent to global warming, and since fossil rfuel combustion is responsible for over three-quarters of it (as well as a significant proportion of the methane and nitrous oxide), the most immediate question to ask is what can be done to reduce, and possibly even to eventually eliminate, the combustion of fossil fuels. This in turn leads us to ask some fundamental questions about energy sources, energy uses and the need (or demand) for energy in convenient forms.

3.1 Uses and sources of energy

There is a fundamental reason why energy, in some convenient form, is essential for the production, distribution and utilisation of commodities and hence for economic and social development. It goes back to a law of physics first discovered by Newton: if you want to move anything (or change the way anything is moving) you have to apply a force to it and in the process transfer energy to it. All agricultural and industrial production processes involve making things move or changing the way they move, and distribution (transportation) does so even more obviously. In industry and agriculture the energy transfers are often clearly observable macroscopic processes; you can *see* things being moved about. In many other situations, energy is being used to change the state of motion of things at the microscopic levels of biology and chemistry. But at whatever level, the same thing applies—no energy, no movement.

The four most important words in the above paragraph are in the first line: **"in some convenient form."** Take, for example, the energy you buy in the form of gasoline—energy stored in the chemical structure of that fuel. You buy it in order to *use* it to some end. You put it into a machine called an automobile which can (under certain circumstances) transport you from one place to another at a reasonable speed and with reasonable comfort and security. In the process of so doing, all the chemical energy in the fuel gets converted into heat. Gasoline, then, is a form of **end-use energy** which you buy to perform a **function,** or service. But gasoline is not the original or **primary** form of that chemical energy. The primary energy form is petroleum, or crude oil. But not all the energy in its primary form is available as end-use energy; energy is needed for a whole series of processes between the emergence of the crude oil at the well-head and the emergence of the gasoline from the pump at the filling station, and that energy has to come from somewhere. As is painfully obvious to any city dweller, by no means all the energy in the gasoline is used to perform the desired function. As you crawl at a few kilometres an hour through the rush-hour traffic, or are stuck in the usual traffic jam, the energy in your gasoline is performing no function at all, other than the useless one of heating up the environment. If you happen to be driving a North-American "gas-guzzler," you will need perhaps twice as much end-use energy to achieve your snail's progress to and from work each day, as you would if you were driving one of the more economical Japanese or European models. If your place of work was just around the corner from where you live or only a few kilometres away along a road unencumbered by heavy traffic, you would get much more functional energy out of your gallon of end-use energy.

Consider one more everyday example. In many countries, most public buildings and houses are heated by electricity. The electricity delivered to your house is a form of end-use energy. What is its *primary* energy source? To simplify matters, suppose that it comes from a coal-fired electrical power station, so the primary (chemical) energy is stored in the coal. (I leave you to reflect for a moment on where *that* came from, and why coal is called a "fossil fuel".) To turn the primary energy in the coal into electrical energy delivered to your house, several processes are needed. The first one is to transform the chemical energy into **heat** energy, by burning the coal in a furnace and transferring that heat to the water in the boiler, thereby producing steam. Then the energy in the steam is transformed by the turbine into mechanical energy (energy of motion of a massive object) and by the generator into electrical energy. Finally, the electrical energy is transported by transmission lines via electricity sub-stations to your home. All these processes involve energy losses, in the form of heat. In some cases the losses can be reduced by good design (of the turbo-generator system, for example). But in one process, where by far the greatest losses occur, no amount of human ingenuity can reduce them by more than a marginal amount. They are a consequence of a fundamental law of physics (the "Second Law of Thermodynamics"). If you want to transform *heat energy* into any other form of energy you have to pay a price (in heat energy that cannot be so transformed) for doing so, and the price is typically quite high—about 40 per cent of the original heat energy will be lost. [As a child, I used to admire the elegant forms of the cooling towers of a nearby power-station and the pretty white plume of steam disappearing down-wind. I wondered what they were for.]

So there will be a very large gap between the primary energy in the coal and the corresponding end-use electrical energy delivered to your home. But you do not buy electricity because it gives you pleasure to see that little meter going round and round as it adds up your next electricity bill. The *function* you want to perform is to heat up the inside of your home and to provide electric lighting. But, as everybody knows, only a proportion of the electrical energy actually warms up the *inside* of your home— the rest simply warms up the little birds on the telephone wires outside. And if you are using standard incandescent light bulbs instead of modern compact fluorescent bulbs, you will be using more than five times as much electrical energy to produce the same amount of light. There are evidently important gaps here too—between *end-use energy* and *functional energy*.

In both these examples (and they could be multiplied many times over) what you actually want is the *service* that energy, in some convenient form, can give you; the energy in its end-use form (gasoline, electricity) is in itself of no value to you at all. Of course, to say that you *want* something is not necessarily to say that you *need* it; you may *want* to drive to work in a vehicle that does only 18 miles to the gallon (traffic-jams apart)—and who can blame you when the motor manufacturers spend millions daily to persuade us all that "status, quality of living—even sexuality—are all tied in with the performance (power, acceleration) of the cars we own,"[12] but you cannot claim that you really *need* to do that.

In his chapter on *The Role of Energy Efficiency* in *GLOBAL WARMING*, Amory Lovins neatly sums up the story of the energy gaps:

> Simply equating (primary) energy use with social benefits telescopes together several distinct relationships which are best kept separate:
> • How much primary fuel is fed into the energy system does not determine how much useful energy is supplied—that depends on the system's conversion and transmission efficiency;
> • How much useful energy is supplied does not determine how much service is performed—that depends on end-use efficiency;
> • How much service is provided does not determine whether what was done with the energy was worth doing.[13]

Added up over whole countries (let alone the whole world), these energy gaps can be enormous:

> The energy wasted* in the United States today costs about twice as much as the federal budget deficit, or more than the entire $10,000-a-second military budget. The amount of crude

---

* "Wasted" in the sense that it is used instead of being displaced by cheaper efficiency options now commercially available and practically applicable and deliverable for doing the same task.

258

oil wasted in 1986 by that year's rollback of US light-vehicle efficiency standards equalled 1985 imports from the Persian Gulf. It also equals the average annual oil output which the Interior Department hoped to achieve over thirty years from beneath the Arctic National Wildlife Refuge.[14]

Merely improving the efficiency of electric *lighting* by using commercially available lighting innovations, could save between a seventh and a fifth of all the electricity now used in the US.[15]

Total installed electrical generating in the US in 1987 was 743 GW. One seventh of this is about 106 GW. The capacity of *all the nuclear power stations in the US* in 1987 was 102 GW (1 GW = 1 gigawatt = 1 million kilowatt).[16]

In spite of the large gaps between primary, end-use and functional energy, there has been an unfortunate tendency in discussions of energy needs/demands—in the press, in pronouncements by politicians and even sometimes in energy policy studies—to forget about them entirely and to concentrate all attention on primary energy only. Thus it is commonplace to read that the per-capita energy "consumption"* of the less-developed countries (LDCs) is x times lower than that of the industrially developed countries (DCs). The figures for 1987 were 744 watts per capita in the LDCs as compared with 5820 watts per capita in the DCs. So in the DCs, the factor (x) was nearly 8. In 1975, this ratio was 435 w/cap, a factor of about 11.**

In a study of global energy needs and sources in 1978, I made a rough guess that, globally, about half the primary energy is lost in conversion processes, and that there is probably a similar factor of at least two between end-use and functional energy, but I did not even try to guess whether these factors would be the same in the DCs and the LDCs.[17]

In the same study, I postulated a future energy strategy that would reduce the ratio of primary to functional energy from 4 to less than 1.5, as illustrated in Figure 4.

Whereas the degree of energy poverty, and hence underdevelopment, of a country relates to *functional energy*, rather than primary energy, the two are, of course, related by the efficiencies of conversion from primary

---

* The energy "*consumption*" is commonly used, but it is in principle incorrect, because energy is in fact *never* consumed; it is converted from one form to another, or transferred from one thing to another. Ultimately, all energy, whatever its source, is converted into *heat* energy.

** It is customary to calculate *rates* of conversion of energy, averaged over a year. A common unit of energy is the kilowatt-hour (kWh). Since there are 8766 hours in a year (on the average, including leap years), 1 kilowatt-year (kWy) is equal to 8766 kWh. If you "consume" energy at the rate of 1 kWy per year, your average rate of energy conversion (or average *power*) for the year is 1 kW.

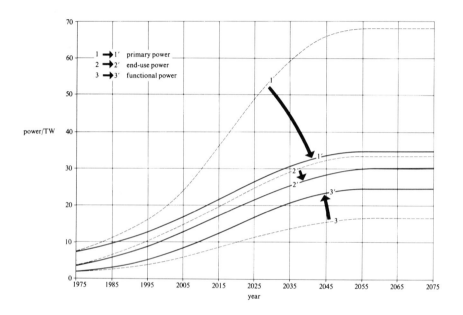

Fig. 4: Reducing the gaps between primary power and end-use power and between end-use power and functional power. The resulting gap between primary and functional power (curves 1' and 3') is much less than before (curves 1 and 3).

The curves are from a global energy scenario in which the total primary power grows to a "steady-state level of about 68 TW (1 TW = 1 terrawatt = 1 million kW). This was based on assumptions about future increases in per capita power in the DCs and the LDCs which now (fortunately!) look like being somewhat high. More recent projections[18] for global power in 2020 are between 19 TW and 25 TW, i.e. much closer to curve 1' than to curve 1.

Source: Open University Science Foundation Course Unit 320

to end-use and from end-use to functional. If these conversion efficiencies in the less developed countries (LDCs) are no better than they are in the developed countries (DCs)—and they are likely to be worse—then the per capita primary energy conversion rate is at least a rough indicator of relative energy poverty.

It is therefore pertinent to compare the levels and trends of per capita rates of primary energy conversion (primary power) in the DCs and the LDCs.

3.2 Primary energy conversion rates

The annual average rate of primary energy conversion in the LDCs rose from 435 W/capita in 1975, to about 644 W/capita in 1980 (i.e., by an average of 8 per cent per year). Between 1980 and 1987 it rose by an average of 2 per cent per year to 744 W/capita (Figure 5).

The trends since 1975 for the principal regions, show that the per capita power continues to rise slowly in Asia and in China, but has remained practically constant, or even decreased slightly in Central and South America and in Africa, which with only 500W per capita in 1987 was still in a state of extreme energy poverty.

The corresponding per capita power curves for the DCs are shown in Figure 6. If you compare these with Figure 5, it is obvious that the gap between the DCs and the LDCs is still very large, though it has reduced somewhat since 1974.

North America shows an appreciable decrease in per capita power from 1980 to 1983, followed by a slower increase. This trend is no doubt due to a combination of several factors: the impact of the 1979 rise in petroleum prices, some improvements in energy conversion efficiencies, and changes in the structure of industrial production in the direction of less energy-intensive industries. Essentially similar trends are shown by Western Europe and Japan, and consequently for the DCs as a whole.

Since the per capita power of the DCs has been about ten times that of the LDCs (11.4 in 1975, 7.8 in 1987), the world trend follows essentially that of the DCs, showing only a slight variation, from 1.86 kW/cap in 1975 to 2.12 kW/cap in 1987.

Does this mean that, world-wide, we have reached a "plateau" in per capita energy conversion and might even see a downturn over the next few decades? I think this inference would be overly-optimistic, unless there are some pretty important changes in energy policies (possibly stimulated by efforts to reduce global warming). The average per capita power in the LDCs is still a factor of two below what even the most optimistic scenario (which assumes major improvements in energy conver-

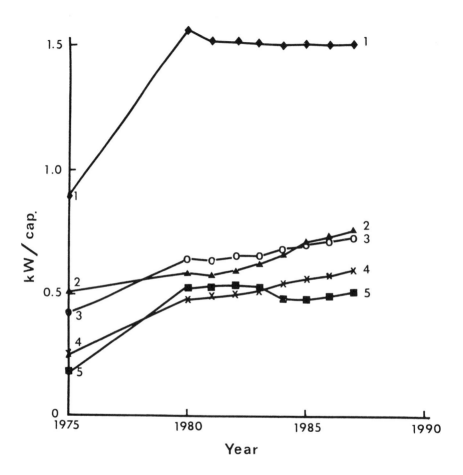

Fig. 5: Average annual rate of primary energy conversion in the LDCs, 1975 and 1980–87. [Source: United Nations Energy Yearbooks 1979–1987]

Key: 1   *Central and South America*
      2   *China*
      3   *ALL LDCs*
      4   *Asia, excluding China, Japan and West Asia (Middle East)*
      5   *Africa (excluding South Africa)*

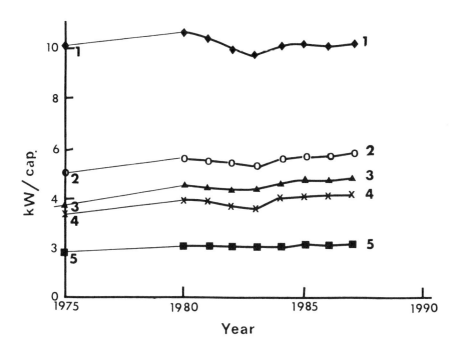

Fig. 6: Average annual rate of primary energy conversion in the DCs, 1975 and 1980–87. [Source: United Nations Energy Yearbooks 1979–87]

Key: 1   *North America*
     2   *ALL DCs*
     3   *Western Europe*
     4   *Japan*
     5   *WORLD*

Note: Oceania, South Africa, West Asia (the Middle East) and Eastern Europe are counted here as DCs, but the individual curves for these countries are omitted for the sake of clarity. West Asia and South Africa are marginal (and mixed) cases. The curve for Eastern Europe coincides quite closely with that for the average over all the DCs.

263

sion efficiencies in the LDCs) suggests will be required if the LDCs are to reach a standard of living comparable to that in Western Europe in the 1970s.[19] The LDCs, especially Africa, have still a very long way to go to escape from the trap of energy poverty.

We need to get some idea of whether the slower rates of growth of per capita *primary* power reflect slower economic growth, or whether they mask a continued increase in both per capita *functional* power and economic development. Some indications can be obtained from the standard index of economic development (at any rate in "classical" economics), namely the GDP, or Gross Domestic Product.

The Gross Domestic Product of a country may be defined as the money value of all the goods and services produced in that country, excluding net income from abroad. It is approximately equal to the sum of the wages, salaries and net profits received by the residents of the country.

3.3   Measuring economic development

The per capita GDP of a country should *not* be taken to mean the same thing as the "standard of living," or "quality of life," of its inhabitants. The standard of living of people clearly depends not only on the sum of wages, salaries and profits, but also on how these are distributed among the people. Furthermore, the GDP measures only the *money value* of goods and services produced and takes no account of the real, longer-term costs of production to nature and to society—the more resources consumed, the higher the GDP figures will be. Per capita GDP is still the generally accepted measure of national well-being, but it tells us nothing about what is growing at the expense of what, about who is gaining or losing, or about the stresses placed upon the environment—and hence the potential for future development—in the process.

With these reservations, GDP per capita is a fairly reliable, if crude, index for comparing industrially developed countries that have capitalist economies, but it is much less reliable for comparing capitalist with socialist countries or industrially developed with industrially underdeveloped countries. Some examples of per capita GDP are shown in Table 4:

Even if we ignore the exaggerated figures for the oil-rich countries, the contrasts are extreme enough: the highest are 100 to 140 times greater than the lowest. Notwithstanding all the limitations of the GDP as an index of development, it is evident that this immense gap will have to be greatly reduced; the problem will be to achieve this without greatly increasing the threat of global warming.

Considering only the contribution of primary energy conversion to greenhouse gas emission (i.e. setting aside for the moment the contributions of agriculture and deforestation), the critical question will be

Table 4   Selected examples of per capita GDP (1980)

	$		$		$
AFRICA	**761**	**ASIA**	**436**	**CENTRAL & SOUTH AMERICA**	**233**
Ethiopia	106	Nepal	139	Haiti	287
Mali	119	Bangladesh	170	Honduras	689
Nigeria	1095	Korea	1637	Venezuela	3941
Libya	3043	Malaysia	1788	Argentina	5454
N.AMERICA	**11723**			**W.EUROPE**	**9034**
Canada	10949			Portugal	2569
U.S.A.	11805			Greece	4163
JAPAN	**9068**			Sweden	14938
				Switzerland	16083
W.ASIA	**4006**			**OCEANIA**	**8495**
Yemen	463			Tonga	645
Turkey	1281			Fiji	1899
Kuwait	20967			N.Zealand	7192
Qatar	34796			Australia	10683

whether industrial development in the LDCs can be achieved with much lower *energy intensities* than those of the DCs during their development phase. Here, *energy intensity* means *the ratio of the rate of primary energy conversion to the GDP.*

As Figure 7 shows, the historical record suggests that the LDCs could, in principle, follow a less energy-intensive path of development. Whether this will happen in practice depends on what policies will be adopted, not only by the LDCs, but also (and perhaps primarily) by the DCs, and by the "development agencies," such as the World Bank, which are dominated by the richest of the DCs.

The energy intensity trend of each of the five industrialised countries was similar: increasing to a maximum in the early stages of industrialisation and then, because of improvements in energy efficiency and materials technology, decreasing. For the same reasons, the later it is reached,

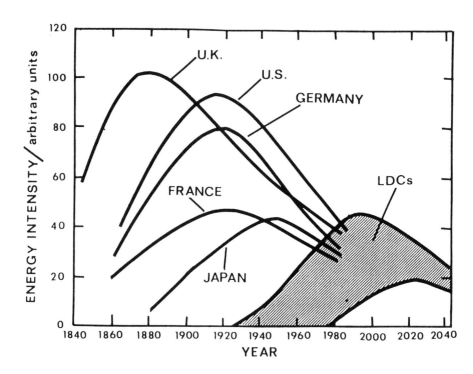

Fig. 7: Historical changes in energy intensity

The historical variation of energy intensity (the ratio of the rate of primary energy conversion to the GDP) is plotted, in arbitrary units, for five industrialised countries, and, speculatively, for the LDCs.
[after Reddy and Goldemberg, Scientific American, *September 1990]*

Table 5   Recent trends in energy intensity

REGION	Year	Primary power W/capita	GDP $/capita	Energy intensity W/$
AFRICA	1975	181	300	0.60
	1980	530	761	0.70
	1987	606	n/a	—
ASIA	1975	252	168	1.50
	1980	480	436	1.10
	1987	606	n/a	—
CENTRAL & S. AMERICA	1975	893	1004	0.89
	1980	1560	2330	0.67
	1987	N1515	n/a	—
N. AMERICA	1975	9992	6525	1.53
	1980	10700	11723	0.91
	1987	10210	n/1	—
W. EUROPE	1975	3812	4176	0.91
	1980	4500	9034	0.50
	1987	4840	n/a	—
JAPAN	1975	3327	4077	0.82
	1980	4000	9068	0.44
	1987	4080	n/a	—

[Sources: United Nations Statistical Yearbooks 1975–1985/86; United Nations Energy Yearbooks 1979, 1983 & 1987]

the lower is the maximum. *If* the LDCs avoid repeating the technological history of the DCs, they may achieve industrialisation at still lower energy intensities.

What have been the actual recent trends in energy intensity?

Table 5 shows the per capita primary power for 1975, 1980 and 1987, and the per capita GDP for 1975 and 1980 (the 1987 GDP figures are not yet available) for three LDC regions and for two DC regions plus Japan. It seems that Africa has still to reach its energy intensity maximum, whereas Asia and Central and South America are already past it, as are North America, Western Europe and Japan. It should be borne in mind, however, that averages over large regional groupings such as "Africa" or "Asia" conceal considerable variations between the individual countries.

Table 6   Primary energy from fossil fuels 1987
(Conventional Fuel Equivalent,/10^3TJ) [% of total]

REGION	TOTAL	Primary Electricity*	Traditional Fuels	Fossil Fuels
AFRICA	12 142 [100]	573 [4.7]	4 388 [36.1]	7 181 [59.2]
ASIA+	34 952 [100]	3 056 [8.7]	6 671 [19.1]	25 225 [72.2]
CHINA	N26 162 [100]	N1 200 [4.6]	1 853 [7.1]	23 109 [88.3]
CENTRAL & S. AMERICA	20 208 [100]	4 071 [20.1]	3 635 [18.0]	12 502 [61.9]
ALL LDCs	93 464 [100]	8 900 [9.5]	16 547 [17.7]	68 017 [72.8]
N. AMERICA	86 240 [100]	13 408 [15.5]	1 243 [1.5]	71 579 [83.0]
W.EUROPE	54 166 [100]	12 869 [23.8]	462 [0.8]	40 812 [75.4]
E.EUROPE	79 890 [100]	6 301 [7.9]	1 055 [1.3]	72 534 [90.8]
JAPAN	15 688 [100]	3 306 [21.1]	7 [−]	12 375 [78.9]
OCEANIA	4 185 [100]	433 [10.3]	157 [3.8]	3 595 [85.9]
ALL DCs	240 166 [100]	36 377 [15.1]	2 934. [1.2]	200 895 [83.6]
WORLD*	333 632 [100]	45 239 [13.6]	19 481 [5.8]	268 912 [80.6]
WORLD**	301 964 [100]	13 571** [4.5]	19 481 [6.5]	268 912 [89.0]

* **Primary electricity**—*(Defined as geothermal, hydro, nuclear and wind) is accounted for in the following manner:*
The primary electrical energy *is converted to conventional fuel equivalent—the quantity of fossil fuels required in a conventional thermal power plant (assuming a 30% plant efficiency) to generate the identical quantity that nuclear, geothermal, wind and hydro-electric plants produce during a given year—by dividing it by the factor 0.3.*

** *In this calculation, the actual primary electrical energy is* **not** *divided by 0.3.*

+ *"Asia" excludes China and Japan, but includes W. Asia (Middle East)*

Source: United Nations Energy Yearbooks, 1979, 1983, 1987.

3.4 Sources of primary energy

About three-quarters of the world's population live in the present LDCs. Because the population growth rates of the LDCs are still much higher than those of the DCs (see section 3.6 for further details), the proportion is likely to reach about nine-tenths by the middle of next century. Since per capita primary energy conversion in the LDCs is bound to increase, even if they are able to incorporate modern conversion efficiencies, it is important to see how much of that energy is likely to come from fossil fuel combustion and thus contribute to further global warming.

Primary energy "consumption" in 1987 (in units of "Conventional Fuel Equivalent") is shown in Table 6 for the principal LDCs and DCs regions, and for the world, together with the subdivision of the total primary energy between fossil fuels, traditional fuels (e.g., firewood), and "primary electricity" (from nuclear, hydro-electric, geothermal and wind sources).

The importance of minimizing primary energy intensity is immediately obvious from the figures in Table 6: in 1987, over 80 per cent of primary energy came from fossil fuels (nearly 90 per cent if "primary electricity" is not counted in "conventional fuel units"—see footnote). In China and Eastern Europe, the proportion is even higher. The dependence of certain countries upon *coal* is of particular concern, because coal emits 21 per cent more carbon per unit of energy produced than oil, and 74 per cent more than natural gas. In China, for instance, 83 per cent of the primary energy from fossil fuels came from coal (and 88 per cent of all primary energy came from fossil fuels). For India (whose population is likely to overtake that of China some time next century), the corresponding figures are 46 per cent and 66 per cent. Unless economic development in China and India is achieved through high efficiencies of energy conversion, and a substantial shift from fossil fuels to other sources of primary energy, efforts to abate carbon-dioxide emissions in other countries are liable to be nullified by developments in these two countries alone.

3.5 Energy and the developing countries

Speaking of the plight of the people in the LDCs, in their major study for the World Resources Institute's **End-Use Global Energy Project (1987)**, **"ENERGY FOR A SUSTAINABLE WORLD,"** Goldemberg, Johansson, Reddy and Williams write:

> It is their grave misfortune to have to industrialize after the era of cheap energy, upon which the industrial bases of the already industrialized countries were built.
>
> Per capita income in developing countries averages one

tenth that in the rich industrialized countries, per capita energy use less than one sixth. Average life expectancy is about 50 years, compared with more than 70 in the industrialized countries. One of every five persons in developing countries suffers from hunger or malnutrition. One of every two has little chance of becoming literate.

If the majority of the world's population that lives in wretched poverty is to achieve a decent standard of living, it will need affordable energy for increasing agricultural productivity and food distribution, delivering basic education and medical services, establishing adequate water-supply and sanitation facilities, and building and powering new job-creating industries. In addressing the world's energy future, therefore, one question stands above all others: will people in developing countries get the energy they need to sustain a higher standard of living, equal, say, to that enjoyed by Western Europeans today?[20]

To this, we must now add another, all-important question, both for the LDCs (which will be more vulnerable to the effects of global warming than the richer countries) and to the world as a whole: can this be done without increasing still further the rate of emission of greenhouse gases, especially CO_2?

The conclusion reached by Goldemberg and his colleagues, as a result of comprehensive and detailed study, is that "large improvements in living standards (in the LDCs) can be made with little increase in energy use *if* planners take advantage of cost-effective opportunities to use energy more efficiently."

Their feasibility study shows primary power in the LDCs rising to only 1.3 kW/capita by 2020, and primary power in the DCs *falling* to 3.2 kW/capita (compare Figures 6 and 7: in 1987 the corresponding figures were 744 W/capita for the LDCs and 5.8 kW/capita for the DCs. As a result, world primary power rises from 10.57 TW to only 11.2 TW, a global average of 1.61 kW/capita. This is achieved essentially by the deployment in both the DCs and the LDCs of *currently available* technologies for improving energy conversion efficiencies, with continued economic development in the DCs as well as accelerated development in the LDCs, raising the average standard of living to the level enjoyed by Western Europe in the 1970s. Their scenario envisages a slight increase only in primary energy from hydro-electricity and from other renewable sources, a moderate increase in nuclear power, a larger increase in energy from natural gas, but corresponding decreases in the contributions of coal and oil.

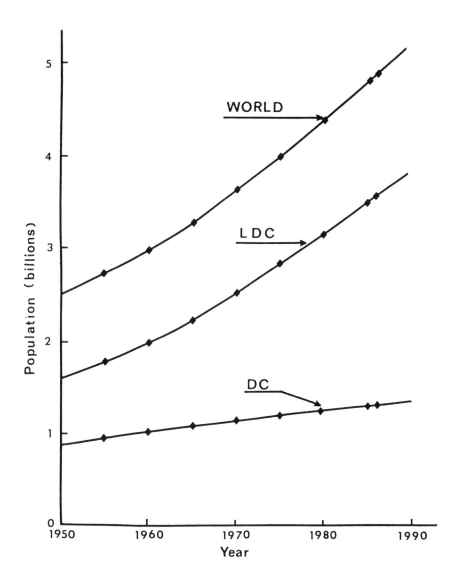

Fig. 8: Population growth 1950–1990
[Source: United Nations Statistical Yearbooks 1972–1985/86]

In the light of more recent studies on the relative cost effectiveness of nuclear power as compared with either energy economy measures or renewable energy sources (wind, photovoltaic, biomass conversion and others), it would be possible to achieve a greater reduction in fossil-fuel use (especially coal and oil) at the same time as phasing out nuclear energy altogether. (See section 4.3.)

3.6 The basic problem—population growth

By extrapolation from the latest available UN population statistics,[21] we can estimate the world's population in 1990 to be just over 5.3 billion, of which just under 1.4 billion are in the DCs and just over 3.9 billion in the LDCs. The population growth curves for the DCs, the LDCs and the world are shown in Figure 8.

The world population is evidently still growing steadily, at the rate of about 1.7 per cent per year. The current growth rate in the LDCs is just over 2 per cent, about the same as it was in the 1950s. It rose to a peak of 2.5 per cent in 1965 to 1970 before declining again to the present level. It is impossible to say from the data available over the past 40 years whether the LDCs' population growth rate has yet started to decline, or to predict when it might do so. The current growth rate in the DCs is about 0.8 per cent. It has been falling steadily since the fifties, when it was 1.36 per cent, and it will most probably reach zero by the year 2000, at which time the total population in the DCs will be between 1.4 and 1.5 billion. According to the United Nations Fund for Population Activities (UNFPA), in its report on "The State of the World Population," published in May 1990, the world population could be 8.5 billion by 2025 and is now unlikely to stabilise below 11 billion, towards the end of next century:

> Fast population growth in poor countries has begun to make
> permanent changes in the environment. During the 1990s
> these changes will reach critical levels. They include con-
> tinued urban growth, degradation of land and water resources,
> massive deforestation, and the build-up of greenhouse gases.[22]

In the period 1950 to 1985, carbon dioxide emissions rose by an average of 3.1 per cent per year. Over the same period, population grew by 1.9 per cent per year.

> Population growth thus accounts for almost two-thirds of the
> increase of carbon dioxide entering the atmosphere between
> 1950 and 1985.[23]

It has similarly been estimated that population growth was responsible for about two-thirds of deforestation (another major source of greenhouse gases) in developing countries. Clearly, irrigation, nitrogen fertilisation, rice cultivation and livestock (all sources of greenhouse gases, particularly methane and nitrous oxide), will also increase in line with population growth in the developing countries. Reducing population growth, especially in the countries with the highest rates of growth,* will be "a crucial part of any strategy of sustainable development."[24]

It has been estimated that the number of couples (in the developing countries) using contraceptives must be increased to 535 million by the year 2000 if population growth is to be kept within the current UN projections. This would mean increasing the expenditure on family planning by a factor of two or three, to about $9 billion a year. Large as this increase seems, it is equivalent to only three days of current world military expenditure.[25]

More than four years ago, in a special section of the Bulletin of the Atomic Scientists on World Population, Paul and Anne Ehrlich stated bluntly:

> Earth is overpopulated today by a very simple standard:
> humanity is able to support itself—often none too well, at
> that—only by consuming its capital. . . . with today's technol-
> ogy, humanity could not support anything like its current num-
> bers without continually using up its nonrenewable resource
> subsidy . . . (and) . . . while exploiting that capital subsidy,
> civilization is continually degrading the systems that supply its
> income.[26]

It is now clear that the most important of all the systems that supply humanity's "resource income" is a stable world climate. It is equally clear that we shall need *today's* technology, and tomorrow's (that of four years ago is not good enough) to support the population we are likely to have next century, if we are to have the slightest chance of avoiding a climatic catastrophe.

It is hard to conceive of a more forthright warning than that in the concluding section of the UNFPA report:

> We are not talking about the interests of distant descendants. It
> is our own children who will inherit a world twice the size of
> our own, who will farm one acre where we have three, and
> who will be denied the diversity of life we have enjoyed. The
> choice now must be to act decisively to slow population
> growth, attack poverty and protect the environment. The alter-
> native is to hand our children a poisoned chalice.[22]

* Annual rates of population growth in the LDCs in the 5-year period 1981 to 1985 were: Africa: 3.4%; Asia: 2.1%; Central & S. America: 2.1%; China: 1.2%.

These are likely to remain pious aims unless we are able to rid our-selves rather quickly of a set of outmoded notions. I agree with the Ehrlichs' view that " . . . the world can no longer afford to believe such myths as that economic growth can be infinite, contraception is immoral and more nuclear weapons will prevent nuclear war." We have recently made a little progress, perhaps, on the last one; let's hope we can make as much with the other two in the next few years.

4.   WHAT CAN BE DONE?

We are clearly confronted by a formidable set of problems: to improve the quality of life in the "developed" countries, especially for the poor, to promote rapid economic development in the less-developed countries, and to do so while drastically reducing the impact of population growth, agriculture and industry upon global warming. The severity of this last re-quirement becomes clear when we try to estimate the effects on global warming of various possible greenhouse gas abatement strategies.

4.1   Can global warming be halted?

In Chapter 4 of *GLOBAL WARMING—The Greenpeace Report,* clima-tologist Mick Kelly identifies "a set of reductions in greenhouse-gas emissions which could halt global warming, thereby providing a neces-sary bench-mark against which targets influenced by political expediency can be judged. On the basis of environmental need, a stable climate sub-ject only to natural variability must be the goal if the security of life on Earth is to be ensured."[27]

The computer models developed in the Climate Research Unit at the University of East Anglia were used to calculate the effects on "effective carbon dioxide concentration",* and hence on global warming up to the year 2050, of three successive strategies:

> First step scenario: the elimination of the production of CFCs
> and all related ozone-depleting chemicals by 1995, and the
> avoidance of substitutes that are greenhouse gases; a halt to de-
> forestation (more precisely, to net emissions of CO_2 from the
> biosphere) by the year 2000.
>
> Second step scenario: in addition to the measures of the first
> step: reduction of energy-related emissions of carbon to 80 per
> cent of the present-day value by the year 2005, and to 50 per

* The effective carbon dioxide concentration takes into account the contribution of all the major greenhouse gases, each individual contribution being specified in terms of the con-centration of carbon dioxide that would enhance the greenhouse effect to the same extent.

cent by the year 2030, after which emissions remain constant at this level.

Third step scenario: the elimination of CFCs by 1995 and the avoidance of greenhouse-gas substitutes (as in the first step scenario); a halt to deforestation by the year 2000, followed by extensive reforestation sufficient to offset the annual emissions of energy-related carbon by the year 2020; a reduction in carbon emissions from fossil-fuel combustion to 30 per cent of the present value by the year 2020; and a reduction in the annual rise in methane and nitrous oxide concentrations to 25 per cent of the present value by 2020 (which would mean holding methane emissions close to present-day levels and reducing nitrous oxide emissions due to human activities by more than a factor of two).

The second step scenario incorporates the proposals from the 1988 Toronto Conference, *The Changing Atmosphere: Implications for Global Security* on reducing carbon dioxide emissions.

The second step scenario was designed to stabilise the effective carbon dioxide concentration by the year 2030.

The realized global warmings by the year 2050 for each of the three scenarios, compared with a "business-as-usual" scenario,[28] are as follows:

Temperature rise by 2050 in °C above pre-industrial level

SCENARIO	Realized temperature rise	Equilibrium temperature rise*
Business-as-usual	2.6 ± 1.1	3.6 ± 1.8
Step 1	2.4 ± 1.0	3.2 ± 1.6
Step 2	2.1 ± 0.8	2.6 ± 1.3
Step 3	1.7 ± 0.8	2.0 ± 1.0

* In the business-as-usual, Step 1, and Step 2 scenarios, the equilibrium temperature will continue to rise during the second half of the twenty-first century, as the greenhouse effect is further enhanced. Only in the fourth scenario, the "stablising scenario" of Step 3, will the equilibrium temperature remain constant.

There is not space in this chapter to explore the implications of the deforestation/reforestation measures incorporated in Kelly's stabilising scenario, or the implications for agriculture of the assumed limitations on the emissions of methane and nitrous oxide.

The feasibility of these measures would depend above all on the effectiveness of population control measures. As for cutting carbon emissions from fossil fuels to 30 per cent of the present value by 2020, this would require a much more drastic reduction of fossil-fuel combustion than that envisaged even in the scenario of Goldemberg et al., which envisaged a reduction in coal use by about 20 per cent, but merely no increase in fossil fuel combustion as a whole.[20]

Kelly says in the concluding section of his chapter: "This particular strategy is not intended as a prescription for dealing with global warming. It serves to illustrate what is physically possible if social, economic and political obstacles are removed."

What energy strategies could achieve such a massive displacement of fossil fuels, and are these likely to be economically and politically practicable?

4.2 Implications for energy strategies

The contributions of coal, oil and gas to carbon emissions in 1987 were: coal 2.178 Gt, oil 1.000 Gt, natural gas 0.418 Gt, making a total from fossil fuels of 3.596 Gt. A 70 per cent reduction therefore means a total cut of 2.517 Gt of carbon emissions from fossil fuels. One scenario that could achieve this cut would be:

Cut out combustion of coal completely:	- 2.178 Gt
Reduce combustion of oil by 60 per cent:	- 0.600 Gt
Increase combustion of gas by 62 per cent:	+ 0.261 Gt

Fuel economies of at least 60 per cent are well within the range of presently available technologies in the automobile industry.[29]

The increased use of natural gas could, for instance, correspond to displacement of electricity by gas for heating buildings, together with some use of gas to replace coal in electricity generation.

The big question is where would the energy replacing that from coal combustion in 1987 come from? In fact, coal provided about 24 per cent of total primary energy. Could this energy (and any additional amounts that might otherwise come from the contribution of coal to any *increased* primary energy requirement in the future) be obtained from some alternative source, or could it be found by improving energy conversion efficiencies, so that functional energy is held constant (or increased as required for economic development) while primary energy is reduced by the amount contributed by coal? In particular, could nuclear power provide the necessary replacement for coal?

4.3   Is nuclear power the answer?

The recent emergence of the greenhouse threat has led to a spate of proposals to "get back on track with nuclear energy,"[30] and "restore the nuclear option."[31] The former Environment Minister for the United Kingdom* pronounced in 1988: "If we want to arrest the greenhouse effect we should concentrate on a massive increase in nuclear generating capacity."[32] In fact, a detailed study published in the same year by Keepin and Kats[30] showed that, even on a set of assumptions that are extremely favourable to nuclear power, to replace the coal-fired component of electricity power production by nuclear power would be impossibly expensive and would not succeed in stopping the growth of greenhouse gas emissions (because of the continued contributions of oil and gas).

Taking a typical "middle-of-the-road" scenario for global primary energy growth,[33] in which primary energy demand reaches 21.3 TW by the year 2025, of which 9.4 TW are supplied by coal, 4.0 TW by oil, 3.6 TW by gas, 2.9 TW by hydro-electric power and 0.7 TW each by nuclear and renewable energy, the analysis showed that to replace the coal by nuclear power would require the construction of more than *five thousand* large nuclear power plants between now and the year 2025—nearly half of which would be located in the Third World. This would mean building, on average, a new 1 GW nuclear plant every two and a half days from now until 2025, at an average *annual* cost of $144 billion, of which the developing countries' share would be $64 billion. Total electricity generation cost would average $525 billion a year, of which $170 billion would be incurred in the LDCs. By 2025, the total installed nuclear capacity would reach 5200 GW, an 18-fold increase over today's capacity. Of this, 2330 GW would be in the Third World, which would mean a 155-fold increase over today's capacity of 15GW. Such a scenario is manifestly absurd. Yet even with this colossal—and impossible—investment, global carbon dioxide emissions would still continue to grow.

In fact, there is not the slightest prospect of global nuclear power growing much above today's level; indeed it is more than likely that it will have ceased growing at all by the end of the century, *even in the absence of another Chernobyl-type accident*. The main reason for the imminent demise of the global nuclear power enterprise is that it is simply not commercially viable. For this reason, above all, there has not been a single order for a nuclear plant in the USA since 1978, while 108 orders for nu-

---

* Mr. Nicholas Ridley, whose propensity for blurting out in public the nonsense he appears to believe in private, subsequently cost him his Ministerial post. It is one thing to burble about nuclear power, it would seem, but quite another to hold forth about "the German character"!

clear plants, including all orders placed since 1973 had, by 1988, been cancelled.[34] Since 1974, the projections of the IAEA (International Atomic Energy Agency) for nuclear capacity installed world wide by the year 2000 have been repeatedly revised downwards—and by 1986 they were nearly 90 per cent lower than in 1974.[35]

Perhaps the most comic recent confirmation of the realities of nuclear power when judged in the market place was the privatization fiasco in Britain. The present British government is an even more ardent supporter of nuclear power (and nuclear weapons) than its predecessors. It is also deeply committed to privatization of practically everything that was once in the public domain. It tried to sell off the nationalized electric power utilities to private investors, including the nuclear power plants (which comprised 11 per cent of total installed electric generating capacity). But nuclear power proved unacceptable to the investors, and had to be withdrawn from the privatization package. The government will now require the (private) utilities to purchase at least 20 per cent of their electricity from non-fossil (effectively nuclear) sources. To subsidise the high cost of nuclear power, a tax is to be levied on fossil-fuel power, and the government has declared that it does not expect to assist in the funding of any new nuclear plant.[36]

Though Edward Teller (unsurprisingly) assures us that "Nuclear power is safe, non-polluting. . . [and] the question of waste is no problem at all,"[37] the fact remains that, with nearly 400 nuclear plants in operation around the world, *there is still not a single long-term waste disposal programme in place.*[38] More than 700 million people live within 160 kilometres of a nuclear plant.[39] The question is not *whether* there will be another nuclear accident at one of these plants (which could easíly be much worse than Chernobyl), but only *where and when*—and one recent study concluded that there is a 70 per cent chance of another nuclear accident within less than a decade.[40] The number of people who will eventually die of cancer as a result of Chernobyl is still undetermined, but it will certainly be many tens of thousands.[41]

There is growing concern about previously unsuspected effects of exposure to low-level radiation, not only on people working in the nuclear industry but also on their children.[42]

Finally, there is the problem of proliferation of nuclear weapons. It was already obvious ten years ago that "we cannot have nuclear power without proliferation, because safeguards cannot succeed either in principle or in practice."[43]

The IAEA's 1986 "forecast" for nuclear power in the year 2000 was about 500 GW. The plutonium production of 500 1GW light-water reactors is about 125 tonnes per year. IAEA "safeguards" can account, at best, for 99 per cent, leaving 1250 kg of plutonium unaccounted for—

enough to make 125 bombs a year. Typical "middle-of-the-road" energy scenarios envisage about ten times the installed nuclear capacity that even the IAEA forecasts.

Nevertheless, the supposed advantages or even "inevitability" of nuclear power have led many to continue their efforts to strengthen the Non-Proliferation Treaty. Now that a whole series of studies have demonstrated that nuclear power is uneconomic, even in the rich industrialised countries, and that it has proved to be an unmitigated disaster in practically all the Third World countries upon which it has been inflicted, it is becoming clearer that the problem of proliferation will before long have solved itself, disappearing into past history along with nuclear power. Unfortunately, the industry's radioactive garbage will outlast this unfortunate episode in human history for quite some time.

If nuclear power has no part to play in the reduction and ultimate elimination of fossil fuel combustion, does the world, especially the Third World, confront a choice between energy poverty and climatic catastrophe?

4.4   Energy efficiency and renewable energy sources

Fortunately, there is an alternative. The most effective, and the most immediately available means of displacing fossil fuels is through the application throughout the energy system of efficient energy conversion technologies. Several recent studies have demonstrated that this solution is not only technically possible but applicable in many circumstances *at a negative* cost. In the United States, for instance, it has been shown that displacing coal-fired power plants by nuclear plants would cost *seven times* as much as displacing them by energy efficiency technologies. Detailed case studies for Brazil, India and Sweden have confirmed that *functional* energy needs can be met, in both the DCs and the LDCs, by the application of *currently available* efficiency technologies.

The case of Sweden is particularly interesting, because it has been suggested that even if the public were to demand a phase-out of nuclear power in the near to intermediate term, there would be no practical way to achieve it in countries that have substantial nuclear power programmes. An example is Sweden, where 50 per cent of the electricity comes from nuclear power, and where a referendum requires it to be phased out by 2010. An analysis of the Swedish electricity sector has shown that "not only is a nuclear phase-out possible in Sweden, but it can be achieved with a 50 per cent *increase* in electrical *services*."[44] At the same time, the GDP increases by 54 per cent, CO_2 emissions are *reduced* by 34 per cent, the cost of electrical services is cut by $1 billion a year, and there is no increase in hydro-power (as required for environmental reasons).

This is achieved by a combination of end-use efficiency, fuel-switching to gas and biofuel and "environmental dispatch" (operating most the power plants that emit the least carbon).[45]

Amory Lovins says in his chapter on *The Role of Energy Efficiency* in *GLOBAL WARMING:*

> This finding implies that practically any other country should
> be able to do even better, because Sweden has a severe
> climate, a heavily industrialised economy and the world's
> highest aggregate energy efficiency to begin with.[46]

For Canada, with only about 15 per cent of its electricity coming from nuclear power, and with a somewhat lower aggregate energy efficiency than Sweden, it should be relatively easy to follow the Swedish example.

There is a widespread belief that renewable energy cannot provide a significant share of primary energy in the foreseeable future. However, this view is based on data and experience that are now out of date. Renewable energy technologies have made striking progress over the past several years (in spite of being starved of government funding for research and development, the lion's share of which still goes to nuclear energy). *Wind power* has matured rapidly, and the cost of electricity generated from wind in the United States has dropped from 25 cents/kWh in 1980 to 7 to 9 cents/kWh in the late eighties (compared with 13.5 cents/kWh for nuclear energy). Electricity generated from *biomass* currently costs about 5 cents/kWh, and the commercialisation of biomass cogeneration technology is expected to generate electricity from sugar wastes for 3.3 cents/kWh within five years.[47]

Solar photovoltaic (PV) technology (which produces electricity from sunlight with no moving parts and no fuel), has also been greatly developed in recent years. The cost of PV electricity has gone down from $1.50/kWh in 1980 to 20–40 cents/kWh today, and is expected to fall to 4 cents/kWh within a few decades.[48]

Yet other renewable energy technologies—such as ocean thermal energy conversion (OTEC) and the catalytic dissociation of water to produce hydrogen—are at earlier stages of research and development and may make significant contributions to primary energy in the early decades of next century.

4.5   *The* Greenpeace *response to the global warming threat*

By way of a summary of the options that seem to be open to us, and to provide a focus for political activity, I shall now summarise the *Greenpeace* response to the greenhouse threat. (See *GLOBAL WARMING*, Chapter 19 for a fuller statement).

1. "The prospects of future environmental security being compromised by global warming are now so real as to make the adoption of a precautionary response imperative—in other words, policy should focus on buying insurance, and policymakers should be clearly aware that waiting in perpetuity for better scientific data entails a real risk of waiting until it is too late."

2. "The main routes to surviving the greenhouse threat are energy efficiency, renewable forms of energy production, an immediate and total ban on the production of all CFCs and related gases, less greenhouse-intensive agriculture, stopping deforestation, and reforestation."

3. "The world community should strive to achieve a "low-energy" future of the kind spelt out by the End-Use Global Energy Project, with a world energy consumption of not much more than around 12 TW by 2025, but spread through the world more equitably than the 10 TW consumed today, so that developing countries can enjoy standards of living akin to those enjoyed in the industrialised countries."

4. "This pattern of consumption should be achieved by massive investment in energy efficiency in the industrialised countries, and large-scale transfer of up-to-date energy-efficient and non-CFC-dependent technologies from the industrialised countries to the developing countries, to enable them to "leap-frog" the kind of energy-intensive, polluting, routes which the developed countries took during industrialisation."

5. "Given suitable investment of funding and resources, the goal should be for the world's entire energy requirement to be produced by renewable forms of energy as soon as possible in the next century."

6. "Expansion of the nuclear power industry, or replacement of existing nuclear power stations when they come to the ends of their operating lifetimes, would involve diverting funds from cost-effective energy solutions to the greenhouse crisis (energy efficiency and most forms of renewable energy production), and therefore, especially when viewed in concert with safety, waste disposal, decommissioning, and nuclear-weapons proliferation problems—should have no role to play in the international policy response."

7. "The detailed mix of policy prescriptions, and their quantification, should be subject to scientific research results during the 1990s, but essential first steps are as follows:
• implementation of immediate cuts in carbon dioxide emissions and the drawing-up of integrated strategies aimed at the phase-out of fossil fuels as early as possible next century;

• no effort to be spared to arrest deforestation and halt the production or use of CFCs, and related compounds such as HFCs.''

8. "The large sums needed to fund these and other anti-greenhouse strategies, plus the expanded scientific research effort which is essential in the 1990s to narrow down the remaining scientific uncertainties, can come from diverting the greater part of the $1000 billion spent on armaments annually, as befits the changing concepts of global security which the late 1980s have heralded.''

5. CONCLUSIONS

There is an urgent need to analyse some of the broader—and more fundamental—questions that arise out of any study of the present, unprecedented human predicament. These include:

> The importance of *political,* as well as economic and technological *decentralisation.* There is no doubt that decentralisation of electricity power generation and the disaggregation of large conurbations will characterise future development. I believe that the concomitant must be a similar decentralisation and disaggregaton of political and economic power.

> Closely related to decentralisation, as opposed to centralism, whether it be "capitalist" or "socialist," is the question of *real* (as distinct from "formal") democracy, by which I mean the actual empowerment of people in the business of deciding their own futures (which should not be confused with putting crosses against alternative party-political options on ballot papers).

> A redefinition of conceptions of socialism, in which both the ownership *and the control* of the means of production and distribution belong *in reality,* not just in constitutional make-believe, to an empowered and informed people.

> A reassessment of concepts of "nation" and "national independence" in a world in which "nationality" has become increasingly irrelevant and national *interdependence* vital to our survival in this global village.

Even a cursory discussion of these questions would require several chapters or even several books—but the purely technological and economic aspects of the global warming problem will not be sufficient to solve it, unless these broader aspects are addressed at the same time.

There is another conclusion that emerges from any serious reflection about the problems of global warming and economic development. It is that the necessary policy decisions are not going to be taken, or implemented, unless due attention is paid *now* to the crucial importance of **education.** The policy-makers themselves, in all countries and at all levels, evidently need education about the realities of our global predicament and about what measures are likely to be cost-effective and practicable. But, educated or not, what they **do** about it will depend on the political pressure of their people. The creation of an informed, educated opinion must therefore be the major aim. It will be important, above all, to reach the young people. It is they who will have to live with the mess we have already made and who will need to know how to clean it up—and how to avoid making it even worse.

It is imperative that the job of educating the world community about global warming and its implications be tackled with methods, media and technologies that belong to the turn of *this* century, not the last. We have to recognise the pathetic inadequacy of archaic means such as books (including this book!), magazines, conferences and seminars. We need to reach people all over the world in their *hundreds of millions.* We have to take education to them, where they are, not expect them to come and fetch it. We must employ modern methods of education *at a distance.*

Fortunately, these methods have been greatly developed over the past few decades, notably by the pioneering work of the British Open University. There exists now an international network of distance education institutions in the framework of the ICDE (the International Council for Distance Education) within which there is a large body of expertise from all parts of the world. I think the ICDE should immediately be invited by the United Nations Environment Programme to assist it in this urgent and crucial undertaking.

Can we yet avert a climatic catastrophe? Perhaps—if we combine the campaign for security in the military sense with the campaign for *environmental security,* and intensify both. But I fear that it will take time for the pressure of public opinion to become decisive at the political decision-making level, and that progress at that level will consequently be both slow and limited, falling far short of what is needed. Possibly there will be climatic excesses in the 1990s even more striking than those that aroused public consciousness of global warming in the late 1980s. Perhaps these events (droughts, storms, excessive temperature extremes) will have a shock effect on public opinion, and this, together with further reduction of the remaining scientific uncertainties, will force governments to start taking effective action. But by then, the unavoidable global temperature rise will be even greater and a larger proportion of human resources will have to be diverted from prevention to protection.

References

1. *Proceedings of the World Conference on the Changing Atmosphere: Implications for Global Security,* 27–30 June 1988 (World Meteorological Organization, no. 710, 1989)

2. The United Nations World Commission on Environment and Development: *Our Common Future* (the Brundtland Report)

3. *GLOBAL WARMING—The* Greenpeace *Report,* Oxford University Press, 1990 [ISBN 0-19-286229-0], Chapter 18

4. Towards a Sustainable World, *Scientific American,* September 1989, pp. 114–120B; see also: Toward a new economic policy, *Bulletin of the Atomic Scientists,* April 1986, pp. 42–44

5. Intergovernmental Panel on Climate Change (IPCC), Report from Working Group 1: Policymakers' Summary of the Scientific Assessment of Climate Change (June 1990)

6. Ref. 3, p. 475

7. *The Greenhouse Effect: Formulating a Convention,* William A. Nitze, Royal Institute of International Affairs, London, September 1990, [ISBN 0-905031-33-4]

8. *The Greenhouse Effect: Negotiating Targets,* Michael Grubb, Royal Institute of International Affairs, London, November 1989, [ISBN 0-905031-30-X]

9. Reference cited by J. Leggett in *GLOBAL WARMING* (Ref. 3): *Biota and Palaeotemperatures,* a collection of papers in the *Journal of the Geological Society of London* (1989), vol. 146, pp. 145–86

10. From the IPCC WG1 Report, Policymakers' Summary, p. 8

11. *GLOBAL WARMING* (Ref. 3), Chapter 5, p. 1313

12. ibid, p. 478

13 ibid, p. 217

14 ibid, p. 206

15 *Energy for a Sustainable World,* Goldemberg, Johansson, Reddy & Williams, World Resources Institute, September 1987 [ISBN 0880-2582]; see also: *Scientific American,* September 1990; pp. 29–36, 39–45

16. United Nations Energy Yearbook, 1987, Table 32, p. 344

17. *Science and the Planet Earth: problems of survival,* in *Science: A Foundation Course,* The Open University, 1979 [ISBN 0-355-80871-5]

18. *Energy in a Finite World—A Global Systems Analysis,* International Institute for Applied Systems Analysis (IIASA), 1981; World Energy Conference—*Energy 2000–2020: World Prospects and Regional Stresses,* 1983, cited in Ref. 15, p. 15

19. see Goldemberg *et al,* Ref. 15

20. Ref. 15, p. 19

21. United Nations Statistical Yearbooks, 1972–1985/86

22. United Nations Fund for Populations Activities: *The State of the World Population,* May 15 1990

23. *New Scientist,* May 19 1990, p. 28

24. UNFPA (Ref. 22), as reported in *The Financial Times,* London, May 15 1990

25. Norman Myers in *The Environment Guardian,* February 23 1990; see also *The Times,* May 17 1990 (on the UNFPA Report).

26. Paul & Anne Ehrlich, *Bulletin of the Atomic Scientists, April 1986*

27. Ref. 3, Chapter 4

28. *Policy Options for Stabilizing Global Climate* (Environmental Protection agency, Washington, DC, 1988), cited in Ref. 3, Chapter 4

29. See, for example, *Scientific American,* September 1990: pp. 55–61 and Ref. 3, Chapter 12

30. Greenhouse Warming: Comparative analysis of nuclear and energy efficiency abate-

ment strategies, Keepin & Kats, *Energy Policy,* December 1988, pp. 538–561, and Ref. 16 therein.

31.   ibid, Ref. 15 therein

32.   Quoted in Ref. 3, p. 296

33.   Cited in Ref. 30, p. 543

34.   "Nuclear power's burdened future," C. Flavin, *Bulletin of the Atomic Scientists* July/August 1987, pp. 26–31

35.   The IAEA's 1986 estimate was 89 per cent below their 1974 estimate—but that was *before* Chernobyl. . . See Ref. 24, p. 26

36.   *Financial Times,* January 29 1990

37.   E. Teller, address to the American Association of Petroleum Geologists, quoted in the *San Francisco Chronicle,* June 7 1990

38.   *Managing the Nation's Commercial High-Level Radioactive Waste* (Office of Technological Assessment, Washington, DC, 1985), cited in Chapter 13 of Ref. 3

39.   C. Flavin, "Reassessing Nuclear Power," in *State of the World 1987,* W. W. Norton, New York, 1987

40.   S. Islam and K. Lindgren, *"How Many Reactor Accidents Will There Be?",* Nature August 21 1986

41.   F. von Hippel & T. B. Cochran, *Bulletin of the Atomic Scientists,* August/September 1986

42.   M. J. Gardner *et al, British Medical Journal,* February 17 1990

43.   Amory B. Lovins, L. Hunter Lovins & Leonard Ross, *Foreign Affairs,* Summer 1980

44.   Ref. 3, p. 311

45.   ibid, Chapter 14

46.   ibid, p. 211

47.   J. Ogden, R. H. Williams & M. Fulmer, *Cogeneration Applications of Biomass Gasifier/Gas Turbine Technologies in the Cane Sugar Industries,* Center for Energy and Environmental Studies, Princeton University, 1990

48.   N. Rader et al, "Power Surge: The Status and Near-Term Potential of Renewable Energy Technologies," *Public Citizen,* Washington DC, May 1989; cited in Ref. 3, Chapter 13; see also J. Ogden & R. H. Williams, "Solar Hydrogen: Moving Beyond Fossil Fuels," World Resources Institute, Washington DC, October 1989

Professor Michael M'Gonigle

CHAPTER 16
Recovering the Root: Militarism and the Ecological Society

PROFESSOR MICHAEL M'GONIGLE AND
DR. SUZANNE ROSE

Recovering the root
Means just this:
The dynamics of peace—
Being recalled to our common fate
In the kinship of all creation.

Tao Te Ching[1]

As we undertake our last revision, we are 10 hours from midnight, January 15, 1991. An unnecessary and incomprehensively dangerous war is about to break out in the Middle East. With people across Canada and around the world, we pray for peace and survival.

This is the next to last chapter of Tom Perry's book. We had planned in this chapter to take what we thought was the larger view—the decline of the Cold War (which itself now also seems in danger of reversal), the

Michael M'Gonigle is a lawyer, political economist and long-time environmental activist. Currently Associate Professor in the Natural Resources Management Program at Simon Fraser University, in British Columbia, he is also Chairperson of Greenpeace Canada. He is a graduate of the Universities of British Columbia and Toronto, the London School of Economics, and Yale University. Dr. M'Gonigle has written extensively in the fields of international and environmental law, political theory and economics, as well as in specific areas of renewable resources, especially forestry and wilderness. His 1979 study of maritime pollution (co-written with Mark Zacher) was awarded the American Soci-

287

Dr. Suzanne Rose

rising concern for ecological survival and, above all, the need to move from wasteful military competition to genuine "whole earth" security. We hope that this larger view will still hold in the months and years ahead. It is most assuredly a correct alternative. But whether it remains a permissible possibility in the face of a manufactured crisis, a devastating war and a resurgent social militarism, is now an open question.

INTRODUCTION
We live at a time when our ability to create mass weapons of war has collided with an urgent need to create a new planetary peace. Everywhere today the buzzword is "sustainable development." Worldwide, the recognition grows that action to protect the earth's environment is needed now if we are to survive very far into the next millennium. It is often remarked that the next 10 years is the "turnaround decade." To achieve a

ety of International Law's Certificate of Merit for its "pre-eminent contribution to creative scholarship."

As an environmentalist, Dr. M'Gonigle represented Greenpeace at the International Whaling Commission from 1976 until 1982. He is a co-founder of Greenpeace International in 1979, and was an attorney at the Center for Law and Social Policy in Washington, D.C. until his return to British Columbia in 1982. In recent years he has been active on wilderness issues in British Columbia, and is co-author (with Wendy Wickwire) of the award-winning Stein: The Way of the River (1988). As a Greenpeace International legal advisor, he is presently active in the pursuit of a global treaty to prevent land-based pollution of the world's oceans. He is presently working on a new book, Ecodevelopment—The Quest for Territoriale. He is married and has two sons.

Born and raised in British Columbia, Suzanne Rose obtained her Ph.D. in Linguistics in 1981, specializing in the Nuuchahnulh (Nootka) language. She then set up a language curriculum for the community-run Ha-Ho Payuk School in Port Alberni, B.C. Concurrently, she returned to university, completing the language curriculum and her B.Sc. in Physical Therapy in 1987. Suzanne spent 1987–1988 in Khartoum, Sudan, setting up and teaching in a community-based rehabilitation training program for displaced women.

Since 1981, Suzanne has helped organize events and produce information for Save Our Seas/Peace Flotilla, Greater Victoria Disarmament Group, Committee for Defence of Human Rights in Peru, and Amnesty International. She has also campaigned against uranium mining and military trade shows. She now works for Greenpeace as a Disarmament Campaigner.

289

new global balance, the United Nations World Commission[2] has called on all nations to address the needs of the environment and those of social equity together. Approximately U.S. $1 trillion is spent globally every year on the military—an amount that exceeds the entire income of the poorest half of humanity, and dwarfs into insignificance any international environmental expenditures. From such a misallocation of resources, the pressing question arises: Is modern militarism compatible with a living planet?

Any serious attempt at sustainable development demands a major re-allocation of resources away from wasteful militarism. Without it, in fact, the prospects for planetary survival are grim. Yet the resistance to change is formidable. Everywhere today massive quantities of natural and cultural resources, and economic capital, are still being thrown at the pursuit of an outmoded concept of military "security." The once-impossible happens, and East Germany joins West; but nuclear testing continues in Novaya Zemlya in the Soviet Arctic, in the deserts of Nevada, and on the French Pacific atoll of Mururoa. The Cold War has seemed intent on dying, and so new challenges like Iraq and even the cocaine trade have conveniently presented themselves—indeed, have been manufactured—as justifications for the continued dominance of the military machine.

In this chapter, we propose to examine briefly the costs of the military to our ultimate security—security provided by a sustainable planet. Militarism inflicts massive costs—on the environment, on the economy through its enormous misallocation of financial resources, and on society through its erosion of the diverse and open institutions needed for a non-aggressive international order. In this paper, we will examine these impacts, especially as they appear in Canada, and what must be done to change our course.

Conversion—from military waste to environmental and social investment—is a critical strategy in the years ahead. But one must also ask: conversion to what? This paper does not espouse simply that the savings from cancelling a nuclear submarine should be redirected into reforestation or cleaning up toxic wastes. Certainly such environmental programs could be more easily financed with the resources now being misallocated into military hardware. But there is a larger challenge ahead, the ecological challenge—to overturn the inherited image of economic expansion, international competition, and global war, with which we have all grown up, and replace it with a more "sustainable" social system. Attaining environmental health and social justice is not something which the military machine can promise. In fact, however, if we are ever to "recover the root," we must treat the cause and not only the symptoms of our military compulsion. How, it must be asked, can we ever make peace between nations without also making peace in our relations with each other and with nature? This is the message of the Tao—that the movement against pre-paring for war must now become nothing less than the movement for building an ecological society.

MILITARISM'S IMPOVERISHED FUTURE
Impacts on Nature

The use of military force to settle disputes and to defend the dominance of one group over another has occurred throughout history. In the West, such force has been used at great cost to land and life. Herodotus mourned the deforestation of the Ionian hillsides to build ships for the pursuit of Greece's overseas glory. Rome rendered the bread basket of North Africa a desert to feed its huge armies of occupation, a desert still growing today. The troops of Europe fanned out across the globe defor-esting the ancient ecosystems and looting ancient cultures to feed a swell-ing industrial civilization.[3]

From countless tribal wars in Africa, to the slaughter of native Indians throughout the Americas, the effects of Western military expansionism have been social as well as environmental. But the legacy of history pales in comparison with the reality of the present. From conventional arms to nuclear missiles, the technologies of today consume unequalled social re-sources and wreak unparalleled destruction on the environment, in peace as well as in war.

With its military budget of over $12 billion annually (8.6 per cent of the nation's federal budget),[4] Canada plays its part in this destruction, and exports it worldwide as well. The impacts of our militarism take many forms—from conventional arms to our lead role in the global nuclear cycle.

As a full-fledged member of both NATO and NORAD, Canada partici-pates in a range of military activities. Even at the level of conventional weapons, the impacts on the environment and its inhabitants are great. Take, for example, the impact of the high-speed low-level test flights. Flying only 250 to 500 feet above the ground at speeds of over 600 miles per hour, the Federal Department of National Defence (DND) has estab-lished a flight path in Labrador and Quebec covering 100,000 square kilo-metres of the traditional territory of the native residents, the Innu.[5]

These flights are extremely disruptive. Adjacent to the Goose Bay base, in the area of Labrador/Quebec called Nitassinan by its Innu in-habitants (meaning "our land"), the residents report ear-shattering noise levels (120–130 decibels), disruption of social calm (sleep disturbances, raised anxiety levels and so on), and major impacts on the traditional life-styles. The Innu report that wildlife suffer disruption of feeding, repro-duction, birthing, young-rearing and migration. They report non-herding caribou, increased fish death, and decreased birth rates. Scientists have confirmed many of these observations. The jets release toxic fuel onto lakes and feeding grounds, and spread toxic fumes over a wide range.[6]

These flights occur over traditional territories, where the natives are attempting to maintain their cultural ways through a direct contact with the nature which sustains them. The Innu have never consented to these activities and have, in fact, actively resisted the militarization of their lands since 1977. As Judge Iloliorte ruled in the court challenge concerning the activities here, the Innu "believe their ancestors predate any Canadian claims to ancestry on this land. . . [N]one of their people ever gave away rights to the land in Canada. . . ."[7]

Instead of openly assessing the impacts of this activity, the Federal Government pressed ahead with plans to expand the NATO base at Goose Bay without public review—plans which would have been the largest military expansion since the installation of the Distant Early Warning system (DEWLine) in the 1950s. As Innu Chief Ashini said of the plans, "Nitassinan will be turned into a war zone, and our nation will be utterly destroyed." Despite worldwide public opposition, these plans were only terminated thanks to the Cold War thaw, and the scaling back of NATO needs.

Meanwhile, DND is still seeking to obtain two additional paths, one sweeping from the Northwest Territories down through the Prairies, and another extending over a 1,400 kilometre land corridor in northern British Columbia.[8] This low-level flight planning is moving forward without the support of the affected residents and without public participation in environmental review.

The impact of Canada's role in conventional arms extends well beyond our borders. Although a seemingly insignificant player in the shadow world of the international arms bazaar, Canada, in fact, exports more than $3 billion in military hardware annually, 80 per cent of all military production sales in Canada.[9] The scale of activity is significant when one considers the uses to which this technology is often put in other countries. Canada sells to the United States, exports which jumped dramatically during the Vietnam War, but also to countries which direct official violence against their own citizens, countries such as Chile, Indonesia, Peru, Philippines, Sudan and Saudi Arabia.

At the time of writing, reports of the effects of Canada's direct involvement in the Gulf are not yet in. But indirectly, Canada's contribution through other countries is significant. In just one example, Jane McAlevey has described the effects of the brief Panama invasion. Due to the bombing of Panama City in December 1989, 30,000 people fled into surrounding areas. As a result, between January and June 1990, they disrupted about 175,000 acres of protected park forests and watersheds.[10] Canadian firms (such as CAE Electronics, Heroux Inc., McDonnell Douglas, and Canadian Marconi) made landing gear, cockpit displays and radar systems for the U.S. military helicopters and aircraft used in that invasion.[11]

By facilitating war in these regions, Canada bears some of the responsibility for the often horrendous consequences which follow. In Sudan, to take another example, a civil war brought on by a repressive regime has again disrupted the ability of age-old tribal cultures to survive on the land, and caused 1.5 million people to converge about the capital, Khartoum, deforesting the local landscape to acquire fuelwood, a landscape already subject to sandstorms, diminishing topsoil, and virtually no rainfall.

In other countries, these imported military supplies have helped strong-arm governments defend the interests of multinational corporations, which are extracting resources over the resistance of local populations. For example, the Federal Government permitted General Motors to sell its Light Armoured Vehicle to the Indonesian government.[12] Advertised by GM as an offensive weapon, prized for its mobility and firepower, the Canadian government permitted its export as a potential "search and rescue" vehicle. Yet Indonesia is the country which has been waging a war in East Timor since the 1960s, with over 500,000 casualties, and is forcibly relocating citizens into the wild lands of Irian Jaya, the infamous "transmigration" program which has devastated so much tropical forest and decimated so many traditional peoples there.

And this is only one example. Others exist with unsettling implications. For example, Canadian Pratt and Whitney motors find their way into helicopters used in "counter insurgency" activities (e.g., helicopter raids on non-cooperative villages), in Guatemala and Peru, two countries with notoriously bad human rights records.[13]

One of the great environmental legacies of the Second World War was the store of deadly chemical and biological weapons. Vast quantities of these were dumped in coastal areas around the world at the end of the war, but many more are stockpiled today. Canada's Defence Research Establishment Suffield, near Medicine Hat, Alberta, had a tremendous supply of germ weapons ready for use during and after World War II. The site has remained in operation, and DND has even released nerve gas into the local environment. In the last few years, DND has proposed, on the one hand, to incinerate 18 tons of chemical agents there, and, on the other hand, to build a facility there to test genetically-altered organisms. Canada is thus embarked on disposing of outdated biochemical agents, while it is busy preparing the next generation of even more deadly and dangerous biological weapons.[14]

It is, however, with nuclear weapons, the most poisonous and danger-ous of all weapons, that Canada comes into its own as a military supplier. From the raw material to the finished product, the Federal Government has been instrumental in the release into the world of the nuclear genie.

To start, Canada is the world's largest producer of the raw stuff of nuclear bombs, uranium. Uranium mines are to be found at Key, Rabbit, Cluff, Wollaston and Cigar Lakes in Saskatchewan (the province has been called the "Saudi Arabia" of the uranium industry), and at other sites in Ontario and the N.W.T.[15] Our uranium from the N.W.T. helped to incinerate Hiroshima and Nagasaki, a role which was secret then and which, under the Atomic Energy Act (1946) is often secret now—all in the interests of "national security."

Although the majority of Canadians have expressed their opposition to Canadian uranium exports unless they are restricted to peaceful purposes, about 85 per cent of our production goes to nuclear weapons states like France, Great Britain, and the United States. This is about one-third of global purchases. Although supposedly for peaceful purposes, the byproducts from nuclear power plants are used to produce plutonium, a key component of nuclear bombs. Indeed, five of every six pounds of uranium shipped to nuclear weapons states end up in military hands.[16]

This continues not only for military reasons, but because of an even simpler reason—uranium is an economic export. Many of the northern mines (and their parent multinationals) are actually subsidized. Mean-while the native people whose water, air and bodies are poisoned by such activities receive substandard medical care, housing, and education from the government.[16] Uranium miners, aboriginal groups, and local residents have for years pointed to the health and environmental effects of present practices—contaminated groundwater, irradiated traplines, increased can-cer rates and other health disorders—to no avail.[18] On the contrary, projec-tions to the year 2000 indicate that some 200 million tonnes of waste (which contain up to 85 per cent of the original radioactivity) will have accumulated in the areas from the uranium milling process, their hyper-toxicity estimated to last for up to 250,000 years. Leaks and spills (one of over 2,000,000 litres of contaminated water in Rabbit Lake in 1989) are common.[19]

The most visible recent political issue in the nuclear debate in Canada has been the government's agreement to test these systems in our air and water spaces: air-launched cruise missiles at Cold Lake, Alberta, and nuclear subs and torpedoes at Nanoose Bay, B.C. And our ports continue to play host to visiting NATO warships which will "neither confirm nor deny" the presence of nuclear weapons on board. These weapons have unbelievable explosive power. For example, one Trident II missile on board an American Trident submarine is equal to about 250 Hiroshima bombs. Despite the lack of debate on the matter, nuclear accidents are by no means rare. In 1968, for example, a B-52 bomber crashed and burst in flames in Greenland, destroying four H-bombs and contaminating a wide area. In the 1950s and 1960s, two bombs were accidentally dropped on Canada, one on the West Coast and one in the St. Lawrence River.[20] William Arkin has reported over 1600 naval mishaps between 1945 and 1988, one-third of these while the vessels were in port.[21] Only four years ago, a Soviet sub burst into flames and explosions, and sank with 34 nuclear missiles and two operational nuclear reactors on board. In 1990, fire raged for 10 hours aboard the U.S.S. Midway, a nuclear-capable aircraft carrier.[22]

Such an event would certainly mar the excitement of the Vancouver Sea Festival and could, in fact, irrevocably contaminate any port. Arkin reports numerous collisions, fires, explosions and sinkings; there are, after all, about 400 operating nuclear reactors at sea. Nine are known to be on the ocean floor. About 20,000 nuclear weapons are on board ships, and should an accident involve one of these, the consequences could be enormous. Professor Jackson Davis has calculated that a shipboard fire involving nuclear weapons at the Esquimalt military base near Victoria would release a vast cloud of radioactive particles which could travel for miles, smothering the provincial capital with cancerogonic toxicity.[23] And this is only one type of accident that could happen.

The final phase of the nuclear weapons cycle is waste storage. Although Canada does not presently store the remains of nuclear weapons, the wind and waterborne pollution from American nuclear facilities have already contaminated this country. Examples of air venting and water releases are common throughout the United States, but the most contaminated site of all, Hanford, Washington, is south of the B.C. border. Between 1944 and 1956, the Atomic Energy Commission secretly authorized the release of 530,000 curies of radioactive 131-I gas into the air from the General Electric-managed Hanford site, some of which may well have drifted into Canada (no studies have been done). The legacy continued, for example, in 1964, when 6,000,000 curies of radioactive waste were dumped into the Columbia River.[24]

In short, throughout every stage of the nuclear weapons cycle—mining, milling, transport, disposals—and their assorted crashes, fires, leaks, and deliberate releases of radioactive plutonium, uranium and other particles have been added to the air, food chain, and our own bodies. And this all results from the testing and development of nuclear weapons in peace, not their use in war. The effects of their actual use are unimaginable. For example, it has been estimated that just *one* bomb dropped between Windsor, Ontario and Quebec City could affect the half of our national population which lives there, causing cancer, immune breakdown, and genetic mutation among the unfortunate survivors.[25]

Impacts on Society

The impact of modern militarism extends beyond its physical harm to our environment and our health. The success of the modern military establishment has been intimately connected with a form of governmental control and industrial development which is anything but sustainable—one which is secretive in the extreme; one which ignores public opinion and avoids democratic debate; one which accords special rights to military suppliers and "fast tracks" for military developments.

Secrecy and special treatment characterize the military. Canadian firms selling to the Pentagon need not disclose many of their contracts. The uranium industry is protected by the Atomic Energy Act which controls not only atomic energy and materials, but information about them. A hundred nuclear weapons could be loaded and ready on a warship visiting Halifax or Vancouver, and the authorities would "neither confirm nor deny" the fact. Nuclear leaks and accidents have been shielded from public scrutiny for decades.

Public consultation and evaluation of the environmental and social consequences of military developments are almost never undertaken. DND refuses to refer the plans for low-level fights in B.C. and N.W.T. to the Ministry of Environment for review. Native land claims and national park boundaries are set aside in the planning of new bases and training areas. Canadians have opposed cruise missile testing, the export of uranium and tritium without guarantees against military use, military exports to human rights violators, nuclear capable ship visits, incineration of biochemical weapons, research into lethal pathogens—all to no avail.

Ironically, this secrecy, discrimination against native groups and local communities, and immunity from public scrutiny undermine the very democracy that the military is supposed to be defending. People are deeply disturbed by the government's collusion in the building of weapons of mass destruction, by the environmentally and socially disruptive practices which it relies upon to do so, and by the desperate lack of imagination of politicians who fail to direct meaningful resources to the real problems of environmental sustainability and social equity. But citizens withdraw into apathy, helplessness, denial or cynicism when they are made powerless to change things. Or they explode in frustration and anger.[26] In such a situation, we clearly face an inversion of social goals as democratic and social welfare values are made secondary to the maintenance, for its own sake, of the military industrial machine.

Impacts on the Economy

In this time of political platitudes about "sustainable development," perhaps the most frustrating aspect of modern militarism is the staggering misallocation of resources involved. Every single day, U.S. $2.7 billion (billion, not million) is spent on the world's military. Two such days would cover the annual cost of the United Nation's long-awaited global anti-desertification program. Three days of global military spending could pay for five years of the UN's tropical forest action plan. Ten days would cover the UN's entire water and sanitation program for a year.[27]

And this is only the beginning. Actually to clean up after the military would also entail monumental costs. In the U.S. alone, there are 20,000 suspected contaminated sites owned or operated by the military.[28] One such site, Hanford, would cost an estimated $57 billion to remedy, ten times the entire budget of the federal U.S. Environmental Protection Agency. The misallocation of priorities is on an epic scale, with military spending in the United States outweighing environmental spending by 60 to 1.[29]

In Canada, military spending in 1989 took 8.6 per cent of the federal budget, and 40 per cent of its discretionary spending (that is, money the government was free to allocate after existing commitments were kept).[30] In contrast, the Department of Environment's budget was only 0.6 per cent of the federal budget. With a budget of over $12 billion, the military is the fastest growing component of the federal budget, after charges for servicing the national debt. The military budget goes up by $500 million per year; in contrast, the national railway which has bound this country together since Confederation was gutted to save $200 million per year. Similarly, the local stations of the Canadian Broadcasting Corporation have been cast off to save $100 million per year, just 20 per cent of the military's annual increase.

Such comparisons are endless. For example, the government spends a full $1.8 billion a year to keep troops in Europe. This is over one thousand times the amount of money saved when the Federal Government cut funding for national women's programs in 1989. Such social programs are an essential component to achieving the sort of "social equity" which the Brundtland Commission concluded was essential to achieving "sustainable development" and environmental balance.

An ecological society must be an efficient society—in its energy use, its use of its renewable resources, and its just treatment of people. The military economy is the opposite of this—it is massively inefficient. Indeed, many studies show that military spending actually costs jobs, when one considers the jobs which might have been created if military expenditures had been directed instead into less capital-intensive social investments. The U.S. Labor Department has shown that $1 billion (1981 figures) invested in military aircraft production would create 14,000 jobs—but would create 16,500 jobs in pollution control, 21,500 in public transit, or 63,000 in education.[31] These areas are all key ingredients of any transition to a sustainable economy, but go underfunded to support arms and generals.

An ecological society must also be a balanced society—consuming now only what it can maintain in the long term. It must be stable and diverse. In contrast, military expenditures produce an overconsumptive, indeed deformed, economic structure. As we have seen, military industries are very capital intensive, and they demand the most highly trained and specialized minds the university system can provide, minds which have been educated at great social expense, but which do not tangibly benefit the society which trained them. As Ernie Regehr has shown, Canadian communities dependent on military industries are vulnerable to sudden changes in military spending and development priorities, and become wedded to maintaining a permanent military product economy—and opposing the sort of economic conversion upon which environmental and social stability depends. But this is a truncated form of industrial development, as many facilities are tied into producing only isolated components for the short-term specifications of the Pentagon.[32]

At a time when everyone is debating the links between the "economy and environment," one should reconsider the effects of our continuing emphasis on military production: reduced funding, labour, and research available for environment, education, public services, mass transit and so on; reduced innovation in civilian industries; a serious reduction in national competitiveness in international markets; and, in general, to both inflation and unemployment throughout the economy. This is exactly the sort of unstable economy which must undermine the environment to gain a short-term advantage, and which will support a foreign war to ensure cheap supplies. Ironically, two of the industrial world's most productive nations, Germany and Japan (nations which are winning the economic war, if you like), have very low military expenditures.

In the face of a fading Cold War and an escalating global environmental crisis, the resources allocated to the creation of a deformed war economy might be better spent in the development of a sustainable new infrastructure of environmental and social peace. This is the appeal of "conversion," of the "peace dividend." But how might such a conversion take place if it really is to make a difference in our prospects for survival into the next millenium?

CONVERSION: CREATING THE SUSTAINABLE SOCIETY
The terrible destructiveness and waste of the modern military machine de-

mand great sacrifices—our health, our environment, our economy, our whole social fabric. Native cultures are overrun to test our weapons, the traditions of our liberal democracy are abused to maintain the secrecy of "national security," and countries around the world are drawn into a grinding cycle of international debt and dependence to maintain their military power. With $16 trillion spent on the military since the end of World War II (can anyone comprehend how truly gargantuan a figure that is?), the economic toll of direct damage and of foregone opportunities is incalculable. In the process of our phantom pursuit of security through power, we have inverted the ends and means—we as a society have created exactly the sort of destabilizing social system which requires enormous military might to protect it. As the economist Kenneth Boulding puts it "National defense is now the greatest enemy of national security."[33]

Until recently, these costs have always been justified by the existence of a threatening enemy—in particular, the Soviet Union, the "evil empire." Just three or four years ago, the expenditure of $12 billion on a fleet of nuclear submarines was justified in this way by Ottawa.[34] That argument should be gone now, since we have repeatedly pronounced the Cold War to be over. Conversion, both in the West and the East, is now the order of the day. But we are not converting, and the Soviet Union may not either.

Instead, for the West, new enemies have presented themselves. For example, as the Russian menace faded for DND planners, the purchase of Canadian subs was instead justified just a couple of years ago as a way of promoting our sovereignty in the Arctic. And today, at the time of the greatest reduction in Cold War tensions since the Second World War, Canada, and much of the Western world, is embarked on one of its largest overseas military ventures, war in the Persian Gulf. Certainly there has been aggression in the Gulf, but the lesson of the Gulf is that the "peace dividend" will not come easily.

In our rush to war, the victims are justice and peace; among the enemies are us, our insatiable greed and our need to control. Behind the military is an industrial complex, an entire economic and institutional structure with an insatiable appetite for more raw resources, with a never-ending drive for growth and expansion, and with a total commitment to competition and strategic advantage. We are driven by a virtually unconscious belief in the pre-sustainability ideology of "Bigger is best." Our economic and political system is now inherently inequitable and vastly over-extended. We have created a global order that is unsustainable, unstable and militaristic.

This system doesn't change easily.

There is no question that the economic resources consumed by the military could, if redirected, play an enormous role in resolving the range of environmental and social crises facing the world. As we have seen above, the figures are staggering. One United Nations publication concluded in 1986:

> A reallocation of say 10 per cent of annual military expenditures (some U.S.$70 billion a year) for sustainable development projects in the developing countries would, within a few years, arrest and reverse soil degradation and desertification, provide clean drinking water and sanitation for all, eliminate illiteracy and some infectious diseases from the world, and alleviate a great deal of chronic poverty prevailing. [This] would also enhance national and regional security and, ultimately, international security and stability.[35]

Without reiterating yet again how military expenditures could be redirected to meet specific environmental and development needs, one example drives home just how comparatively few financial resources are being allocated to such needs. The example is the Federal Government's long-awaited Green Plan, a five year plan for environmental cleanup and restoration with a total price tag of $3 billion. This amounts to 5 per cent of the annual Canadian military budget—2½ weeks worth. As a percentage of GNP the military budget in Canada is approximately 15 times as large as our foreign aid and development programs. The comparisons are endless—the entire federal commitment to cleaning up Canada's air, water and land over five years is $850 million, or less than 7 per cent of just one year of our military consumption. Planned spending for soil conservation, sustainable agricultural, forestry and fisheries development, and water quality research ($350 million over five years) is just less than .25 per cent of the military budget for the corresponding period.

Such comparisons could be repeated endlessly. But the problem is not really what enormous good could be achieved with the "peace dividend." Nor is there really any question whether such a reallocation would achieve greater international peace and stability than comparable military spending. The real issue is how to overcome the institutions opposed to making this conversion happen.

To date, in the face of the omnipresent justification of the Cold War, the peace movement has been a resistance movement—stop testing, stop building, stop concealing. There are, of course, drawbacks to a campaign based largely on calls for limits to unacceptable military activities or destructive practices. For one thing, the movement is largely reactive, while the government takes the initiative. For another, popular participation is largely illusory, with citizens excluded from setting objectives and from any meaningful involvement in future planning. The fading of the

Cold War has, however, changed all that. Now the "peace dividend" can be seriously articulated as a practical policy, one that is in keeping with Canada's historic reputation as a "peacekeeper." To achieve that, however, the peace movement must begin to articulate a positive program that encompasses both a strategy for reducing our military dependence and a vision of how we might create a stable society without the need for weapons of mass destruction.

CREATING THE ECOLOGICAL SOCIETY

Conversion entails both dismantling the institutions of war and building the institutions of peace. On the first level, the Canadian government could undertake dramatic steps towards such dismantlement, for example, by ending the $250 million annual subsidy to arms manufacturers through termination of the Defence Industry Productivity Program (DIPP). Conscience Canada encourages taxpayers to withhold the portion of their income taxes devoted to military spending.[36] The Women's International League for Peace and Freedom and Project Ploughshares provide alternative budgets where military expenditures have been reallocated to meet real social needs. And the military can be restructured. Indeed, DND actually experimented with conversion when it successfully transformed some of the 17 terminated Cadin-Pine Tree Line radar stations into a retirement home, a training centre, a jail and native community housing.[37]

In the United States, Congressional representatives have proposed comprehensive conversion bills for over 20 years. For example, one bill would have required that military bases and production sites set up conversion committees to document a site's resources and propose new products, markets, and renovations. The bill would also require the government to provide occupational retraining and assistance to military-dependent communities, funded by a tax on military sales.[38] Similarly far-reaching bills have been proposed in the Ontario legislature and the House of Commons, but none has been enacted.[39] Municipal planning for local industrial conversion is increasing especially in many large American cities.

In Sweden, studies were undertaken on the economic effects of and strategies for conversion, and they found that impact was less than imagined, and more easily dealt with. What was needed was comprehensive planning and financing, something which only the central government could provide. In this light, military conversion could well serve as a model for the larger ecological conversion necessary to bring environmental and social peace to the planet.[40] A national Citizen Inquiry in Peace and Security has been launched for 1991 and it will, in part, address conversion proposals from across Canada.

The ultimate answer to militarism is to reduce the need for it. To begin this task requires the difficult recognition that the present economic system which the military defends and promotes worldwide is simply not sustainable. The evidence for that conclusion is all through this book. But in considering how to respond to this situation, we must turn around that term "sustainable development." If we do not presently have a sustainable infrastructure, then we need to build one—to "develop sustainability."

There are numerous aspects to this. All those troops in the Gulf are there, at least to a degree, because North Americans don't have rational and efficient transportation systems. Canada is the most energy wasteful country on earth, and one way to turn away from war is to restructure our energy systems, indeed our entire society, around energy efficiency, conservation and renewables. Instead, recycling and resource conservation programs are starved, and we continue to prowl the globe for more resources and more money to develop them. Rather than doling out more money to secure our international control, we should redirect our federal budget into a massive international effort to aid impoverished countries to achieve sustainability. One expenditure could be to help repair the environments of so many Third World countries that have been ravaged (with all the attendant security problems) to support our wasteful ways. Another expenditure could be to reduce some of the $25 billion which these governments owe to Canadian chartered banks, especially as a significant portion of Third World debt was incurred to finance military expenditures and unnecessary environmental destruction. By reducing the need for these countries to service high debt loads, they could instead attend to local needs which will achieve local stability.

We are far from any of these goals; we are told that the money is not available. It is scandalous that, for example, only $100 million per year is being allocated in the new Green Plan for something called "global environmental security." This includes trying to tackle the *real* threats to our security—such as the diminishing ozone layer, and the growing greenhouse effect. Yet the budget allocated to all these global problems would not have bought half of one of those prized nuclear submarines over which so much political blood was spilled only a couple of years ago.

The money isn't there because the understanding isn't there. Above all, the end of the arms race, and the conversion which could ensue, will not occur without a larger change in social values. In developing sustainability, we literally need to "reinvent society." We need to build a new infrastructure in virtually every facet of life—from energy to food, from native rights to international development—to make society in the third millennium more self-reliant (and, therefore, less expansionary), more just (and, therefore, less aggressive), and thus, hopefully, more sustainable. To create this new industrial and, indeed, cultural structure would be a massive undertaking. But it would have surprising economic benefits—stimulating many new jobs and creating a much higher quality of life—that would more than offset any losses from the decline of the old infrastructure.

To create such a world, we need new concepts of security as well. For example, the Brundtland Commission has advocated the concept of "common security," that is, security based on the security of others—making peace happen by working to better conditions for one's potential enemy. Military security here cannot be divorced from the economic, social, and environmental well-being of one's own society, and those of others.[41] Indeed, as we become more and more aware of the severity and depth of the ecological crisis, we need a concept of security which acknowledges that crisis. We need here to "transform the root" by modeling society not on the violation of the planet, but on respect for its ecological laws—the laws of diversity, interdependence, and balance. This demands what one environmental/peace activist calls "whole earth security," a security provided not by state or military power, but by environmental reclamation and stability, social development and justice, and by the economic conversion that makes it possible.[42]

CONCLUSION: TOWARD A COMMON MOVEMENT

In short, when one talks about the environmental impacts of the military, one must think of the whole planet and the unsustainable, militarily dependent societies which we have created on the planet. Our security "problem" today is not a military problem. Rather a security problem exists with militarism itself—with its waste, its dominating institutions, and its resistance to change. Similarly, our environmental problems involve not just specific issues of air and water quality, but related issues of military misallocation and institutional greed. To dismantle, convert and rebuild is our task; in such a task, the goals of the environmental and peace movements are one.

References and Notes

1. The Tao is an ancient Chinese text ascribed by some to Lao-Tze in the 6th century B.C., but dating at least from the third century B.C. The work has the status of an almost biblical text, a central message of which is that human activities must follow a simple and gentle path in tune with nature's way.

2. *Our Common Future,* 1987, New York: Oxford University Press.

3. See Johnson Hughes, *Ecology in Ancient Civilizations,* Albuquerque: University of New Mexico Press, 1975.

4. Charles Caccia, "The Environment as a Security Issue," *Policy Options,* VII:8, October 1990, 2628.

5.   Mike Chandler, "Haste Makes Waste: The Government Pushes for NATO in Labrador-Quebec," *Native Issues,* VII:1, August 1987, 59–65.

6.   K. M. Manci *et al.,* "Effects of Aircraft Noise and Sonic Booms on Domestic Animals and Wildlife: A Literature Synthesis," National Ecology Action Center Report, 88/29, Fort Collins, Colorado, June 1988; and, Daniel Ashini, "Innu Opposition to Low-level Flying," *Native Issues,* VII:1, August 1987, 5–21.

7.   "Canada has no 'magical' title to Innu land, judge rules," *The Canadian Peace Report,* Summer 1989, 7–8.

8.   Silvia Schriever, "Ear-piercing low-level flights are headed for B.C.," *Times-Colonist, Victoria, B.C.,* Victoria, B.C., October 9, 1990, 2.

9.   Ernie Regehr, *Arms Canada,* Toronto: Lorimer, 1987; and "Canadian Sales to the Pentagon," *Ploughshares Monitor,* March 1988, 12–15.

10.   "Another Panama Victim: Environment," *Nuclear Times,* VII:2, Summer 1990, 8–9.

11.   Ken Epps, "Recent Canadian Military Exports," *Press for Conversion,* Issue #3, 1990, 12.

12.   Carolyn Musselman-Wigboldus, "Canadian Military Sales to Indonesia," *Ploughshares Monitor,* June 1988, 10; and, "Canadian Military Equipment Bloodied in Indonesia's Genocidal War Against East Timor," *Press for Conversion,* Winter 1989/1990, #1, 21.

13.   Ken Epps, "Engineering Injustice," *Ploughshares Monitor,* June 1988, 16–18.

14.   Diana Chown, "Those Toxic Chemicals in Alberta," *Peace Magazine,* VI:111, June 1990, 12–31.

15.   Suzanne Rose, "Uranium: The 20th Century Curse," *Priorities,* May 1986, 3–4; "Uranium," *National Film Board,* 1990.

16.   John Willis, "What's Next for Canada's Uranium Mining Business?", *Peace Magazine,* June/July 1989, 22–23; Paul McKay, "Adding Fuel to the Fire," *The Upstream Journal,* June 1988.

17.   Diana Leis, "The Collins Bay Blockade," *Briarpatch,* July-August 1985, 5–9.

18.   Rosalie Bertell, *No Immediate Danger,* Toronto: Women's Education Press, 1985.

19.   "Contaminated water leaks from Sask. (sic) uranium mine," *Times-Colonist,* Victoria, B.C., November 9, 1989.

20.   Ed Offley, "The day a nuclear bomb fell on Canada," *Seattle Post-Intelligencer,* October 25, 1990, A:4; Robert Norris and Thomas Longstreth, "U.S. Nuclear Weapons: Danger in our Midst," *The Defense Monitor,* X:5, 1981.

21.   William Arkin, *Naval Accidents: 1945–1988,* Neptune Papers No. 3, Washington, D.C.: Greenpeace/Institute for Policy Studies, June 1989.

22.   William Arkin and Joshua Handler, "Nuclear disasters at sea, then and now," *Bulletin of the Atomic Scientists,* XLV:6, July/August 1989, 20–24.

23.   W. Jackson Davis, "Nuclear Accidents on Military Vessels in Canadian Ports: Site-Specific Analyses for Esquimalt-Victoria," Environmental Studies Institute, University of California, Santa Cruz, 1987.

24.   Dana Coyle, "Deadly Defense: Military Radioactive Landfills," Radioactive Waste Campaign, New York, 1988; Seth Shulman, "Toxic Travels: Inside the Military's Environmental Nightmare," *Nuclear Times,* VII:3, Autumn 1990, 20–32; Michael McCally, "What the Fight is All About," *Bulletin of the Atomic Scientists,* XVXI:7, September 1990, 11–23.

25.   Don Bates *et al.,* "What Would Happen to Canada in a Nuclear War?", in Ernie Regehr and Simon Rosenblum, *Canada and the Nuclear Arms Race,* Toronto: James Lorimer, 1983.

26.   Joel Kovel, *Against the State of Nuclear Terror,* Boston: South End Press, 1983.

27.   Such figures are found in: Ruth Sivard, "World Military and Social Expenditures, 1989," in *State of the World: 1989*. (Washington, D.C.; Worldwatch Institute) New York: Norton, 1989; Swedish International Peace Research Institute (SIPRI), *1990 Yearbook,* Sweden; Donald Snow, "Ecology Wars," *Nuclear Times,* Spring 1990, 40–48.
28.   Seth Shulman, cited at Ref. 24.
29.   Charles Caccia, cited at Ref. 4.
30.   David Langille, "'Defense Cuts' Camouflage a Spending Increase," *Press for Conversion,* Winter 1989/1990, 15 at 28.
31.   Michael Renner, "National Security: The Economic and Environmental Dimensions," Washington, D.C.: Worldwatch Institute, Paper #89, May 1989.
32.   For a discussion of these issues, see: Alex Michalos, "Militarism and the Quality of Life," *Canadian Papers in Peace Studies,* No. 1, University of Toronto, 1989; and Seymour Melman, *The Demilitarized Society: Disarmament and Conversion,* Montreal: Harvest House, 1988; Ernie Regehr, "Economic Conversion in the Canadian Context," *Press for Conversion,* Spring 1990, 10, as well as other works by Regehr.
33.   Quoted in Donald Snow, "Eco Wars," *Nuclear Times,* Spring 1990, 43.
34.   "Action Plan—Stop the Subs," and "Why We don't need Nuclear Subs," *The Canadian Peace Report,* Spring 1989.
35.   Essam El-Hinnawi, "Disarmament, Environment and Sustainable Development: A Time for Action," Nairobi, Kenya: United Nations Environment Program, 1986, 12.
36.   "Prior: Supreme Court Denies Hearing," *Conscience Canada Newsletter,* No. 41, Spring 1990.
37.   Ken Epps, "Closing the Pinetree Line," *Ploughshares Monitor,* March 1988, 16–17.
38.   Mel Duncan, "Local Planning in Minnesota," *Nuclear Times,* VIII:2, Summer 1990, 14–17; Verna Fausey, "Tennessee Coalition Tackles the Federal Budget," *Nuclear Times,* Autumn 1990, 51–52.
39.   Bill 17, Ontario Legislature, November 10, 1987; Bill C-256, House of Commons, September 26, 1989.
40.   See especially Michael Renner, "Converting to a Peaceful Economy," in Lester Brown (ed.), *State of the World, 1990,* New York: Norton, 1990.
41.   For a discussion of these issues, see: Hanna Newcome, "Collective Security, Common Security and Alternative Security," *Peace Magazine,* VI:4, August 1990, 8–10; Mary and Richard Kaldor, *Dealignment: A New Foreign Policy Perspective,* New York: United Nations University, 1987.
42.   Patricia Mische, "Ecological Security in an Interdependent World," *Breakthrough,* X:4, Summer/Fall, 1989, 7–17.

Postscript: A Plea for New Ideas from Readers

Peacemaking in the 1990s: A Guide for Canadians is meant to stimulate its readers both to think imaginatively and to act constructively for peace. The book is certainly not intended to be an encyclopedia on war and peace issues. All of the contributors and the editor are deeply concerned about preventing the human suffering of warfare and avoiding the privations caused by wasting natural and human resources preparing for war. All of us want to see our planet's fragile environment protected. But between us we unfortunately do not have all of the expertise needed to accomplish these aims.

Here is where readers of this book can play a very important part. We need your creative thinking and additional knowledge, as well as your political activity. For instance, you will have noticed that Professor Michael Wallace in Chapter 6 calls for strengthening the United Nations system, and that C. G. "Giff" Gifford in Chapter 5 goes into detail about providing "fire brigade" military units to the U.N. to stamp out threatening conflicts between nations. But what should be done when the United Nations is forced by one or more domineering powers to do their bidding, without regard to what is best for maintaining world peace?

A current example of this problem is the Persian Gulf War. After the Security Council of the U.N. promptly undertook in August 1990 to exert collective sanctions against Iraq to force its withdrawal from Kuwait, certainly a welcome U.N. initiative, the whole character of this action has been gradually subverted by one domineering power, the United States. First, under American pressure, the Security Council was persuaded to abandon economic sanctions as a relatively slow but non-violent way of forcing Iraq to withdraw from Kuwait. Then an artificial deadline (January 15, 1991) was set, after which military action by the U.N. was authorized, thus hampering diplomatic negotiations which might have avoided a war. And finally, now that a devastating war between Iraq and the U.N. "coalition" forces—predominantly American and British—is underway, the aims of the war have subtly been changed from getting Iraq out of Kuwait to destroying Iraq's industrial and military potential, and getting rid of Saddam Hussein. These changes in aims have clearly been forced by the American administration and do not reflect sober deliberations by the United Nations. If the U.N. has indeed lost control of the situation in the Persian Gulf, how do we now get a cease-fire in the war, and how do we get meaningful negotiations restarted? I hope that some readers will come forward with new ideas for really strengthening the United Nations.

Several contributors to this book have stressed the vital importance of achieving a comprehensive nuclear weapons test ban (CNTB) treaty. Such a treaty would greatly lessen the danger of a global nuclear war, would impede the lateral spread of nuclear weapons to small countries, and would create an international atmosphere conducive to all sorts of further disarmament agreements. Yet at the Partial Nuclear Test Ban Conference at the United Nations headquarters in New York in January 1991, Canada's Ambassador for Disarmament, Peggy Mason, abstained on a vote to convert the Partial Test Ban to a Comprehensive Test Ban. Her explanation is that Canada must move slowly, step by little step, toward that goal, and that it would have been pointless for Canada to support a CNTB so long as the United States is still firmly opposed to halting nuclear weapons testing. When is Canada going to develop its own independent foreign policy, and when are we going to have the guts to enunciate it? And is there no urgency about this issue? In my view, we are extraordinarily lucky that Saddam Hussein had not developed his own nuclear weapons while Canada procrastinated on whether or not to become a serious member of the group of nations opposing nuclear testing.

Canada exports one to three billion dollars of arms and military equipment each year, about 75% to the United States and 25% to Third World countries. When asked recently whether Canada should not immediately cease all sales of arms to other countries, a prominent Canadian civil servant answered testily that we will continue selling arms abroad, and added that it would be very unfair to deprive developing countries of arms which they are unable to manufacture for themselves! How long will it take our Federal Government to understand that the deliberate arming of Iraq over the last 10 years by at least 5 nations has had everything to do with Saddam Hussein's belligerence? Do readers of this book still feel that there can be gains made towards more decent societies through the barrel of a gun? Or is more harm done by brutalizing and killing, and would it be better to prohibit all international sales of arms to avoid putting power into the hands of other potential dictators?

You have noted that several of the contributors to this book call for "conversion," and make the point that more jobs are created by investing money in socially useful production than in military production. At a time when the unemployment rate in Canada as a whole is over 10%, we must think in terms of how to create new jobs when we curtail military production. As editor, I regret that we have not been able to treat conversion in this book with more precision, proposing concrete plans for providing goods and services that Canadians need, without geographically displacing and socially disrupting large numbers of workers and their families. What should we do with the thousands of people who ought no longer be working at Canadian Forces Base Summerside on P.E.I.; or those flying low-level bombers at Goose Bay, Labrador; or those building the guidance systems for cruise missiles at Litton Industries in Ontario; or those still experimenting with chemical warfare in Suffield, Alberta; or those developing submarine warfare at Nanoose Bay, B.C.? We don't want to see these people forced into the ranks of the unemployed, or forced to move away from friends to other parts of Canada. I hope that some readers of this book will come up with imaginative and workable conversion plans for these communities.

All the contributors to this book have striven for accuracy in their presentations, and we think that being careful about the truth is just as important in working for peace as it is in doing science. We have tried to avoid bias and dogmatism. I particularly recommend Chapter 13 by Dr. Alan Philips, where he tries to weigh facts carefully for and against the use of nuclear fuels for the generation of electricity. Good physicians carefully weigh the balance between the good and the harm that particular treatments may cause their patients. In peacemaking, where disputes between peoples and nations are often extremely complicated, we need to use the same careful judgment. When the Persian Gulf War is over, for example, what sorts of steps should Canada take to decrease the intense hatred for the West that is likely to pervade the Islamic world?

This book contains a lot of *substantive* material about peacemaking, but less than it might about the *tactical* problems of how to get the Government of Canada to listen to the views of ordinary Canadians who crave peace and disarmament. An exception is Chapter 12, where Councillor Libby Davies stresses the useful part which municipal governments can play. There are endless alternatives for action that peacemakers can take, some of them more effective than others. How much good does it do to accumulate thousands of signatures on petitions to Ottawa, or signatures on printed postcards? How do these techniques compare to hand-written individual letters from constituents to their Members of Parliament? In protest demonstrations, how can peace people make as many friends as possible? How can organizers avoid behaviour that alienates neutral observers, such as rowdiness and obstructing traffic?

Perhaps the most important area where imaginative tactics are badly needed is in picking candidates for election to Parliament who have well-formulated ideas on how to promote peace. Our experience over and over has been that if we wait until a federal election is called, the agenda has already been set by the major parties, and it does *not* include discussion of steps that could be taken to preserve world peace. We contributors to this book do not have all the answers; but we feel sure that some of our readers can develop effective ways of encouraging peace-minded people to seek nomination for office, and of forcing declared candidates to state their positions on peace issues.

Perhaps the most important thing all of us can do is to be bolder in talking to our friends, neighbours, and colleagues at work about peace issues. Instead of fearing to be thought different, or guilty of bad manners, when we discuss seriously what Canada ought to do to preserve peace and encourage disarmament, we should take pride in having exercised the most important functions of humanism and good citizenship.

On behalf of the contributors to this book, I welcome all comments, new ideas, or disagreements from readers.

March, 1991
Thomas L. Perry, M.D., Editor.

Selected books from
Gordon Soules Book Publishers Ltd.

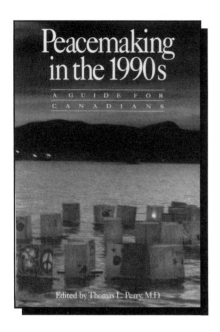

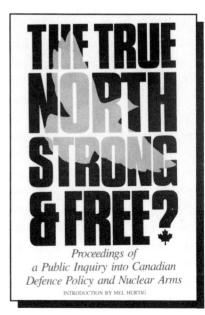